THE
FORBIDDEN
APPLE

THE FORBIDDEN APPLE

A CENTURY OF SEX & SIN IN NEW YORK CITY

KAT LONG

BROOKLYN, NEW YORK

Printed in the United States of America.
10 9 8 7 6 5 4 3 2 1

Ig Publishing
178 Clinton Avenue
Brooklyn, NY 11205
www.igpub.com

Library of Congress Cataloging-in-Publication Data

Long, Kat.
  The forbidden apple : a century of sex and sin in New York City / Kat Long.
      p. cm.
  Includes bibliographical references.
  ISBN-13: 978-0-9815040-0-1
  ISBN-10: 0-9815040-0-0
  1. Sex--New York (State)--New York--History. 2. Sex customs--New York (State)--New York--History. 3. New York (N.Y.)--Social life and customs. I. Title.

  HQ18.U5L65 2009
  306.709747'10904--dc22

                          2008051195

For my family

CONTENTS

INTRODUCTION

New York City has always loved contradiction. As a visitor to Manhattan in the late nineteenth century observed, "If the city contains the gaudiest, the most alluring, and the vilest haunts of sin... New York is also the centre of everything that is good and beautiful in life."[1]

This book will illuminate the sexual history of this city. But first, what is a sexual history? Alfred Kinsey revealed in *Sexual Behavior in the Human Male* in 1948 that the sexual histories of individuals feature unmistakably universal similarities. A place can also boast such universal similarities. Over a period of time, residents of a particular place can express, evaluate, and retrofit their sexual ideologies indefinitely, and eventually that process comes to be identified with that place.

New York City is such a place. Its residents have argued over innumerable sexual issues, and expressed radical ideas so forcefully through the centuries, that the city has become synonymous with sexual opportunity, chance, and change. I distill New York's sexual history as the war between two opposing forces: those who want to uphold a traditional yet disintegrating sexual and moral order, and those who want to break out of the past into new forms of sexual thought and provocation. I will illustrate individual battles in this war such as anti-prostitution campaigns, public health attempts to eliminate venereal disease, and Supreme Court fights against censorship. I've chosen to focus on the peculiar quasi-legal space in which these battles took place to expose the motivations of each side in fighting for or against the expansion of sexual expression.

Of the original thirteen colonies in America, only New York was founded as a hub of trade rather than a refuge from religious persecution or a family fiefdom. Through commercial exchange with the Old World came diverse peoples, ethics, and tastes—a cultural blend found nowhere else in the world. Far ahead of their time, the original Dutch settlers based their laws on enlightened principles of equal justice, racial parity, religious freedom and the collective ability to turn the other cheek. Religious Puritan asceticism and social homogeny, on which the New England colonies had been founded, had little place in the thriving mix of merchants, sailors, traders, their families and the attendant industries.

Despite its unique liberalism, New York was not completely disconnected from European standards of sexual propriety. Once the Dutch provisionally ceded the colony to England in 1664, the English governors declared street prostitution an offense against honor and reputation, and charged perpetrators with vagrancy or disorderly conduct that entailed harsh punishment. In 1738, one accused streetwalker was publicly whipped thirty-one times and banished from the colony; in 1753 five "ladies of Pleasure" received fifteen lashes each and banishment.[2] In addition, the government condemned miscegenation, adultery, and "unnatural acts"— including but not limited to sodomy and homosexuality—as immoral. The ruling class used its social power to suppress transgressions by the masses. This loose hegemony continued into the mid-nineteenth century, even as the commercialization of sex increased.

In antebellum New York, as Timothy Gilfoyle notes in *City of Eros: New York, Prostitution, and the Commercialization of Sex, 1790-1920*, erotic display and commerce, in the forms of prostitution, the presence of houses of ill repute, trade in explicit pamphlets and photographs, and popular entertainment, were as much a component of urban life as regular church attendance. No organized efforts to stem this industry lasted very long, partly due to a lack of incentive on the part of middle—and upper-middle class—men, the group with the funds and influence to create such a movement. They were, in fact, the industry's main customers, with the tacit approval of their peers.

Furthermore, socially-minded philanthropy did not carry the admirable caché it would come to later in the nineteenth century. Responsibility for reforming "fallen" women, when someone did take it, fell to religious societies or missions. Generally, missionaries set up group homes for prostitutes who repented (that was a requirement for entry), and worked to convince them to live a respectable life. But they did not act to reform prostitutes who did not want to repent, nor did they focus their energies on preventing the causes of prostitution.

After the Civil War, the city underwent a physical and spiritual transformation. I have chosen to begin this book at this crucial turning point: when New York City emerged from Wild West-style mayhem into a modern, orderly, and—above all—moral metropolis.

The 1873 Act of the Suppression of Trade in, and Circulation of, Obscene Literature and Articles of Immoral Use (also known as the Comstock Law), the nation's first federal law against obscenity, marked this seismic shift toward establishing public moral standards. The indefatigably righteous energy of Anthony Comstock, as well as the American public's desire to correct a society bent out of moral shape by the Civil War, made the law possible. I chose to begin the narrative at the time of the Act's passage because it marks the birth of the modern movement against vice and the first delineation between the "good" and "evil" sides on the moral battlefield.

With the Comstock Act passed into law, social, religious, and municipal forces in New York joined to create an organized moral-reform movement. This "preventive society," as Gilfoyle has written, was concerned with bettering the condition of the poor and morally destitute through charitable organizations such as the Society for the Prevention of Crime and the Society for Prevention of Cruelty to Children. In this rush to right the masses' moral compass, boundaries regarding morally acceptable commerce and behavior were redrawn. The groups redefined elements of the city's sexual culture, heretofore unthreatening to the social order, as indecent, dangerous, and evil. So while the Civil War had fostered a brisk trade in "French postcards," prostitution and erotic entertainment in the city, its influential citizens afterward turned to ameliorating the perceived moral collapse resulting from war.

The social reform organizations of the late nineteenth century established a pattern, which is evident well into the twentieth century. By condemning sexual commerce as immoral and calling for its destruction, twentieth century religious leaders successfully appealed to public opinion for support, which in turn influenced the policy decisions of the city government. The mid-century conservative moral leader Cardinal Francis Spellman, for example, had the ears of both the city's huge Catholic population and its mayoral administrations. Moral crusaders used this consolidated power to attempt to eliminate all—not just illegal—sexual expression from the city.

This set of factors, too, created a pattern that has been evident well into the twentieth century, as rogue individuals and groups in New York sought to counteract the overwhelming prudery of the religious/municipal alliance. The Minsky brothers infiltrated the sacrosanct artistry of Broadway theatre with their populist burlesque extravaganzas in the thirties. Samuel Roth and Ralph Ginzburg fearlessly challenged the censorship of sexually explicit books in the sixties and altered the literary landscape of the city. Gay sexual culture evolved in the seventies after decades of active repression by moralizers in government, medicine, and the press.

For every victory won by moral reformers, however, citizens fought back with the tools of spectacle, protest and dissent. In Comstock's time, the Victorian ideals of sexual conduct—premarital chastity, rigid gender roles, male authority and female subjugation within marriage—created a vacuum for the expression of desire. Men of all economic classes, with sexual needs that could not be satisfied within the confines of marriage, found fulfillment in the booming marketplace of "commercialized vice"—an enormous and efficient sexual economy composed of brothels, nightclubs, and erotic entertainment. Most citizens devoted their energy to vice: profiting by it, indulging in it, or fighting its insidious autogenesis.

The Forbidden Apple will show the significant battles in this ongoing struggle and demonstrate that the agents for good and evil, in New York especially, are symbiotic. As Southern journalist James D. McCabe, Jr. observed in 1882, "It is said that New York is the wickedest city in the country. It is the largest, and vice thrives in crowded communities...yet, if it is the wickedest city, it is also the best on the Continent. If it contains thousands of the worst men and women in our land, it contains thousands of the brightest and best of Christians."[3]

New York City's cycle of sexual revolution and conservative backlash has reverberated through other cities, helping to shape culture in the United States. Americans look to New York as a microcosm of the country as a whole, squeezed onto an island thirteen miles long, with cultural philosophies and social movements magnified and their effects condensed.

But there is no end to the cyclical war between perceptions of good and evil. We have seen it at the close of the twentieth century; we see it now at the beginning of the twenty-first. "As everyone knows," said police chief William McAdoo in 1906, "the city is being rebuilt, and vice moves ahead of business."[4]

1.

THE DASTARDLY DO-GOODERS
1873-1918

In 1906, Anthony Comstock finally got his man. It had taken at least four attempts, but he nabbed Charles Conroy at last, his nemesis, the criminal who had allegedly ruined the innocence of thousands and unintentionally handed Comstock his destiny.

Thirty-eight years before, while working in a dry-goods shop on Warren Street in lower Manhattan, Comstock was shown a book by a fellow clerk—a book the clerk blamed for his unwelcome contraction of a venereal disease. Outraged that his friend was thus corrupted, Comstock sought out the publisher of the book, one Charles Conroy. After purchasing a similarly outrageous item at Conroy's shop in the neighboring basement, Comstock brought the police and had Conroy arrested. But that was not the end of the story.

Six years later, in 1874, Comstock caught up with Conroy again. By now Comstock was the federal postal inspector, and he collared Conroy at the Newark, New Jersey post office as he was mailing dirty pictures. As he escorted the felon to jail, Conroy suddenly "stabbed him in the head, inflicting frightful wounds, the last stab cutting a gash from the temple to the chin."[1] Comstock recovered, but was thereafter badly scarred (though he considered the scar a badge of honor).

Ten years after the attack, Comstock happened to pass by Conroy's picture-stand at 701 Broadway and again took the opportunity to arrest him. Conroy fought back again, attempting to punch Comstock in court,

but a bailiff intervened. At his final arrest in 1906, Conroy, age seventy, offered no resistance to Comstock, age sixty-two.

Charles Conroy, an unrepentant two-bit pornographer—whose name
even the *New York Times* couldn't get right, mistakenly reporting him as
John or James Conroy in his arrest notices—inadvertently kick-started
Anthony Comstock's career as the most influential moralizer in American
history.

Resplendent in bushy white muttonchops, a severe black suit, starched
white shirt and stiff collar, Anthony Comstock stood as a righteous figure
over a city steeped in physical and moral chaos. Yet his beginnings were
appropriately humble for a man who made a career of pious humility. Both
his father, Thomas Anthony, and his mother Polly were direct descendents
of the first Puritans of New England and owned substantial farmland, with
two sawmills in New Canaan, Connecticut. Anthony Comstock was thus
born, on March 7, 1844, into the landed gentry, but spent his childhood in
ascetic study, reading Bible stories and tales of moral courage.

At the outbreak of the Civil War, while Comstock enlisted in the
Union Army and saw minor combat, his most enduring feat of heroism
was to convince some of his fellow soldiers to follow his path to purity. "As
we entered the Barracks a feeling of sadness came over me and it seems
as though I should sink when I heard the air resounding with the oathes
of wicked men," Comstock wrote in his diary. "[But], as I read [the hymn
entitled 'Waiting'] such a light and relief came over me that I resigned to all
of my trials…3 out of 7 [soldiers] that accompanied me Pledged themselves
to me that they would not swear, drink nor chew tobacco while we were in
the army (for 3 yrs.)."[2]

After the war, Comstock settled in New York City, an unusual choice
for someone who was "saddened" by his proximity to vice. He lived in a
variety of cheap lodging houses in lower Manhattan and Brooklyn while
working in the dry-goods shop, and saved his wages until he was able to
purchase, with a $500 down payment, a small house at 354 Grand Avenue
in Brooklyn's Fort Greene neighborhood.

Thus settled, Comstock set about procuring a wife. Margaret Hamilton, an old maid at thirty-seven, was ten years his senior and the daughter of a Presbyterian elder. M., as Comstock called her in his diary, would become a subordinate and unfailingly gracious partner to her fire-and-brimstone husband.

All was not well, however, within Comstock's purview. In June 1871, six months after settling on Grand Avenue, he noticed several nearby saloons staying open on Sundays, ignoring the Sabbath. He promptly called the police, who refused to close them down. "I am determined to act the part of a good Citizen and wherever a man breaks the laws I will make him satisfy the laws demands if in my power," Comstock wrote defiantly in his diary.

As was his wont, Comstock didn't stop at forcing people to obey the law; he attacked businesses and individuals whom he felt violated his own sense of decency. His imperious attitude made people listen, while an absolute devotion to his duty as self-appointed moral watchdog won over skeptics. "O how I loathe the actions of corrupt officials in our city," he wrote. "This is a murderous age. Crime stalketh abroad by daylight and Public officers wink at it. Money can buy our judges and corrupt our juries. But God helping me, it shall never buy or sell me."[3]

THE CHALLENGE OF THE CITY

"What Paris is to the Frenchman, or London to the Briton, New York is to the Americans," wrote James D. McCabe Jr., a journalist from Virginia, in his exhaustive 1882 survey of the city, *New York by Gaslight*. "One of the chief characteristics of New York is the rapidity with which changes occur in it. Those who were familiar with the city in the past will find it new to them now."[4]

After the Civil War, the whole country strained under the burden of rebuilding the shattered economy, as well as reestablishing the national identity. Reckless speculation led to inflation, while the overextended steel and railroad industries defaulted on federal loans of hundreds of millions of dollars. As historian and Comstock biographer Margaret Leech noted in 1927, "it was a period of melodramatic crime, of corporate theft, of extravagance, of specious prosperity."[5]

In New York City, pervasive corruption infected every level of government and society, pioneered by the Tammany machine. Formerly an obscure Democratic club, Tammany Hall's political power accumulated in the 1870's under the guidance of Bowery street thugs turned small-time gang leaders turned local bosses. They excelled in election-rigging, back-slapping fraud and ethnic favoritism. Tammany decided the fate of politicians in New York City based on their enthusiasm for graft. Tammany bosses handpicked mayors and city aldermen; police and fire companies answered only to them. William "Boss" Tweed directed Tammany to its height of power by handing city contracts over to favored supporters, personally pocketing taxpayer dollars, and unashamedly pandering to the Irish working class vote. His blithe disregard for ethics was such that his name still connotes malfeasance on a gargantuan scale.

Reform candidates who opposed Tammany were shut out of municipal government, which enraged muckrakers and the press. McCabe challenged, "Go to the City Hall, or to any of the various departments, and you will find the majority of the persons present in official capacity…risen from the slums to their present position by the power—not of intellect or ability, but of politics."[6]

By baiting the poor masses' interests against the wealthy classes—and the political power of the huge Irish population against that of other ethnic groups—Tammany exploited a political powder keg. Deeply-rooted, often violent conflicts were common between immigrants and so-called native (white Protestant) Americans, Catholics and Jews, the very rich and the very poor. Local bosses exacerbated the situation.

Prior to 1883, 85 percent of all immigrants to America hailed from the northern European countries (Ireland, Germany, and Scandinavia), but after that year, new immigrants started pouring in from southern and eastern Europe, notably Italy, Greece, Russia, and the Balkans.[7] During the 1880s, twice as many immigrants were arriving at Castle Garden, the depot for new arrivals, as in any prior decade; 1,562,000 of these were Russian Jews fleeing the pogroms in their native country. "The most densely populated portion of New York is the region embraced by the Seventh, Tenth, and Thirteenth wards, which lie upon either side of East Broadway and

Grand Street,"reported McCabe in *New York by Gaslight*.[8] "In 1870 these wards contained 119,603 inhabitants…in 1875 the population numbered 135,456."[9] Hundreds of thousands of people were literally crammed into an area measuring only a few acres. Twenty-five years later, the Jewish ghetto housed 640,000 people per square mile, the highest such density of humanity in world history.[10] The depot for immigrants had to be moved to Ellis Island in New York Harbor to accommodate all of the new arrivals.

Poverty was the one thing a majority of immigrants had in common. Tenement houses were erected to shelter the poor from all corners of the globe, as comfort became a distant afterthought, despite one-half of Manhattan's entire population living in such accommodations.[11] Conditions were so squalid that Jacob Riis, a police reporter for the *Evening Sun* newspaper and himself a Danish immigrant, took his camera into the slums and photographed the horrific scenes. Riis observed 128 children scattered among forty families in a single Bayard Street tenement, "that for a yard has a triangular space in the centre with sides fourteen or fifteen feet long, just room enough for a row of ill-smelling [privies]."[12] Riis, like his reform-minded peers and patrons, was convinced that such abject poverty created a population that was both physically and morally stunted.

Contemporary leaders blamed the awful conditions in tenements for the explosive growth of prostitution in the late nineteenth century. A representative of the Tenement House Association in 1903 declared that inhabitants of the city's forty thousand tenements had nothing to hope for but a life of "disease, poverty, vice and crime, where the marvel is not that some children grow up to be thieves and prostitutes, but that any become decent men and women." He did note, however, that a fine of one thousand dollars imposed on erstwhile landlords eliminated some of the immorality.[13]

Out of this maelstrom emerged moral leaders like Comstock and his intellectual counterpart Dr. Charles Parkhurst, a Presbyterian minister, who recognized the average New Yorker's exasperation with graft, public indecency and the abysmal standard of living. Both men acted as agents of social reforms, leading the growing movement to correct the problems caused by mass immigration, widespread poverty, and government indifference. Late nineteenth century reformers—often the wealthiest members of society—

formed numerous organizations to combat drunkenness, child labor, work-place dangers and overcrowding in tenements at Comstock's and Parkhurst's behests. Industrial magnates also signed on to fund groups against prostitution and pornography, which eventually brought down a vast web of police complicity in the commercial sex industry. After this success, many believed rampant prostitution had been controlled.

The vast divide between the rich and the poor in New York directly corresponded to a similar divide between the virtuous and the vulgar. New York's richest businessmen and most influential clergy members provided the moral movement with steady funding. In return, donors received unassailable peer recognition as concerned servants of the Lord, willing to save innocent youth as Jesus had saved sinners. Wealth therefore came to be associated with virtue, as the relationship between rich patrons and reform groups like the New York Society for the Suppression of Vice grew tighter. This arrangement had an unfortunate side effect: the actual poor of New York City had little say in the policies and initiatives meant to help them.

By contrast, poverty became synonymous with immorality. It also meant laziness, a lack of hygiene, alcoholism, attendance at bawdy theaters and brothels, and generally any incident of bad judgment. Thus hobbled, the poor were easy prey for Tammany leaders, who exploited ethnic divisions and sentiments for votes. Tammany became the nemesis of reform-minded benefactors, leading to a race for the souls of the masses.

But the world was changing quickly. Comstock's avowed enemy, birth-control booster Margaret Sanger, was already strategizing for a widespread campaign for contraception, hoping to bring about the liberation of women of all classes from the restrictive bonds of marriage and children. Her ideas were revolutionary, coinciding with the growing Socialist movement and the declining influence of Comstockian morality. Comstock and Sanger's long-running war of words symbolized the polarity of sexual mores in the first decade of the twentieth century: while his Victorian view of womanhood was waning, her vision of a powerful, sexually aware movement of women was gaining steam.

"A LIFE OF SHAME"

Prior to the twentieth century, women were left entirely out of the power grab, no matter what their social status. Women of lower economic status were shunned by the upper classes because of their need to support families with work outside the home, which presumably bred moral deficiencies; middle- and upper-class women were prevented from earning their own wages by the prevailing distaste for female industry. Caught in this catch-22, women counted among the most desperate people in the growing metropolis of New York. Prostitution loomed as a constant and dangerous last resort. The five thousand prostitutes who worked the Tenderloin, the nightlife district centered at Fifth Avenue and 23rd Street, tried to blend with the melée, yet their shame and degradation were easily spotted by average citizens. "Glancing swiftly and keenly at the men they pass are a number of flashily-dressed women, generally young, but far from attractive," James McCabe sighed. "They are the 'Street Walkers,' one of the most degraded sections of the 'Lost Sisterhood.' Woe to the man who follows after one of these creatures!"[14]

The Victorian ideal of womanhood clashed violently with the reality of prostitution. Comstock, especially, ascribed a divine purity to women, equal to the purity of children: innocent, unblemished, morally clean, yet always susceptible to evil forces. Women's intellectual capacity was considered similar to that of children. On one hand, should she get into trouble, a woman was to be pitied for she knew not what she did; on the other hand, as she was impressionable and had a childlike curiosity about new things, a woman was deemed wicked and sinful if she took too readily to evil influences. Of course, women were constantly trapped between the impossible ideal and the irreversible moral nadir. "It has often seemed to me one of the most dark arrangements of this singular world that a female child of the poor should be permitted to start on its immortal career with almost every influence about it degrading," wrote the children's advocate Charles Loring Brace in his 1872 study, *The Dangerous Classes of New York; and Twenty Years' Work Among Them.* "For there is no reality in the sentimental assertion that the sexual sins of the lad are as degrading as those of the girl. The instinct of the female is more toward the preservation of purity, and therefore her fall is deeper."[15]

Immigrant women often ended up as prostitutes after arriving at Ellis Island with little money, skills, or knowledge of the English language. The brothels of New York roughly mirrored the ethnic makeup of the city, with a staggeringly diverse population of cultures, languages, religions, and customs. One study assessed 464 prostitutes and found that 30 percent were French, 20 percent Jewish, and 6 percent German immigrants; the rest were a mix of Irish, African-American, and other groups.[16] Some customers had their favorites among the races: French prostitutes, for example, were considered kinkier than others and more willing to indulge their more perverse customers. McCabe marveled at the ease with which sex was sold, remarking, "men who at home are models of propriety seem to lose all sense of restraint when they come to New York."[17]

To maximize their income, prostitutes sometimes entertained up to twenty customers a night. Some girls worked sixteen-hour shifts with little rest. In 1900, the going rate for sex with a Tenderloin prostitute was only fifty cents, about the cost of a burlesque show. The ledger from one brothel illustrates one resident's exhausting schedule: sex with 273 men in two weeks (an average of nineteen a day), for which she earned $136.50. Half of her earnings went to the brothel's owner, while the other half was used to pay for room and board.[18]

One of the many red-light districts of the 1890s—so called because brothels hung red lanterns outside their doors for easy identification—was located in the vicinity of Greene, Mercer, Wooster, and Crosby Streets (now the heart of Soho), and populated with immigrants from China, Africa, and Europe.[19] Slightly to the east, the Bowery carved a broad path from Chatham Square to Astor Place and possessed a distinctly different character than polyglot Soho. German was the predominant ethnicity of this street, and Bowery merchants were in the rag trade or ran cheap hotels and saloons. Novelist Stephen Crane wrote "Overhead elevated trains with a shrill grinding of the wheels stopped at the station, which upon its leg-like pillars seemed to resemble some monstrous kind of crab squatting over the street."[20] McCabe observed, "On the Sabbath…the most infamous dens of vice are in full blast."[21]

Only the Bowery provided entertainment for more unconventional tastes: male prostitutes could be found as easily as female, and relatively openly for the Victorian age. The Slide at 157 Bleecker Street catered directly to gay men, even hiring perfumed, rouged "fairies" as live amusement.[22] Tourists determined to see the seamier side of New York City made a mandatory stop at the Slide or the Black and Tan on Bleecker, owned by Slide proprietor Frank Stephenson. There, outré sexual hi-jinks were de rigueur as that dive specialized in matchmaking white women with nonwhite males. Nearby on West 4th Street, the bar at the Golden Rule Pleasure Club offered bottom-of-the-keg swill laced with dope, along with male prostitutes dressed in petticoats and tight bodices.[23]

Columbia Hall at 392 Bowery (better known to the cognoscenti as Paresis Hall, in honor of the medical term for syphilitic insanity) was an open secret as a hangout for male prostitutes. A report in 1899 recorded a visit by city vice investigators: "That is a place where fancy gentlemen go…a place where male prostitutes resort. That is a well-known resort for male prostitutes; a place having a reputation far and wide, to the best of my knowledge. I have heard of it constantly…These men that conduct themselves there—well, they act effeminately; most of them are painted and powdered."[24] The inspectors also noted numerous city and state politicians present, taking in the sights. A contemporary gay patron of Paresis Hall, "Jennie June," wrote in his autobiography of "preachers in New York pulpits of the decade would thunder Philippics against the 'Hall,' referring to it in bated breath as 'Sodom!' They were laboring under a fundamental misapprehension. But even while I was an habitué, the church and the press carried on such a war against the resort that the 'not-care-a-damn' politicians who ruled little old New York had finally to stage a spectacular raid…the 'Hall's' distinctive clientele were congenital goody-goodies, incapable (by disposition) of ever inflicting the least detriment on a single soul. But the 'Hall's' distinctive clientele were bitterly hated, and finally scattered by police, merely because of their congenital [homosexuality]."[25]

All the social classes could be found mingling in the Tenderloin traps, from the opera house to side-street dives and bordellos along Broadway and westward. Opium dens were a favorite hangout of prostitutes and their customers alike, as the house drug took the edge off life's ugliness. Opium, commonly smoked by Chinese laborers, proved just as addictive for white locals. Dens were established in the Tenderloin in proximity to the brothels. Though illegal, one pound of Persian opium cost $125 to $150,[26] and even after it was banned in 1891, 93,667 pounds still made it into the country to meet growing demand.[27]

To Comstock and his followers, sex was a gateway to all other forms of vice. Meanwhile, Victorian moralizers assumed a woman was either as innocent as a child or wicked enough to choose that life of shame. A man's role was to protect womanhood, yet moral crusaders were reluctant, even helpless, to suggest that prostitutes might be saved from their fates. Once "fallen," there was no getting back up.

A SAVIOR EMERGES

Socially prominent New Yorkers longed to see the city return to civility after the Civil War, and as a result, a wave of righteousness swept over the upper classes, who displayed their concern for the huddled masses with their checkbooks. Groups hastily organized to battle these lapses of morality with compassion and decency. The Young Men's Christian Association (YMCA), the most powerful of these, was founded by well-known citizens. Morris K. Jesup, its president, was a self-made financier, manufacturer, and one of the founders of the American Museum of Natural History. Cephas Brainerd, the Secretary-General, was a top attorney and lecturer at New York University. Influential Secretary Robert R. McBurney, an Irish immigrant, shepherded the YMCA from its infancy to a semi-autonomous branch network with national headquarters in a custom building of his own design.

In 1866, the organization had printed up a memorandum whose title succinctly explained the YMCA's modus operandi: *A Memorandum Respecting New York as a Field for Moral and Christian Effort Among Young Men; Its Present Neglected Condition; and the Fitness of the New York Young Men's Christian Association as a Principal Agency for its Due Cultivation.* The survey's writers observed young, wayward men who spent their idle time in billiard halls, gambling dens, saloons and brothels, and wished to help these men achieve their God-given place at the head of family and community. But, among New York's many temptations, erotic magazines sold freely on the streets posed a danger to the achievement of this goal. As the memorandum warned, "The debasing influence of these publications on young men cannot be over-estimated; they are feeders for brothels."[28]

Thus, the YMCA and Anthony Comstock had a common enemy. In typically florid prose, Comstock wrote in his 1880 book *Frauds Exposed*, "This cursed business of obscene literature works beneath the surface, and like a canker worm, secretly eats out the moral life and purity of our youth, and they droop and fade before their parents' eyes."[29] In 1871, Comstock was invited to meet with Jesup and McBurney to discuss each others' strategies and form an alliance. Comstock shrewdly yet humbly mentioned that he had the contacts necessary to infiltrate and destroy the small presses that published these erotic books. Soon, under the auspices of the YMCA, he organized the Committee for the Suppression of Vice, whose sole purpose was to eradicate obscene literature. Impressed, Jesup gave Comstock $650 for the committee and an "in" to the moneyed classes that would sustain his crusade.

As an agent for the Committee for the Suppression of Vice, Comstock set his sights on the United States Congress, the one legislative body with the power to permanently banish all obscene literature. A variety of state laws banned obscenity to some degree, but the United States did not have a Constitutional definition of what literature could and could not be protected by the First Amendment as free speech. Comstock sought to make the distinction himself, and his definition of obscenity was vast:

> It consists of books, pamphlets, tracts, leaflets, of pictures engraved on steel and wood, of photographs, cards, and charms, all designed and cunningly calculated to inflame the passions and lead the victims from one step of vice to another, ending in utmost lust. And when the victims have been polluted in thought and imagination and thus prepared for the commission of lustful crime, the authors of their debasement present a variety of implements by the aid of which they promise them the practice of licen-

tiousness without its direful consequences to them and
their guilty partner.[30]

In short, Comstock considered obscene any written material that de-
picted sex, birth control, remedies for venereal diseases, abortifacients, sex
toys, or the instruments for committing any of those acts.

In late January 1873, Comstock took the train to Washington D.C.
armed with a proposal to ban all obscene articles. At the behest of Representative Clinton L. Merriam (R-NY), Comstock took the floor of the
House of Representatives, displaying his exhibits of obscene articles to the
legislators. Many were impressed, others were simply disgusted. At the end
of the day, Comstock triumphantly reported back to New York headquarters of his success.

Throughout the month of February, Comstock kept busy lobbying
powerful senators and the Washington elite. His early supporters included
Representative Merriam and Senators William Buckingham (R-CT), Dan-
iel D. Pratt (R-IN), Adelbert Ames (R-MS), Cornelius Cole (R-CA), and
Vice President Schuyler Colfax. "All were very much excited, and declared
themselves ready to give me any law I might ask for," Comstock wrote in
his diary[31]

Comstock's bill introduced airtight laws against mailing and advertising sexually explicit material, and included "for the prevention of conception" to expressly indicate birth control methods. Merriam and Senator
William Windom (R-MN) introduced the bill in the House and Senate,
respectively. While making its slow progress through committee debates,
Comstock sat on pins and needles. Wooing skeptical lawmakers whenever
he could, he attended a White House audience with President Ulysses S.
Grant, where he found Washington society ladies "brazen" and "extremely
disgusting."

Good news came toward the end of the month: Windom informed
Comstock that $3,425 had been appropriated in the bill for a Special Agent
to the Post Office, and Comstock would be appointed to the position. But
time was running out. Congress would adjourn on March 4, yet the bill was
still stuck in committee, though his supporters promised every day that it

would come to the floor for a vote. Comstock alternately fumed at certain Senators for their hesitation, then willed himself to accept it as God's plan, then decided the Devil must be tempting him to believe he was defeated. He stayed awake into the wee hours of March 2—the Sabbath—until he believed all hope for the bill's passage was lost.

Later that day, however, Comstock received word that the bill had passed. With only thirty dissenting votes in the House and a nearly unanimous vote in the Senate, the bill was sent to Grant's desk, and signed into law with unheard-of alacrity. "O how can I express the joy of my Soul or speak to the mercy of God," Comstock rejoiced.

From that day forward, anyone who distributed or was found in possession of "an obscene book, pamphlet, paper, writing, advertisement, circular, print, picture, drawing or other representation, figure, or image on or of paper of other material, or any cast instrument, or other article of an immoral nature, or any drug or medicine, or any article whatever, for the prevention of conception, or for causing unlawful abortion, or shall advertise the same for sale, or shall write or print, or cause to be written or printed, any card, circular, book, pamphlet, advertisement, or notice of any kind, stating when, where, how, or of whom, or by what means, any of the articles in this section...can be purchased or obtained, or shall manufacture, draw, or print, or in any wise make any of such articles, shall be deemed guilty of a misdemeanor."[32] Once convicted of breaking this law, one could expect to be "imprisoned at hard labor in the penitentiary for not less than six months nor more than five years for each offense, or fined not less than one hundred dollars nor more than two thousand dollars."

Basking in victory, Comstock returned to New York City a powerful lobbyist for morality and the first and only federal agent with the authority to censor all mail in the United States. His newfound notoriety, however, and penchant for hurling Biblical invective at everyone, regardless of the consequences, did not sit well with the YMCA. A series of terse discussions led Comstock to take the Committee for the Suppression of Vice out of the YMCA and rename it the New York Society for the Suppression of Vice (NYSSV). Again, Comstock counted society's elite among the NYSSV's supporters and members: Samuel Colgate, millionaire head of the Colgate company; publisher Alfred S. Barnes; William E. Dodge, Jr., a mining and timber mogul, and John M. Cornell, a philanthropist.[33] He was able to sway them with a tally of his success at the head of the Y's Committee: 134,000 pounds of indecent books seized and destroyed; 194,000 pounds of obscene photos and pictures destroyed; and 14,200 pounds of printing plates, 60,300 indecent rubber articles, 5,500 naughty playing cards, and 3,150 boxes of pills and patent medicines confiscated.[34]

From the NYSSV's inception in 1873 to 1880, Comstock and his cronies arrested ninety-seven abortion providers and suspected sellers of birth control. One of those arrested would prove to be his most notorious case—Madame Restell, a well-known provider of pills and potions to upper-class ladies for the relief of "feminine troubles." In reality, Restell was no French matron—she was Ann Lohman, a former midwife from the East End of London—but her vocation gave her a certain je ne sais quoi. Though her trade was obviously illegal, she openly advertised her wares in prominent newspapers. She was something of a celebrity, and her services to the wives and mistresses of New York's leading citizens shielded her from arrest. Madame Restell conducted consultations in her grand Fifth Avenue mansion at the corner of 52nd Street, and wisely never met with single women; that would have clearly marked her as peddler of abortions. Rather, her female clients brought male benefactors with them, or she met with young men privately.

One day, Anthony Comstock came calling in the disguise of a worried husband. He begged her for the pills and elixirs she gave to women inconvenienced by pregnancy. Madame Restell hesitated. She had been considering getting out of the business and joining society proper. But Comstock impressed upon her that he, his wife, and existing child already had one foot in the poorhouse and another child would throw them over. She reluctantly handed over the contraband. Comstock pounced. The police were waiting around the corner.

Madame Restell knew that Comstock could not be bought off, but she offered him forty thousand dollars anyway. He refused. However, the idea of prison did not suit Madame Restell. Though she would be, at worst, convicted of only a misdemeanor (under Comstock's own law), the prospect of five years hard labor was not agreeable to the sixty-seven-year-old. After arraignment, back in her Fifth Avenue palace, she slit her throat in the bathtub.

Despite the suicide, the Restell case should have been an absolute victory for Comstock in the newspaper editorials. Instead, his method of entrapment met with disapproval. The *New York Sun* commented, "Whatever [Restell] was, she had her rights, and the man who cunningly led her into the commission of a misdemeanor acted an unmanly and ignoble part…he deceived and wheedled her into a crime."[35] As we have seen with his arrests of Charles Conroy, Comstock's questionable tactics often provoked anger in those he persecuted. In one instance, as he exited a Brooklyn courthouse, Comstock was attacked by a doctor he had labeled an "abortionist." "He came behind me and spit in my face," Comstock recorded in his diary. "Then, as I turned, he struck me with his cane causing the blood to flow freely from my head. I knocked him down and then took him by the Collar and handed him over to the Marshall."[36] That was not the first nor the last time Comstock would defend the Lord with his fists.

In the court of public opinion, the Restell case reinforced Comstock's reputation as a bully; among the clergy, who generally looked down on trickery and deceit, his credibility was severely damaged. He had become such a polarizing figure that he would never again enjoy the uncritical support of the YMCA or that of his comrades.

PARKHURST'S CRUSADE

Besides the YMCA and the NYSSV, several other groups were actively engaged in ridding the city of one or more supposed evils. The Women's Christian Temperance Union advocated prohibition, while the Anti-Saloon League tried to close down the bars that prostitutes used as places of business. The Society for the Prevention of Crime formed in 1878 to bring down gambling dens, saloons, and prostitution. The latter had little lasting effect until 1891, when the Reverend Dr. Charles H. Parkhurst became its president and visionary.

Parkhurst was Comstock's physical opposite: slight, myopic, bookish. Morally, however, they were equals. Parkhurst's early life also mirrored that of Comstock—he was a New Englander of Puritan stock, born in 1842 in Framingham, Massachusetts. His father was a farmer and a schoolteacher, and Parkhurst grew up in a household that prized religious education. Yet

unlike Comstock, Parkhurst was naturally studious and graduated with
honors from Amherst College in 1866. He then studied theology and philosophy in Germany, and became a professor of Greek and Latin.

In 1880, Parkhurst became pastor of the Madison Square Presbyterian
Church at the corner of Madison Avenue and East 24th Street, in the heart
of the Tenderloin. From his daily observations, he came to discover that
houses of prostitution, gambling halls, and saloons were operating next to
his church. Parkhurst then watched for years as local beat cops, totally under
Tammany's control, infiltrated the seedy underworld and shook it down on
a spectacular scale, rather than arrest the perpetrators. Infuriated by the brazen lawbreaking among people entrusted to uphold order, Parkhurst blasted
the Tammany-backed city administration in an 1892 sermon: "[they are a]
damnable pack of administrative bloodhounds, polluted harpies and a lying,
perjured, rum-soaked, libidinous lot."[37]

When asked by the press to produce actual proof of his accusations
against politicians, Parkhurst unfortunately had none. For the next two
weeks, he went about collecting evidence, aided by Charles W. Gardner, a
detective and seasoned patron of the Tenderloin dives. In his 1894 book,
The Doctor and the Devil, or the Midnight Adventures of Dr. Parkhurst, Gardner recalled taking Parkhurst to "the worst vice that New York holds...I
led the way to the Golden Rule Pleasure Club," on West Third Street in a
four-story tenement....The basement was fitted into little rooms, by means
of cheap partitions, which ran to the top of the ceiling from the floor. Each
room contained a table and a couple of chairs, for the use of customers of
the vile den. In each room sat a youth, whose face was painted, eye-brows
blackened, and whose airs were those of a young girl...The Doctor instantly
turned on his heel and fled from the house at top speed."[38] Parkhurst was
less leery of observing standard-issue brothels and parlor-houses, however,
where he customarily had a few glasses of beer with Gardner as they collected their evidence.

On the night of March 11, 1892, Parkhurst, Gardner and John Irving, a
member of Parkhurst's congregation, visited a house of assignation at 31 West
27th Street belonging to Mrs. Hattie Adams. Parkhurst initially stayed behind
to assemble a disguise. Arriving at 11 P.M, Irving and Gardner were ushered

into the parlor by Adams and seven ladies of the evening, who served the men several rounds of beer. After Parkhurst arrived, Gardner asked the girls to commence the "circus" the men had come to enjoy, which involved a mirthful game of naked leapfrog (Gardner, in a potential conflict of interest, was the frog) and the French cancan danced *sans vêtements*.[39] During the show, Parkhurst looked stunned—too stunned, Adams thought, for someone who professed to enjoy the services of a brothel. Still, she accepted $15 for the show.

Parkhurst revealed the results of his personal investigation in an incendiary sermon to packed pews the following Sunday, basing it upon the theme of Psalms XII: "The wicked walk on every side, when the vilest men are exulted."

> 'I believe [the] administration to be essentially corrupt, interiorly rotten, and in all combined tendency and effect to stand in diametric resistance to all that Christ and a loyally Christian pulpit represent in the world,' he began. 'I have here a list of thirty houses, names and addresses specified, that are simply houses of prostitution, all of them in this precinct. These thirty places were all of them visited by my friends or my detectives on the 10th, and also on the 11th of March, and solicitations received on both dates. One of these places I spent an hour in myself, and I know perfectly well what it all means…The house is three blocks only from the spot where I am standing now,' he thundered. 'To say that the police do not know what is going on and where it is going on, with all the brilliant symptoms of the character of the place distinctly in view, is rot.'[40]

Although Parkhurst did not mention Adams' brothel by name, police nevertheless arrested her that afternoon. On April 7, 1892, the Reverend appeared as a prosecution witness in her trial, recalling his undercover visit. But his sensational account was met with confusion. Under cross-examination from Adams' lawyer, Parkhurst revealed that he had failed to recognize Adams when she went to his church later that Sunday to protest. Her lawyer suggested that Parkhurst must have visited some other house of ill repute, not Adams'.

The following day, Hattie Adams took the stand in her own defense. She emphatically denied operating a disorderly house, instead claiming to make ends meet by running a legitimate boardinghouse for women adjacent to her own home. She also "swore very positively that she had never in all her life seen such a dance as Dr. Parkhurst testified."[41]

While the all-male jury might have been inclined to believe Parkhurst's word over Adams,' the verdict was split, with four jurors for Adams, and only two for Parkhurst. The case was retried in May 1892, and this time, Adams was found guilty and sentenced to nine months' imprisonment on Blackwell's (now Roosevelt) Island. Pleading for mercy, Adams told of her ill-fated marriage at seventeen, the subsequent years of physical abuse and adultery on the part of her husband, and a divorce that left her penniless. Running her boardinghouse, she testified, was her only means of support. Pitiful as it was, the judge only smiled, not believing a word.[42]

For Parkhurst, the Adams case was a twofold victory. Not only did he succeed in holding up Hattie Adams as an example of the wages of sin, but he also exposed—through sermons and trial testimony—the awe-inspiring web of police corruption that had allowed Adams and others like her to operate brothels without fear. Parkhurst's information was used as the basis for the 1894 New York State Senate commission's investigation into NYPD corruption and policy dealers (gamblers who ran illegal lotteries, also known as the numbers racket). Known as the Lexow Commission, the investigation reached from the lowest of street-level swindles to the highest offices of law enforcement.

Police Captain William S. "Big Bill" Devery, a conspicuous character even among his fellow officers, had organized a complex graft operation, which was detailed in the Lexow report. Devery and an accomplice, Patrolman Edward Glennon, had coerced numerous pimps and gangsters to fork over retainers totaling thousands of dollars. Henry Hoffman, "who kept a disorderly house at 180 Allen Street," paid $500 per year for the privilege, plus $100 each month as long as Devery was captain of the 11th precinct. Charles Prien, proprietor of a house at 28 Bayard Street, doled out $25 for the privilege and $50 a month afterwards. Kate Schubert of 144 Chrystie Street paid an initial $500 plus $50 a month. Karl Werner of 6 Delancey Street agreed to the same arrangement. In the span of a month, Devery and Glennon could shake down nearly $2,000—at a time when a patrolman's annual salary was $1,200.[43] And that was only the tip of the iceberg.[44] Many lower-ranking officers were dismissed as a result of the investigation, but the higher-ups were allowed to retire with full pensions or, in Devery's case, be promoted to Chief of Police in 1898.

While police officers under pressure from Parkhurst and the Lexow investigators stepped up surveillance of disorderly houses, the prevailing attitude among the force continued to be ambivalence, if not outright derision. The same year, 1892, Police Superintendent Thomas Byrnes commanded his officers to sweep the red-light districts and record the locations of brothels, but expressed doubt about the social benefits of this protocol. Byrnes wondered whether "good results are obtained by the closing up of such houses and the scattering of the inmates…[or if] it might be better for the health and morals of the city to localize houses of this character in certain well-recognized quarters where the evils could be regulated by police supervision."[45] Localization would also make for easy exploitation, of course.

THE COMMITTEE OF FOURTEEN AND THE RAINES LAW

The fleeting nature of the Lexow Committee's improvements infuriated followers of the moral movement, who now realized that the police were consummately untrustworthy and that institutional reforms were, ultimately, ineffective. By 1900, reformers were also fighting the popular entertainment industry, in addition to prostitution and police collusion. To strengthen their impact, the Anti-Saloon League joined several other reform groups in 1905, assuming semi-legal authority to raid brothels and arrest suspected prostitutes and their pimps, independent of corrupt precincts and Tammany Hall influence.

Like the YMCA and the NYSSV before it, the Committee of Fourteen, as the coalition became known, counted among its members the cream of New York society. Of the fourteen, six were clergy members, including Reverend Lee W. Beattie, pastor of Madison Square Church House at Third Avenue and 30th Street (appointed by none other than Charles Parkhurst). Other notable colleagues included George Haven Putnam, president of G.P. Putnam's Sons publishing house; William S. Bennet; the U.S. Representative from New York; and Mary Simkovitch, a prominent social reformer and the sole woman on the committee.[46]

The Committee of Fourteen's primary objective was to eliminate the so-called commercialized prostitution that was financially supported by the hundreds of saloons scattered throughout Manhattan. To accomplish this goal, the Committee would need to first close down the particular places where vice occurred, known as Raines Law hotels. Then, they would have to consolidate remaining hotels in designated districts, away from respectable neighborhoods, thereby establishing a way of making reforms permanent.[47]

Sex, a commodity always in demand, was mostly sold in the Raines Law hotels. Passed in 1896 and named after New York State Senator John Raines, the law permitted hotels to sell alcohol on Sundays, but did not extend that right to bars and saloons. By definition, a hotel was any establishment with at least ten rooms and a restaurant. To avoid losing valuable Sunday business to hotels (as Sunday was typically the only day off for working people to drink), saloon owners swiftly added curtains and cots to their backrooms, served morsels of stale bread, and rented beds by the hour.

The Raines Law was an excise regulation meant to limit the saloons' ability to sell alcohol, but it fostered an explosion of ersatz hotels catering almost exclusively to prostitutes. Before the Committee of Fourteen's existence, a reformer named William H. Baldwin Jr. commented, "Any one who is familiar with conditions in New-York must admit that the effect of the Raines law has been to provide unexampled accommodations for prostitution…many of the Raines law hotels are themselves the scene of the most insidious and therefore most effective solicitation…[they] are very frequently the place where the growing boy is introduced to immorality." Worse than that, "the Raines law hotels provide the greatest known facilities for seduction;" that is, of young girls into prostitution.[48]

The Committee of Fourteen, in a departure from the NYSSV's method, focused on the johns who visited these hotels as well as the prostitutes who used them as their places of business. By 1906, the Committee had managed to persuade police to raid more than one hundred Raines Law hotels, and took this evidence to court in an effort to have the law amended. Judges, however, usually dismissed the cases. Like Comstock and Parkhurst, the Committee of Fourteen realized that their best hope lay not in simply trying to ban the hotels, but to make it impossible for them to do business. Comstock and Parkhurst used shame as a weapon, while the Committee used something more practical: licensing. With the help of the state Brewers Association (which also wanted to clean up its public image), the Committee used the saloons' liquor licenses as a bargaining chip. The Committee and brewers dictated how and when liquor could be sold by regulating the licensing of the saloons, and saloons had to obey the restrictions to keep their licenses. If the scheme worked, not only would prostitution disappear, but the public would be saved from the other vices that stemmed from alcohol.[49] Liquor licenses were issued and renewed every year, giving the Committee ample time to investigate New York's saloons and recommend which should stay open and which should close.

The plan worked. By 1912, nearly all of the Raines Law hotels were out of business or, at least, operating in a morally-appropriate manner. Dance halls, burlesque theaters, and tenement barrooms that offered some form of sexual entertainment were also shuttered. While the Committee of Fourteen's success proved that manipulation of licenses was an effective means of regulating public decency, the group—and indeed, no group—was able to permanently stem the invention of tempting entertainment.

"MOVING PICTURE EVILS"

The unsettled forces of licentiousness and reform in the Tenderloin prompted savvy entrepreneurs to stake a claim in territory that wasn't so scrutinized—namely, the rough environs of Longacre Square, where 42nd Street, Broadway, and Seventh Avenue met in a triangle. "Thieves' Lair," as it was known, boasted plenty of undeveloped real estate. In 1904, *New York Times* publisher Adolph Ochs convinced Mayor George McClellan to rename the area Times Square in honor of the paper's new headquarters, which undoubtedly infuriated William Randolph Hearst's *New York Journal* and Joseph Pulitzer's *New York World*.[50] Adding to the area's allure, the Interborough Rapid Transit system had broken ground on the first citywide subway, with a central station planned for 42nd Street and Broadway.

By the turn of the century, Times Square featured Oscar Hammerstein's Olympia, the largest and most opulent amusement palace in a city of amusements, flanked by restaurants, the Knickerbocker and Astor Hotels, and a string of theaters—the New Amsterdam, Selwyn, Liberty, Empire, and Victory—on 42nd Street. Early motion pictures played alongside the live theater—Oscar Hammerstein had even convinced Thomas Edison to play his short films at the Olympia to warm up the audience. Movies' popular appeal surpassed even that of vaudeville, the working-class leisure activity of choice at the time. Admission prices, at ten cents for adults and five cents for children, were less than those of the average vaudeville show. The number of theaters (usually storefronts with film projectors and a few chairs) and nickelodeons (where viewers put a coin in a slot and peered into a hand-cranked projector) had grown from fewer than fifty in 1900 to more than five hundred by 1908.[51] Between two-hundred-thousand and four-hundred-thousand New Yorkers went to the movies every day, lured by such scintillating shorts as *Sea Waves, The Butterfly Dance, Little Egypt*, and spellbinding flicks like *Kaiser Wilhelm Reviewing his Troops*.[52]

Most importantly, the novelty of animation appealed especially to children and teenagers. By 1911, as many as 225,000 children went to the movies every week, creating a perfect storm of immoral temptation: darkened rooms, mixing of the sexes, and erotically-charged moving pictures. Naturally, the New York Society for the Suppression of Vice—still headed by the indomitable Anthony Comstock—went on the warpath.[53] Even in the early days of the moral movement, Comstock had shrewdly linked his anti-vice crusade to the preservation of children's moral purity, and the movies provided an ideal opportunity for him to prove his argument.

The Society for the Prevention of Crime (no longer led by Charles Parkhurst, who had resigned in 1908) and the Society for the Prevention of Cruelty to Children (which counted Cornelius Vanderbilt, Andrew Carnegie, John J. Astor, John D. Rockefeller and J.P. Morgan among its directors) raised alarms over the danger of the pictures and the poorly-ventilated, hazardous theaters.[54] "Moving picture evils for young children continue unabated," the SPCC'S annual report of 1913 began, "notwithstanding the society's unceasing activity in prosecuting cases arising through the 'movies,' the demoralization of children goes steadily on."[55] The report noted theater managers' common practice of paying adult "guardians" to escort unaccompanied children into the shows.

The reform groups were especially concerned over the content of the movies, which generally consisted of a modern fable between good and evil, with a moral lesson at the end. One would think that Comstock and company would appreciate such character-building entertainment, but in typical films, the moral was only reached after a whirl of visual stimulation and erotic nuance, as stories of love played with seduction and taboo. The SPCC and NYSSV were worried that impressionable audiences of women and children would be vulnerable to such temptations. Both groups believed that films about female sexuality and independence had the potential to encourage women to abandon marriage, motherhood, and obedience. In addition, boys would inadvertently receive instruction about committing petty infractions, disrespecting women, and submitting to the lure of crime as an adult. And young girls, perhaps the population in most danger, might be led astray toward prostitution, adultery, abortion or lesbianism. Even men were not immune; movies supposedly acted as a stimulant for rape and assault.

The fear of movies' bad influence on children morphed into a genre of movies *about* the bad influences on children in a treacherous city. In 1913, producers churned out a rash of "sex problem" films—movies that showed predatory pimps, fallen women and kidnapped innocents in a graphic tableaux allegedly meant to warn women and children about prostitution.[56] While sex problem films were nominally educational, the real thrill lay in how the evildoers met their fated end.

Going a step further, the subgenre of "white slave" pictures employed sensational story lines of sexual coercion and kidnapping of innocent (read: white) women by foreigners, told in the melodramatic gestures of silent film. The hugely popular *A Traffic in Souls* played in twenty-eight movie theaters in New York City in 1913, grossing $450,000—or nine million nickels.[57] "White slave" movies also caused controversy in the pages of the *New York Times*. On December 9, 1913, Universal Studios' *The Inside of the White Slave Traffic* opened at the Park Theater near Columbus Circle. The final slide of the film announced that "its purpose was to teach a great moral lesson," but before that slide, audiences saw "a representation of the sensational ways in which it has been alleged from time to time the so-called White Slavers work. These include drugged drinks, taxicab abductions, the machinations of professional procurers, the interior of brothels, the daily life of a cadet, and the life-story of a 'typical White Slave'."[58] At the sold-out premier, two-thirds of the audience were women, many between the ages of sixteen and eighteen.

The Inside of the White Slave Traffic also attracted unwanted attention from police inspectors and social workers. Alfred P. Hamburg, manager of the Park Theater, was served a summons for showing a moving picture that was "likely to impair the morals of young girls."[59] The summons was dismissed after a selection of social reform leaders, including noted suffragist Carrie Chapman Catt, viewed the film and pronounced it appropriate for impressionable minds. But three days later, the Park Theater was raided by a half-dozen officers and Deputy Police Commissioner Newburger.[60] They seized the film, shut the theater, and ordered it to cease exhibition. Police also had a warrant for the arrest of Samuel H. London, the film's producer and president of the Moral Feature Film Company, who was also a former "white slavery" inspector for the U.S. government. Before the warrant could be delivered, however, a mêlée erupted outside the theater as a crowd of five hundred women rushed toward the door, waving the green tickets they had purchased for the 9:30 PM screening. Police on horseback were called in to quell the disturbance, but word of the raid spread up and down Broadway. Soon, a throng of several thousand had amassed at the theater protesting the shutout, though they dispersed when police reserves were summoned.

Deputy Commissioner Newburger, furious at the film's popularity, blustered, "The pictures are vicious and are intended to cater to morbid imaginations...I am prepared to put an end to this production and others of its kind."[61] On Christmas Eve 1913, Newburger and a squad of officers moved in on the Bijou Theater on Broadway between 30th and 31st Streets, in a re-enactment of the Park Theatre raid. (The Bijou had been showing *The Inside of the White Slave Traffic* to packed houses after the Park had closed.) This time, two female members of the Wage Earners' Anti-Suffrage League had complained about the film.

A few days later, an injunction was issued sparing both the Park and Bijou further police harassment, and each returned to exhibiting the picture to insatiable audiences. But the reprieve would be short-lived. A State Supreme Court Justice eventually ordered the Park Theater closed, despite the argument from the attorney representing *The Inside of the White Slave Traffic*, who reminded the court that "several well-known women and physicians had seen the white slave pictures and decided they were a good thing for the community."[63]

The Bijou Theatre eventually washed its hands of *The Inside of the White Slave Traffic* and began showing less notorious films. In response to the controversy, in 1914, the National Board of Censorship of Motion Pictures devised a set of guidelines for judging each movie's levels of sex and violence. Films were rated by their likelihood of scaring young children with gory scenes, cruelty to animals, or violent crimes. Sexual situations between men and women were acceptable only if the scene showed love and fidelity. The board only allowed infidelity and adultery if the adulterers met tragic ends—picking up a venereal disease, or being exposed as a cheating spouse. Male characters couldn't wink at, nudge, ogle, or grope the film's heroine, and even kissing was restricted to a chaste peck.[64] Scenes containing ardent passion, nudity (no matter how tasteful), adultery and prostitution, or scenes taking place in dance halls and houses of assignation were strictly forbidden.[65] Similar guidelines applied to drug use, insanity, murder, suicide, and homosexuality.

In its zeal for suppression, the National Board of Censorship of Motion Pictures thoroughly examined such long-forgotten titles as *Hell's Hinges*, *Is Any Girl Safe?*, *Our Sinful Daughters*, and *This Naked Age*.[66] Ironically, *The Inside of the White Slave Traffic* was censured for not portraying *enough* of the dangers of the white slave trade. A board member suggested that the movie should have "shown what happened to the girl in the end; her becoming a drug-fiend hag, a sufferer of venereal disease; a suicide; a specimen for the doctor's dissecting table; and finally filling a grave at Potters Field."[67]

MARGARET SANGER V. COMSTOCK

As the century progressed, the moral absolutism favored by Comstock seemed increasingly antiquated, a quaint Victorian style of social reform that depended on outraging the upper classes (and guaranteeing their financial support) with tales of working class vice and moral decay. There was little thought, if any, given to empowering the working class to help itself. That was about to change.

New York City was a hotbed of radical thought in the 1910s. The Socialist Party of America, the International Workers of the World (IWW), and assorted anarchist groups found receptive audiences among the Jewish and European immigrants and intellectuals in New York City, particularly in Greenwich Village. Of primary importance to radicals was equality of the sexes; without gender equality there could be no economic, political, or social equality. Necessarily, the process began with achieving sexual equality: if women were sexually subjugated by men, in marriage and in childbearing, any further steps toward parity would be meaningless.

Margaret Sanger was the loudest voice of women's emancipation. She had moved with her husband William Sanger and their two children to New York City in 1912 from White Plains, New York, where she had been attending college for nursing. Working in the slums of the Lower East Side, Sanger observed mothers with large families, unable to properly care for their children and suffering from the physical effects of multiple pregnancies. (Her own mother had been pregnant eighteen times, borne eleven children, and died of cervical cancer.)

The suffering Sanger witnessed in the slums affected her acutely. In addition to her nursing, she began writing a column, "What Every Girl Should Know," in the Socialist newspaper *The Call*, a blatant effort to educate young women about sex and marriage and to counteract women's endemic ignorance of their own bodies. Sex was not shameful or immoral, she argued, but ignorance about sex was a sin. "Students of vice, whether teachers, clergymen, social workers, or physicians, have been laboring for years to find the cause and cure for vice, and especially for prostitution... upon one point they have been compelled to agree: Ignorance of the sex functions is one of the strongest forces that sends young girls into unclean living," Sanger wrote in her sex-education compilation *What Every Girl Should Know*.[68] The pamphlet went on to describe in a conversational tone the basics of adolescence, puberty, sex and pregnancy.

An ardent Socialist, Sanger couldn't resist concluding that women's sexual ignorance was a byproduct of male political and economic dominance. "It is impossible to separate the ignorance of parents, prostitution, venereal disease, or the silence of the medical profession from the great economic questions that the world is facing today," she stated. "Until the evils of capitalism are swept away, there is no hope for working girls to live a beautiful life during their girlhood...that a woman can live in the family relation and have children without sacrificing every vestige of individual development. There is no hope that prostitution will cease, as long as there is hunger." Manmade evils will perpetuate, Sanger wrote, "until women rise in one big sisterhood to fight this capitalist society which compels a woman to serve as a sex implement for man's use."[69]

Sanger was convinced that a woman's sexual emancipation was inextricably tied to her economic emancipation, and the greatest cost to women, as she observed through her ongoing work among poor immigrants, was the financial burden of too many children. *Choosing* motherhood in the 1910s was an unheard-of concept. Women did not choose to be mothers, but were expected to embrace pregnancy in the natural course of their lives, even those who worked outside the home or had other responsibilities to attend to. A childless, married woman was abnormal, a tragic figure who was either unable or unwilling to fulfill her human duty. Sanger reasoned that women would not be free citizens unless freed from unwanted pregnancies and children, and the associated mental and physical costs.

In March 1914, having found *The Call* too conservative for her needs, Sanger began publishing her own journal, aptly titled *The Woman Rebel* and funded by the Greenwich Village feminist socialite Mabel Dodge. In the first issue, Sanger clearly stated her aim, with not a small amount of derision for the current attitude propagated by Comstock et al. towards women. "All this slushy talk about white slavery, the man painted and described as a hideous vulture pouncing down upon the young, pure and innocent girl, drugging her through the medium of grape juice and lemonade and then dragging her off to his foul den for other men equally as vicious to feed and fatten on her enforced slavery—surely this picture is enough to sicken and disgust every thinking woman and man, who has lived a few years past the adolescent age. Could any more repulsive and foul conception of sex be given to adolescent girls as a preparation for life than this picture that is being perpetuated by the stupidly ignorant in the name of 'sex education'?"[70] She added, "It will also be the aim of the *Woman Rebel* to advocate the prevention of conception and to impart such knowledge in the columns of this paper. Other subjects, including the slavery through motherhood; through things, the home, public opinion and so forth, will be dealt with."[71]

Sanger aggressively advocated birth control—a term she coined—to alleviate poverty and all of its unpleasant consequences: mothers in ill health or dying from too many pregnancies, miscarriages, or abortions; underfed and undereducated children; unemployed, absent, or abusive husbands. There was, at the time, only one alternative to unwanted births, which was abortion, which Sanger denounced: it was "so common as to be almost universal, especially when there are rigid laws against imparting information for the prevention of conception…to force poor mothers to resort to this dangerous and health-destroying method of curtailing their families is cruel, wicked, and heartless, and it is often the mothers who care most about the welfare of their children who are willing to undergo any pain or risk to prevent the coming of infants for whom they cannot properly care."[72]

Sanger toured the country giving lectures about birth control, which were well-received, and putting out the word that she was planning to open a clinic to dispense information and methods for contraception. Her Socialist Party connections and the network of IWW chapters were the conduit through which she alerted the working class to the birth control option, as well as engaging radical intellectuals and anarchists (such as Emma Goldman) to agitate for birth control as a free speech principle.[73] Predictably, such talk infuriated Anthony Comstock—amazingly, at age seventy-one, he was still actively prosecuting people for sending obscene material through the mail in his capacity as Postal Censor. Sanger was delighted to attract his attention, as, from a left-wing perspective, it was a bona fide stamp of approval. Even better, Sanger was indicted in 1914 under the Comstock Act, specifically for mailing copies of *The Woman Rebel*. Before abdicating to Europe and therefore escaping trial, she wrote *Family Limitation*, a tract explaining contraception, and had one hundred thousand copies mailed across the country.[74]

Since Margaret Sanger was in exile, Comstock sunk his talons into William Sanger. As was his wont, Comstock used deception to entrap Sanger into committing a crime. NYSSV agent Charles Bamberger called on Sanger at home one day and said he was "Mr. Heller," the husband of one of Mrs. Sanger's friends. Sanger refused to give him a copy of *Family Limitation* until "Heller" convinced him that he would have it distributed among the poor. Sanger "hunted among his wife's effects, found and gave him the pamphlet," telling him not to say where he got it.[75]

Sanger was arrested, and at the trial refused to question any witnesses. "I do not deny that I gave the pamphlet," he said on the record. "I frankly admit it. Nor will Mr. Bamberger, the Comstock agent, deny he came to me under false name and obtained the pamphlet under false pretenses. I admit I broke the law, and yet I claim that, in every real sense, it is the law and not I that is on trial here today."[76] The anarchists in the audience cheered and waved their handkerchiefs in support.

Comstock followed by loudly declaring that he had been threatened with assassination if he tried Sanger for obscenity, though he did not elaborate as to who had made the threat or why. The judge was growing impatient. "Such persons as you who circulate such pamphlets are a menace to society," he shouted to Sanger. "If some of the women who are going around and advocating equal suffrage would go around and advocate women having children they would do a greater service." He sentenced Sanger to thirty days in the Tombs or a $150 fine, and noted he would personally prefer to throw Sanger to the lions.

Ironically, just four days after this triumph, Comstock died, which allowed Margaret Sanger to return to New York and convince the government to drop its obscenity charge against her. She celebrated by opening, as promised, the country's first birth control clinic at 46 Amboy Street in Brownsville, Brooklyn, in October of 1916. She printed flyers in English, Italian and Yiddish asking, "Mothers! Do you want any more children? If not, why do you have them? Do not kill, do not take life, but prevent."[77] Hundreds of women lined up as Sanger and her sister, Ethel Byrne, for a ten-cent registration fee, gave out diaphragms and showed the curious women how to use them. After ten days, police closed the clinic and arrested Sanger and Byrne, who gladly served thirty-day sentences to publicize their cause.

"NOT A NECESSARY EVIL"

Interestingly, while Sangers' style of direct confrontation on behalf of birth control was grabbing headlines, many communities had ceased to tolerate another sexual activity associated with women: prostitution. Because of the efforts of the Committee of Fourteen, by the early 1910s, there were few ordinary saloons that would serve liquor to a known prostitute, or any unaccompanied woman for that matter. The Committee proudly announced in 1916 that the vice rackets of the Tenderloin had been busted, and the "men who lived on women scattered—some of them even driven into legitimate employment."[78]

The results of the Committee of Fourteen's effort gave support to a new method of fighting vice, as science, practicality, and efficiency in dealing with the problem of prostitution took the place of the moral outrage and censorship of figures like Comstock. Beyond enforcing his eponymous law, which was obviously still useful, birth control suppression and abortion prevention were not high on the anti-vice agenda; instead, prostitution and its primary consequence—venereal disease—were the top priorities for the new wave of social reformers. This "Progressive" ideology, developed by social scientists, physicians, and educators rather than clergy, focused chiefly on social hygiene. A term that literally meant public cleanliness, this new philosophy relied on social progress rather than a sense of moral decency. "Physical hygiene, sex hygiene, and social hygiene"[79] through advances in medicine, sex education, and social welfare were now considered the keys to solving social problems, a theory that was antithetical to the views of the anti-vice crusaders.

At the same time, physicians' attitudes toward venereal diseases had evolved since the Victorian era. Back then, physicians had believed the chief cause of the two most common venereal diseases, gonorrhea and syphilis, was excessive sexual intercourse. Amusingly, Victorian doctors prescribed marriage as a sure cure; if that failed, a non-amusing solution, ingesting mercury, was thought to help. In 1905, a Progressive New York City physician named Prince Albert Morrow determined the actual rates of venereal disease among the population. Using data supplied in part by the military, he contended that "as many as eighty of every one hundred men" in the city had had gonorrhea at some point in their adult lives, and 5 to 18 percent had had syphilitic infections,[80] which led to an estimated 10 percent infecting their wives.[81] Most of those men were thought to have contracted venereal disease from prostitutes. To the Progressives, the prevalence of venereal disease was evidence of the sure collapse of Victorian-style morality: an estimated 75 to 90 percent of prostitutes had infections, according to surveys.[82] Morrow coined the term "social disease" to describe venereal disease because it was largely spread through the social evil, prostitution.

The ideology of the social hygiene theory helped form a proper movement in response to the Page Law of 1910, a New York State law that required venereal disease testing of all prostitutes picked up for solicitation and, if found infected, incarceration until they were deemed non-contagious. Supporters insisted that prostitutes were entitled to medical care like anyone else, and that the law didn't change the fact that prostitution was illegal. A loud chorus of opponents, including feminists and members of social hygiene organizations like Prince Albert Morrow's newly-founded American Society for Sanitary and Moral Prophylaxis (ASSMP), argued that the law amounted to state-sponsored prostitution, in the French fashion. Feminists in particular were incensed that the law punished only women; there was no corresponding law requiring testing of male customers. Underlying that view was the fear of hundreds of newly-healthy prostitutes being returned to the streets after the enforced quarantine. In fact, some considered the popular assumption that prostitutes carried venereal diseases a deterrent to the johns who were thinking of soliciting them. In that way, venereal disease actually acted as a prophylactic against public immorality.[83] However, Morrow declared, "The fatal defect of every sanitary scheme to control disease has been that the masculine spreader of contagion has been entirely ignored as mythical or practically nonexistent; the woman has been regarded as not only the chief offender against morality but the responsible cause of disease."[84]

The Page Law controversy brought the medical reformers and the anti-vice crusaders together for the first time in a common front. Two prominent groups, the American Vigilance Association and the American Federation for Sex Hygiene, formed the American Social Hygiene Association (ASHA) in 1913. The merger was engineered by John D. Rockefeller Jr. in hopes of adding businesslike efficiency and corporate legitimacy to the social hygiene movement. Rockefeller appointed Charles W. Eliot, formerly of Harvard, as president; daily operations were managed by James Bronson Reynolds, a New York anti-vice attorney, and William F. Snow, a well-known physician. Rockefeller provided $5,000 per year for the group between 1913 and 1916, and $10,000 from 1916 to 1918.[85]

Rockefeller also proposed a permanent organization to develop public policy in line with the social hygiene movement's objectives. With millionaire banker Paul Warburg and powerful lawyer Starr Murphy, he created the Bureau of Social Hygiene in 1911, with headquarters at 61 Broadway. More than any other New York group, the Bureau was instrumental in shifting the tone of anti-vice efforts from exclusively moral, à la Comstock, toward practical reform based on medical research and environmental factors that contributed to the spread of venereal disease.

To support its theories, the Bureau produced the first major study from a social hygiene perspective, George J. Kneeland's *Commercialized Prostitution in New York City*, and three follow-up reports in 1915, 1916 and 1917. Despite the Committee of Fourteen's success in closing the vast majority of Raines Law hotels by 1912, there were still numerous other venues for prostitution. The Bureau of Social Hygiene investigated a total of 1,831 "vice resorts" in Manhattan that year, categorized into tenement apartments (1,172), massage parlors (300), parlor houses (142), furnished room hotels

(112) and hotels (105).[86] The huge immigrant populations in New York City posed a conundrum for the social hygiene movement, as overcrowding in the tenement blocks where most immigrants lived was thought to foster both physical and moral perversion.

By 1917, the Bureau reported a vast decrease in all types of "vice resorts" due to "new standards in safeguarding public health, in establishing public decency, and in protecting public morals."[87] The cheap parlor house "may at this date be considered extinct in Manhattan," the Bureau concluded, and while tenement houses were much more numerous than any other type of resort, they reported that 417 out of 518 had been put out of business over the previous year. There were only eleven massage parlors left, and those were no longer falsely advertising their services. One Bureau investigator in Harlem asked a cabbie to take him to a neighborhood street plied by prostitutes. The cabbie replied, "There's nothing doing…if you take a chance with anybody, it's a fifty to one shot you'll get three years for your trouble."[88]

Not surprisingly, the pimps and proprietors of the disorderly houses vanished along with their businesses. Reported the Bureau, "one prominent member of the former 'vice trust,' who, shaking his head very earnestly, said in May of [1917], 'I'm afraid things are today and will be forever this way, as far as New York is concerned. The people are educated. There was a time when they used to say, New York can't get along without blood money. That's poppy-cock; look at New York today. New York is done!'"[89]

2.

MODERN MADNESS

1919-1929

By 1919, social reformers had destroyed the apparatus that had enabled commercialized prostitution to prosper, while a network of home-grown watchdog groups, from the YMCA to the American Social Hygiene Association, had been established to ensure that commercialized vice never again had the institutional support of politicians and police. At the same time, Progressives encouraged an attitude of moral rigor and maintenance of physical health that was adopted by the city's leaders. These developments led many to believe that New York was now virtually free of vice. However, three events would crush this hard-won order and shape the coming decade.

The first, the passage of the 14th Amendment to the U.S. Constitution, gave women long-sought suffrage and added the potential power of nearly thirty million women over the age of twenty-one[1] to the political realm (nearly two million in New York City alone[2]). Secondly, the almost simultaneous ratification of the 18th Amendment—popularly known as Prohibition—outlawed the sale of intoxicating liquors, which had been a goal of the social reform movement since the Committee of Fourteen assailed the Raines Law hotels in 1905. Third, and most importantly, the Great War ended in Europe, altering forever the outlook of the young people who came of age in the 1920s. "A whole generation had been infected by the eat-drink-and-be-merry-for-tomorrow-we-die spirit...their torn nerves craved the anodynes of speed, excitement, and passion," wrote Frederick Lewis Allen in his memoir *Only Yesterday: An Informal History of the 1920's.* "They found themselves expected to settle down into the humdrum routine of American Life as if nothing had happened, to accept the moral dicta of elders who seemed to them still to be living in a Pollyanna land of rosy ideals which the war has killed for them."[3]

MODERN TIMES

The achievement of women's suffrage capped the feminists' long struggle for equality. Even if, as some suffragists complained, women didn't immediately know how to wield their newfound clout, they were nevertheless provided with a sense of self-determination and social esteem that coincided with the efforts of many industries to lighten their domestic burdens. Newly-invented household appliances like electric washing machines and irons lessened the grind of housekeeping, canned foods and delicatessens cut down on meal preparation, and mass-produced clothing in department stores freed women from hours of sewing. In addition, the young New York woman often chose to acquire a job, which gave her a source of income independent from her husband's and a place in society when she might have previously been consumed with domestic chores in the isolation of her home.

These developments made female sexual emancipation possible. Now out in the world, women were exposed to the theories of Freud then sweeping the popular newsstand—that sex was the guiding force of all human action, the libido dictated one's motivations unconsciously, and that mental stability rested on the indulgence of one's sexual desires. Psychoanalysis lent an air of sophistication to a woman's life. Freud's theories were distilled by a flurry of sex magazines and publications devoted to movie stars. Predating the pulp novels of the 1950's and 1960's, the rags of the postwar years titillated readers with shockingly-true tales of moral missteps: *Indolent Kisses, The Confessions of a Chorus Girl,* etc.[4]

Perhaps the magazines weren't what the feminists had desired as the fruits of their labor, but the effects of another woman-led movement made racy novelettes seem like child's play. While suffrage had been achieved by liberal women's radical vision of gender equality, the ratification of the 18th

Amendment represented a victory for the conservative women-led temperance lobby, the last stragglers of the social reform movement of decades past.

As the Committee of Fourteen's smashing of the Raines Law hotels showed, alcohol had long been considered the catalyst for the breakdown of the family, poverty, violent crime and an absence of religious virtue. The Anti-Saloon League (still kicking after a quarter-century) and the Women's Christian Temperance Union repositioned the social hygiene argument to push for passage of the Volstead Act, which would enforce the 18th Amendment's ban on consumption or manufacture of alcohol. World War I had given the "drys" the ideal platform for the abolition of liquor: they appealed to Americans' patriotism by urging them to conserve grain; exploited public opinion against Germany, and tacitly, its beer; and encouraged a belt-tightening ethic to help America win the war.[5] Thus tied to the war effort, the Volstead Act passed after less than two days' debate in Congress. After ratification by the states in October 1919, the resulting enforcement of the 18th Amendment to the U.S. Constitution prohibited "manufacture, sale, or transportation of intoxicating liquors."[6] It appeared that the morality police had finally won.

In New York City's restaurants, guests staged memorial services for their beloved booze. "A large congregation joined…in the exhibition of sorrow. Black was the prevailing color—clothes, table cloths, even the walls, while the casket was filled with black bottles."[7] At a party at Healy's Restaurant at Broadway and 95th Street, mourning celebrants took home miniature caskets as souvenirs. The *New York Times* opined, "Here and there enterprising restaurateurs capitalized the demise of John Barleycorn with wet funeral ceremonies, but the spontaneous orgies of drink that were predicted failed in large part to occur on schedule."[8]

It was predicted that the banning of liquor would cause widespread economic havoc: thousands of brewers and bottlers would be shut down, saloons and dance halls would lose business, and innumerable stores of liquor in warehouses would have to be destroyed. In Brooklyn alone, which had two thousand liquor licenses the previous year, "75 percent of the liquor men…would immediately go out of business," lamented the *Times*.[9] Restaurateurs, who made most of their profits from the sale of alcoholic drinks, knew that even the choicest sirloin wouldn't keep customers at the tables like a crisp martini. A manager named Joe at the Black Cat restaurant, a mainstay of the radical Greenwich Village set before the war, cynically stated the obvious. "Look at this place. Bare walls, a few lanterns, an iron stove. Do you think people will come here to see that…you take the drink away from them and they don't come."[10] Morosely, he sighed, adding, "all the places in Greenwich Village will close up. There won't be any Greenwich Village."

Joe's fears proved largely unfounded, however, as Prohibition was generally ignored in New York City, and plenty of bootlegged whiskey and gin would flow through Manhattan's fifteen thousand speakeasies over the next decade. Eventually, Prohibition came to shape New York society. Everywhere, one might see "hip flasks uptilted above faces both masculine and feminine…the speakeasy, equipped with a regular old-fashioned bar, serving cocktails made of gin turned out, perhaps, by a gang of Sicilian alky-cookers (seventy-five cents for patrons, free to the police), [and] well-born damsels with one foot on the brass rail, tossing off Martinis." Of course, drinks were expensive and of highly questionable quality when made of bathtub gin, demon rum, hooch, or "smoke" in 1920's parlance.

Social hygiene advocates were thrilled with Prohibition during its first year of enforcement. As an example of its success, a Chelsea intersection that previously hosted a bar on each of the four corners now had "three coffee houses, each known as 'The Coffee Pot'."[11] However, the social reform crowd was battling a generation whose mentality was far removed from that of their parents. The modern horror of World War I had obliterated the lingering Victorian social structure in New York once and for all. Soldiers and those on the home front disdained Victorian ideals of gender, sexuality, and social mores. The men and women of the "lost generation" rejected the conventions of their parents and questioned every established rule and emotion as never before. They found American culture limited compared to that of Europe, and emulated the continental attitude toward socializing and, especially, sex.

The war had also brought the threats of venereal disease to public discussion, and with that came startlingly frank explanations of human sexuality that had previously been fit only for medical journals. Young men and women of marriageable age transgressed old gender roles in public in ways that were unthinkable only five or ten years previously. (Going to saloons, for instance, had been the privilege solely of men and prostitutes before the war.) Sexual roles and marriage evolved from a more-or-less economic transaction to a partnership in which women demanded sexual equality and satisfaction and men strived to please their wives' wishes. Social and sexual taboos seemed outdated to young people accustomed to a damned-if-you-do, damned-if-you-don't outlook. These attitudes resulted in greater sexual knowledge, equalization of men and women in the social sphere, racial mixing, and breaking of sexual taboos such as homosexuality. New York City was the epicenter of the rebellious spirit of the "Roaring Twenties," with its extremes of political sentiment and social hedonism, sex, drugs, jazz, fads, crazes, and turn-ons.

'NEW IDEALS OF SEX'

During World War I, the military had conducted mandatory American Social Hygiene Association lectures, where soldiers were told that gonorrhea and syphilis (and the prostitutes that carried them) were greater dangers than any submarine attack or cloud of mustard gas. Each recruit also received an American Social Hygiene Association pamphlet entitled *Keeping Fit to Fight*. "Every prostitute (whore) has [venereal diseases] sooner or later, because she catches them from some of the hundreds of men she sells herself to," the booklet warned. "Most professional prostitutes (about 90%) have one or both diseases all the time...Women who solicit soldiers for immoral purposes are usually disease spreaders and friends of the enemy."[12]

The effect of the educational campaign was, for the most part, the opposite of what the government intended. Instead of being warned away from soliciting sex, soldiers got an earful of helpful advice about where to find prostitutes, what they might do with them, how much they charged, and what to do if you did picked up the clap or syphilis. The military's VD campaign's unintended accomplishment was an increase in frank sexual information for the civilian population.

Young women, having been taught that babies were miraculously manifested by cabbages and that sitting too close to ones' suitor would result in pregnancy, were profoundly affected by the more open sexual atmosphere. Instead of getting their information from military lectures, they consulted the popular marriage manuals and sex-advice pamphlets that were circulating throughout society. The 1918 manual *Married Love: a New Contribution to the Solution of Sex Difficulties*, which advocated sexual equality within marriage, sold hundreds of thousands of copies before being banned in the United States. Its author, suffragist Marie Stopes, argued for women's sexual and personal autonomy: "A woman's nature is set to rhythms over which man has no more control than he has over the tides of the sea,"she wrote.[13]

Margaret Sanger, ever the radical, took the sentiment even further in her 1920 treatise *Woman and the New Race*. "The need for women's lives in not repression, but the greatest possible expression and fulfillment of their desires upon the highest plane possible. They cannot reach higher planes through ignorance and compulsion. They can attain them only through knowledge and the cultivation of a higher, happier attitude toward sex. Sex life must be stripped of its fear...Out of our increasing sex knowledge we shall evolve new ideals of sex."[14]

Taking the conservative angle, New York City socialite Emily Post published *Etiquette* in 1922. Amidst advice about letter-writing, funerals and "the country house and its hospitality," Post attempted to put a socially-respectable polish on the new familiarity of men and women. "In nothing does the present time more greatly differ from the close of the last century, than in the unreserved frankness of young women and men towards each other," she admitted. "Those who speak of the domination of sex in this day are either too young to remember, or else have not stopped to consider, that mystery played a far greater and more dangerous role when sex, like a woman's ankle, was carefully hidden from view, and therefore far more alluring than to-day when both are commonplace matters."[15]

By 1922, ankles and much more were no longer hidden. In Greenwich Village, the "long-haired radical men and short-haired radical women"[16] adopted feminist theories of sexual equality in every sphere, from the home to politics to intellectual pursuits; influenced by Freud and the sexologist Havelock Ellis, they believed equality facilitated an atmosphere of indulgence to both male and female desires. Feminists of the Village—Margaret Anderson and her partner Jane Heap, publishers of the *Little Review;* journalist Louise Bryant, avant-garde artist Elsa von Freytag-Loringhoven, even relatively staid Margaret Sanger—were recognized as the vanguard of sexual modernity: intelligent, vocal, unhampered by social and sexual convention.

Free love was advocated as an antidote to the bourgeois confines of matrimony, and it was aided and abetted by access to birth control, premarital sex, and the acceptance of women taking lovers to whom they weren't married.[17] It was also dependent on the honesty of men and women to one other, a minor value in the marriages of previous generations but essential to the contemporary Socialists and anarchist intellectuals like John Reed, Mabel Dodge, Eugene O'Neill, Emma Goldman, Ben Reitman, Louise Bryant, Elizabeth Gurley Flynn, Carlo Tresca, Hutchins Hapgood and Neith Boyce who traded partners with one or more of their comrades. Such alliances were formed on sexual desire as much as intellectual admiration and political belief.

However, despite its supposed radicalism, as early as 1919, the free love movement of the Village was lampooned as quite chic to support, even if one was not actually interested in pursuing it. "It's very, very unfashionable to be the least bit conservative these days, and very, very fashionable to be radical!" claimed an article in the *New York Times* magazine. As the twenties wore on, free love became less a radical stance against the bourgeoisie and more the typical M.O. of the young.

THE CULT OF YOUTH

The bohemians' sexual-equality philosophy was adopted by the masses in the mid-1920's, lessening the social and cultural barrier between genders. "She does what she likes, whatever he thinks about it. In her vanity bag there is every virtue except obedience," sniffed a contemporary essay. "And for the first time in the history of her sex therefore, a woman is all that she wants to be, except a man. And sometimes she is almost that."[18]

The equanimity of socializing was matched by a relaxation in the standards of dress for both sexes, but most daringly for young women under thirty—the flappers—who set the style standard for the decade. Nearly every aspect of clothing was a repudiation of the conservative dress of the war years. Dancing the Charleston, the Black Bottom and the Lindy hop in jazz clubs, a flappers' main preoccupation, was impossible in the ankle-length skirts and corsets of the previous generation. Hem lines shot up accordingly. In 1923, the distance of a skirt's hem from the floor was about 10 percent of a woman's height—roughly six or seven inches. In 1924, the distance jumped to 20 percent (fourteen inches); in 1925, 25 percent (about seventeen inches). From 1927 to 1929, hems stayed resolutely just above the knee.[19]

Dancing was also the catalyst for doing away with the corset once and for all. A boyish figure, with a flattened chest and undefined waist, was now the ideal; a similarly boyish hairstyle was *de rigueur*. Bobbed hair became the universal symbol of the "new woman," no longer exclusive to the radical set of the Village. "For a brief period the hair was not only bobbed, but in most cases cropped close to the head like a man's," reported Frederick Lewis Allen in *Only Yesterday*. And no ensemble was complete without a flask and cigarette.

Cosmetics and beauty products exploded in the 1920's, as wearing makeup was the signature of women who ridiculed the naked faces of their mothers' generation. "Women who in 1920 would have thought the use of paint immoral were soon applying it regularly as a matter of course and making no effort to disguise the fact."[20] Black kohl was used to create a smoky halo around the eyes to imitate popular cinematic sex symbols like Pola Negri, Louise Brooks and Clara Bow. Dark red lipstick was applied in a heart shape called the "Clara Bow." Flappers used rouge to give their cheeks a teenager's glow. "That we have abandoned the theory of our grandmothers is obvious…[a proper woman] was so sure of herself and of him too that she did not need to depend on powder and lipstick. It was her complexion and only her complexion that was visible. But today the complexion is all that you cannot see."[21]

The cumulative effect of the short skirts, cropped hair and dramatic makeup was that of youth, even pre-adolescence, simultaneously alluringly sexy and tomboyish. Women affecting the flapper look emulated boyish silhouettes and boyish behavior; rather than daintily stepping out for tea with their suitors, they were in the bar, knocking back gin in mixed company. After Prohibition, both sexes had something to rebel against equally. "A spirit of deliberate revolt…in many communities made drinking 'the thing to do,'" wrote Frederick Lewis Allen. In addition to the ubiquitous hip flask, cocktail parties and private events with alcohol resulted in "the general transformation of drinking from a masculine prerogative to one shared by both sexes together.…They wanted to be—or thought men wanted them to be—casual and light-hearted companions; not broad-hipped mothers of the race, but irresponsible playmates."[22]

In this respect, the flapper could not have been further culturally removed from her feminine predecessors—the suffragists, the anti-saloon campaigners, the moral reformers—who relied on conservative dress, comportment and morals for social acceptance. The post-war woman was not the epitome of "fruitful maturity or ripened wisdom or practiced grace. On the contrary: the quest for slenderness, the flattening of the breasts, the vogue of short skirts (even when short skirts still suggested the appearance of a little girl), the juvenile effect of the long waist—all were signs that, consciously or unconsciously, the women of this decade worshiped not merely youth but unripened youth."[23]

"GAY AND DELIGHTFUL"

As gender roles broke down both in the home and in public, racial barriers too began to blur. White youth's fascination with black culture and jazz prompted nightly excursions up to Harlem, where the anything-goes attitude toward sex and nightlife went far beyond that of the Village. "Harlem is the one place that is gay and delightful however dull and depressing the downtown regions may be," wrote the novelist Max Ewing.[24] During the war, blacks from the agricultural south had migrated to New York for plentiful and lucrative work, settling in Harlem. Black intellectuals W.E.B. Du Bois, Marcus Garvey, and Alain Locke; writers Langston Hughes, Zora Neale Hurston, Countee Cullen, Claude McKay, Richard Bruce Nugent, and Richard Wright; as well as actor Paul Robeson all moved to Harlem in the early 1920's, creating a dynamic crucible of music, poetry, plays and politics. Harlem became, in the popular imagination, "the Negro Capital of the World."[25]

As night fell in Harlem, the neighborhood became a whirl of lights, jazz, and abandoned rules. White flappers and sports out for a night on the town may have thought themselves terribly outré for having dinner and applauding a scantily-clad chorus line at one of the neighborhood's legendary nightspots, but in reality, most slummers only signed up for the tour of Jungle Alley, the famous strip of whites-only nightclubs on 133rd Street between Lenox and Seventh Avenues. Black performers at the Cotton Club, Connie's Inn and Small's Paradise, in turn, knew what the white audiences expected to see as a representation of Harlem's anything-goes spirit.

The Cotton Club—even the name evoked the Jim Crow South— opened in 1923 and featured Harlem's finest musicians, Charleston dancers, and a chorus line for the middle-class audiences. Cab Calloway praised the virtues of the light-skinned girls in the club's signature tune, *She's Tall, She's Tan, and She's Terrific*;[26] and Duke Ellington and singers Ethel Waters and Adelaide Hall also graced the stage. The interior resembled a white New Yorker's fantasy of the old South accented with artificial jungle trees; diners could order soul food as well as more genteel menu items.[27] White customers could observe the socially daring mix of races in the same building, yet be assured that every black person in the club was a bartender, hostess, or musician, there to serve them. Despite their supposed radicalism, most whites still condescendingly saw blacks as the primitive other—sexually uninhibited, culturally transgressive— in short, the antidote to middle-class WASP values. To white bohemians, Harlem represented an oasis of sexual freedom and erotic abandon, but this self-conscious rebellion only amounted to a sort of sexual colonialism.

This contrasted with the side of Harlem that whites rarely experienced: the working-class speakeasies and house parties, often gleefully raunchy, in which blacks could socialize freely. At one point in the mid-1920's, law enforcement officials estimated that there were ten speakeasies to the block in Harlem. Working class blacks made up the bulk of the crowds, as jazz trios played in the dank and narrow subterranean spaces, prodded by the revelers, who packed in so tightly that hardly anyone could dance in the ankle-deep pools of alcohol. *The Saturday Evening Post*, of all publications, recognized the egalitarian atmosphere of the speakeasies. "Here, in low-ceilinged stifling basements, in lofts, in former stables, ex-gambling dens and sumptuous damask-draped dance ateliers, bootlegging kings, gamblers, the nouveau riche, the restless, the lonely, the neurotic rub shoulders with members of the sporting and criminal fraternity and joggle one another in the dance," it reported. "The scene, with its cheap, sensational decorations, the crashing band, the vulgar dancing, the stifling air compounded of alcoholic emanations, cheap perfumes and stale tobacco smoke and the thinly veiled sensuality which underlies it all, grips one by the throat."[28]

To raise rent money, enterprising promoters in Harlem threw private parties in their own apartments, turning their residences into speakeasies for the night. Partygoers heard about the events from handbills passed out on the street, and each person paid an admission fee ranging from ten to fifty cents for all the bootleg hooch one could drink. Card games, Charleston contests and a revolving line-up of the neighborhood jazz players made up the entertainment.[29]

The buffet flat, another African-American contribution to New York nightlife in the 1920's, was a semi-permanent after-hours club in a private apartment that offered sexual pleasures "cafeteria-style."[30] Viewers and participants chose what they liked and dove in. "They had a faggot there that was so great people used to come there just to watch him make love to another man," remembered Ruby Smith, blues diva Bessie Smith's niece.[31] Hazel Valentine, an entrepreneur who ran a buffet flat on 140th Street, featured audacious acts by an overweight drag queen with the enigmatic name of Clarenz.[32]

Harlem's most famous socialite and hostess was A'Lelia Walker, the richest black woman in America. Her mother had built a beauty empire made up of products to "de-kink" African-American hair and powders to lighten complexions; perhaps her immense pride in her race stemmed from that ironic source. Walker was the quintessential "jazz baby," who spent her millions on parties, drinks and music. She loved to highlight her transgression into the ruling class—at one soiree, she allegedly served her African-American guests a sumptuous meal with champagne while giving her white guests bathtub gin and chicken wings.[33]

Among the rent parties and speakeasies existed a community of sexually-ambiguous writers and entertainers. Comparatively few Villagers—poet Hart Crane, novelist Djuna Barnes and critic/Harlem booster Carl Van Vechten (who was married)—were openly gay, and the bohemians' occasional same-sex dalliances were considered par for the course in their nonjudgmental, free-love philosophy. Conversely, many of Harlem's writers and thinkers were gay, including Langston Hughes, Countee Cullen, Wallace Thurman, Claude McKay, and Alain Locke. They were, however, less focused on enacting a radical sexual ideology than promoting racial equality and pride. Recalled writer Richard Bruce Nugent, "I have never been in what they call 'the closet.' It has *never* occurred to me that it was anything to be ashamed of, and it never occurred to me that it was anybody's business but mine."[34]

The writers and poets were somewhat protected from public criticism by virtue of their "artistic" (a contemporary euphemism for gay) pursuits—but it was in the raunchy, wistful blues clubs in which gay identity found its powerful voice in the 1920's. Songs of protest and bewilderment at the changing times, the blues used literate lyrics to reveal the unadorned realities of black life, based on a simple one-four-five chord progression. Singers exposed their disenchantment with the misfortunes of modern life, with which young white audiences immediately identified; blacks, however, bemoaned the empty promises of the post-war North.[35]

The blues divas cultivated an environment of sexual ambiguity in Harlem's night world. Whether in risqué lyrics, often personalized from the original words; in costume; or by their residencies at Harlem clubs, the popular entertainers' knowing acceptance of homosexuality created a space for spectators to acknowledge their own sexual identity. Bucking sexual convention was also an extension of young people's desire to cast off the principles of their parents' generation, dovetailing with the blues' message of disillusionment.

Some performers were actually gay, while others played up their bisexual inclination to augment their public image. Singers Ethel Waters and Alberta Hunter specialized in jazz and popular songs and rose from Harlem clubs to careers on Broadway, necessitating a certain level of sexual discretion. On the other hand, Ma Rainey, Bessie Smith, and Gladys Bentley preferred the unvarnished environs of the smoky, boozy clubs and speakeasies to illustrate their hard-luck lyrics and knowing double-entendres. The latter three developed sexually-nonconformist personae and replaced traditional blues lyrics with personal tales tailored to the knowing audience.

Ma Rainey was apparently coy about her bisexuality off-stage, yet on-stage sang gay lyrics that left nothing to interpretation. Born in Columbus, Georgia in 1886, her real name was Gertrude Pridgett; she wisely changed it when she married Will "Pa" Rainey in 1902. The Raineys traveled the South headlining minstrel tours for twenty years until the blues of the region finally caught on in the nightclubs of the North. Ma Rainey mentored other female performers, such as Bessie Smith; carved her own way in the newly-formed recording industry; and claimed affinity with bulldaggers (contemporary slang for masculine lesbians). One wonders if the Rainey marriage was simply a professional partnership, since her relationships with women were well-known, and Bessie Smith even bailed her out of prison when she was arrested during a lesbian orgy in 1925. Rainey's signature song, one of a hundred that she recorded in the 1920's, was *Prove It On Me Blues*—an unusually candid monologue about preferring women to men. She admitted she "went out last night with a crowd of my friends/they must have been women, 'cause I don't like no men/wear my clothes just like a fan/talk to gals just like any old man." She knows she's crossing a social boundary, and she's proud of it. But she dares anyone to chastise her for crossing that line: "they say I do it, ain't nobody caught me/they sure got to prove it on me."[36]

Bessie Smith was less candid in her lyrics but consistently lived up to her reputation as an ardent lover of booze and women, in that order. She joined Ma Rainey's traveling show when it passed through her hometown of Memphis when she was just a teenager, and followed Rainey up to Harlem, where she found acclaim in the clubs. The most successful blues singer and recording artist of the 1920's, her triumphant artistry was marred by a volatile personality, her hot temper frequently triggered by drinking. In 1926, she and one of her chorus girls, Lillian Simpson, became lovers, to the chagrin of Bessie's husband Jack. Vicious knock-down drag-outs ensued. However, Smith never recanted her earthy, independent and iconoclastic mien: one of her most telling songs was titled *T'aint Nobody's Bizness if I Do*.

Though never attaining the financial success of Ma Rainey or Bessie Smith, the extraordinarily dexterous pianist and singer Gladys Bentley was the only blues diva of the era to tailor her shows almost exclusively to a gay audience, and she was the only performer who never hid her sexual orientation behind the conventional mask of heterosexual marriage. Instantly recognizable in her stage costume of white tux and top hat, Bentley made it up to New York from Philadelphia in 1923 at the age of sixteen and honed her chops in Harlem's rent parties, eventually being offered a headlining slot at Harry Hansbery's Clam House, a smoky gay speakeasy in Jungle Alley. Instead of merely exploiting bisexual chic like her peers, Bentley reveled in lesbian double-entendres, obscene parodies of blues standards and high butch style onstage and off. She was notorious enough to elicit a mixed white and black audience (including Carl Van Vechten, her ubiquitous champion) and to merit numerous items in the Harlem gossip columns. Though few of her recordings contain the risqué gay lyrics for which she was famous, she evidently had a powerful effect on her audiences—Eslanda Robeson, the wife of actor and singer Paul Robeson, claimed she'd "never be the same" after seeing a performance.[37]

END OF THE PARTY

If any time in the twentieth century cried out for a tempering influence, it was the 1920's. However, for most of the decade, the forces that had once constituted the front against vice were conspicuously absent. There were several reasons for this. First, there was no powerful, Parkhurst-like figurehead to lead the movement from the pulpit. Secondly, no anti-vice institution came forward to fill the postwar vacuum left by the Anti-Saloon League and the American Social Hygiene Association. And, most importantly, there was no desire on the part of the government—i.e. the police or the mayor—to enforce Prohibition. As a matter of fact, as Parkhurst had earlier deduced, vice could not have been so widespread without the collusion of the police and city officials.

In early 1924, in response to a scandal involving twelve police officers who were "on the payroll of the proprietors of certain 'speak-easies' in Harlem,"[38] Police Commissioner Richard E. Enright appointed Deputy Chief Inspector Samuel G. Belton as head of the Special Service Division, the squad charged with keeping a lid on illegal activity associated with Prohibition. To his dismay, however, Belton quickly discovered that a tangle of restrictions and the unwillingness of the public to obey the unpopular dry laws prevented him doing much to stem the rising tide of illegal speakeasies. As an example, uniformed officers were not allowed to enter speakeasies where they suspected liquor was being sold; instead, they had to notify supervisors of their suspicions. While Belton's men visited more than four thousand speakeasies and made 17,226 arrests on various vice and dry law offenses in 1924, the officers' ability to collect evidence was nearly impossible, as they were not allowed to enter establishments without their commanders. In the end, evidence was obtained on less than half of the speakeasies, resulting in their closure. In addition, Belton had appealed to the Feds to close 12,551 places for Volstead violations, but only 275 were eventually shut down.[39]

Belton's chief problem was that judges wouldn't grant warrants to search suspected speakeasies unless the police produced concrete evidence of violations. But without warrants, obtaining the necessary evidence was extremely difficult. Belton was also discouraged by the speakeasies' ingenious plans to stay one step ahead of the police. He complained of owners dumping flasks of liquor in vats of water when police hustled into the room. "In many of these cases, the plainclothes men previously had obtained search warrants on evidence of violations which they had succeeded in getting," reported the *New York Times*, "but they were unable to make concrete cases in the Federal Courts because of their failure to produce the liquor."[40] Even the least sophisticated speakeasy had some kind of bell system set up to warn patrons.

The situation worsened when James "Jimmie" Walker took office as mayor in January 1926. Walker was a Tammany man who had a proven track record in the State Senate of sponsoring bills for causes such as permitting baseball, boxing matches and movies on Sundays.[41] His many pals in show business and his laissez-faire lifestyle made him the perfect symbol of the times, but poorly prepared him for the job of mayor, which didn't seem to bother him one bit. Instead of capitulating to pressure from the morality police, he dismissed do-gooder efforts to rid newsstands on 42nd Street of salacious film magazines, reportedly quipping, "I never knew a woman who was hurt by a magazine."[42] Walker, who was married, spent his quality time with a soubrette named Betty Compton, eventually leaving his wife for her. His fondness for New York's nightlife was legendary.

With Walker in office, the NYPD's motivation for cracking down on nightlife evaporated; there was no reform administration breathing down their necks and public opinion was with the bootleggers. But like a Phoenix rising from the ashes, the Committee of Fourteen finally mustered their forces and launched a return volley.

Though the group had drifted without a clear motive since ridding the city of Raines Law hotels, the flagrant violations of Prohibition and the police's blatant disregard for order gave it new life. In a time honored tradition, the Committee dispatched its own vice inspectors into the Harlem speakeasies, and its findings were shocking (to some). The Committee's annual reports for 1926, 1927 and 1928 professed alarm at the explosion of commercialized prostitution enabled by speakeasies and dance halls. Reminiscent of the pre-war white slave panic, the reports revealed a widespread "traffic in hostesses,"[43] run by amateur kidnappers and coercive pimps who drew feeble-minded girls into their web of gin and jazz. The reports also belied fears over the disappearing hegemonies of race and class in New York, stating that Harlem's speakeasies "are attracting young men and young women of a class who never would have visited the old-time Raines Law hotel."[44] The Committee seemed especially concerned with the exploitation, as well as the fraternizing, of girls in Harlem, noting that whites appear to flock to Harlem's nightspots not out of generous spirit but "morbid curiosity."[45]

The Committee also noted a 32 percent increase in the number of "delinquent" women appearing in court in 1926 as compared to 1925, and a

51 percent increase in cases involving wayward minors, most originating in Harlem's dens of iniquity. "It is common knowledge that Volstead law has been responsible for the springing into existence in the City of New York of numerous so-called night clubs and speak-easies. Prostitution has been quick to take advantage of these new conditions by using such places as rendezvous, and we again have the old and vicious connection of prostitution and alcohol."[46] The *New York Times* lamented that nightclubs and speakeasies had "developed a situation which is worse that those existing under the old Raines Law," which had, of course, been the Committee of Fourteen's original *raison d'etre*.

The Committee also revealed another insidious method of female entrapment, the "hostess problem," decrying the employment of young, attractive women in order to "increase[e] the sales of liquor, food and other drinks; incidentally she is to provide aesthetic, social and sexual entertainment for the men customers."[47] To the Committee, any form of female employment that was based on sex appeal was immoral, even if the woman performed no illegal acts—one might assume the Committee believed employment for women was itself dangerous and likely to lead women into vice.

Of the 157 liquor dens the Committee infiltrated in 1927, it associated 132 of them with some form of prostitution or hostess rustling, and of 441 women seen in said dens, 66 percent were of that vocation. An editorial in the *Times* agreed that the commercialized vice of the late 1920s was a "more serious social menace than in the old days of the Raines Law hotel."[48] The speakeasy had, for better or worse, established itself as a social institution in the city. Though the total number of speakeasies in New York was impossible to know, considering their ephemeral nature, Police Commissioner Grover Whalen estimated that by 1929 there were 32,000 speaks in the city—after nearly nine years of Prohibition enforcement. "Nowadays, all you need is two bottles and a room and you have a speakeasy," he noted.[49] However, only two hundred police officers were dedicated to fighting Prohibition crimes, which provided a ratio of one cop for 160 bars, saloons, dancehalls, nightclubs and back-alley stills. It was thus physically impossible for the vice squad to monitor an underworld that employed ingenious schemes to evade the law, creating the ideal environment for the thriving trade in hostesses, dime-a-dance girls and booze.

The Committee's last report on the hostess racket in Harlem was published on October 14, 1929, confirming what police already knew: that "night clubs and speakeasies now furnish an overwhelming majority of [commercialized prostitution] with Harlem as the head and front of this type of offending."[50] The Committee's inspectors were again sent in with the purpose of collecting evidence of prostitution and other forms of vice, and the results were as expected. "Only 9 percent of the total number of investigations by the committee's staff was made in night clubs and speakeasies, [but] that small number yielded 78 percent of all the prostitution violations."[51]

While the Committee of Fourteen was busy conducting its investigations, the party was beginning to wind down in Harlem. The hard-living necessary for blues authenticity had exacted a heavy toll on singers like Ma Rainey and Bessie Smith. After a declining career during the Depression and a mutually abusive marriage, Smith was killed in a car accident in Mississippi in 1937 at the age of forty-three. Ma Rainey, after retiring from showbiz in 1935, died of heart disease in 1939. Only Gladys Bentley enjoyed a long career in Harlem's clubs, including several years headlining the Clam House and the Ubangi Club, another popular speakeasy. In the late 1930s she moved to the West Coast and, fearful of McCarthyism, totally renounced her lesbian identity in a 1952 article in *Ebony* titled *I Am Woman Again!* where she claimed to have married a man and become a devout Christian. Most telling of her transformation was an appearance on the TV show *You Bet Your Life* with Groucho Marx in the mid-1950's, where she wore a silk evening gown and large button earrings.

At the same time that the sexual ambiguity of the female blues performers—so central to Harlem's exhilarating atmosphere—was going out of style, an organized anti-vice front was finally being organized from the pulpit, led by the Reverend Dr. Adam Clayton Powell, the esteemed leader of Harlem's Abyssinian Baptist Church on 138th Street. Powell addressed the vice surrounding his church in a sermon called "Lifting Up the Standard of the People," delivered on November 3, 1929. Though meant to encourage

African-Americans to look beyond the lure of sex and immorality as a matter of racial pride, the sermon was memorable for its exposé of what Powell termed "sex-perversion" (i.e. homosexuality) among some black preachers in Harlem.

Powell had built his career on preaching self-sufficiency, education and civil rights; unlike Parkhurst and Comstock, vice and moral filth were not his obsessions, which made his "attack on vice in high places,"[52] all the more unusual. In his autobiography *Against the Tide*, Powell offered a rejoinder of sorts. The sermon "was not even against natural sins among men and women, but abnormal sins…Why did I preach against homosexuality and all manner of sex perversions? Because, as every informed person knows, these sins are on the increase and are threatening to eat the vitals out of America."[53]

Among blacks in Harlem, the presence of homosexuality was a blow to the quest for respectability. Deviance from the middle-class ideal was a direct threat to blacks' pursuit of whites' appreciation, and the putting down of such deviance was admired by white boosters. George Foster Peabody, the philanthropist and white benefactor of African-American institutions, wrote, "I was much pleased to observe the straightout talk which Dr. Powell gave with such force and emphasis, and such good response respecting the purging of the Ministry."[54]

On the other hand, Langston Hughes, a gay Harlemite himself, blamed white boosters like Peabody and white tourists for the demise of Harlem's black realness and sexual performance. "I was there. I had a swell time while it lasted…[but] how long could a large and enthusiastic number of people be crazy about Negroes forever?" Hughes wrote in his eulogy of the Renaissance, *When the Negro was in Vogue*.[55] The influx of bohemian whites had forced black Harlemites to the margins of their own community, and Hughes felt their writing and art suffered from efforts to please their white audiences. Commercial packaging of the black experience in 1920s Harlem necessarily diluted its meaning.

It was, however, an event entirely out of the hands of the artists, preachers and tourists that, in Hughes' words, "sent Negroes, white folks, and all rolling down the hill toward the Works Progress Administration."

"THE STREET OF VANISHED HOPES"

They immediately called it "Black Thursday." On October 24, 1929, investors exchanged a record thirteen million shares of stock on Wall Street, more than three times what was traded on an average day. Traders panicked and sold off shares blindly throughout the morning, but the market did not close down as a stop-loss measure, and bounced back by the bell. Investors hoped the worst was over. But the following Monday, stock prices were slashed, resulting in more than nine million shares exchanged and the Dow Jones Industrial Average plummeting 13 percent. The next day, October 29, almost seventeen million shares changed hands and the market dropped another 12 percent, "swept downward with gigantic losses in the most disastrous trading day in the stock market's history."[56]

Shareholders across the country were gripped with a growing sense of dread, but in New York, investors went down to Wall Street to witness the disaster for themselves, each in his or her own personal agony. "Wall Street was a street of vanished hopes, of curiously silent apprehension and of a sort of paralyzed hypnosis yesterday," remarked the *New York Times*. "Men and women crowded the brokerage offices, even those who have been long since wiped out, and followed the figures on the tape. Little groups gathered here and there to discuss the fall in prices in hushed and awed tones."[57] By November, $30 billion of the $80 billion worth of stock that had been listed on the board the previous September had been liquidated.

The Roaring Twenties were over.

3.

BURLESQUE AND THE BISHOP
1930-1940

The twenties began with a roar and ended in a gasp, as the crash and the resulting economic depression radically altered the character of the city. "Nowhere had America's Great Depression struck harder than in New York City," the historian Robert A. Caro wrote forty years after the horror.[1] Common images of the time, seen today in bleak black and white photographs: men and women shuffling along breadlines that stretched for blocks; children scavenging for food at city dumps and in the gutters underneath pushcarts; mobile soup kitchens in the heart of Times Square; and, as an insult to the anti-saloon battles of the Progressive era, men sleeping on the floors of bars for the price of a drink. By 1932, ten thousand of the city's twenty-nine thousand manufacturing concerns had shut down, while one out of three employable men and women was out of work; those still employed saw their salaries halved, or worse. One of the consequences was a welfare roll containing 1.6 million New Yorkers, out of a total population of 7 million.[2]

The statistics of misery, though shocking, hardly described the squalid conditions that people had to endure. Families began to double up in single-family apartments, causing the kind of overcrowding last seen thirty years before in the slums of the Lower East Side. The muddy plain behind the Metropolitan Museum of Art became the site of Manhattan's largest shantytown. "Hoover Valley," named in honor of the despised president, housed hundreds of destitute families in makeshift huts made of metal siding and discarded billboards. Brooklyn's "Hoover City" had six hundred residents living in squalor on Cadman Plaza, while smaller settlements grew in Riverside Park and on West Houston Street.[3] Those who couldn't find a roof slept in public places, from bus stations to open sidewalks.

With regards to the Depression's effect on morality, there was initially a belief that the necessity of shared sacrifice in the face of hardship might help to strengthen the bonds of family. At its regional conference in 1932, the American Social Hygiene Association happily reported that the economic catastrophe had brought new focus to the importance of marriage and homemaking among the general population. The family was the bulwark against the rising tide of troubles, and "the next generation will know better how to keep the hearth clean-swept and the flame bright," opined Dr. Edward L. Keyes, the Association's president. "Sexual maladjustment seems to be the largest single cause of incompatibility in marriage, and education and inspiration in this respect should be the largest single source of prevention and relief."[4] In this case, the suggested remedy for said maladjustment was not institutionalized programs of frank sexual education, as the Association had advocated during the disease-ridden days of World War I. Instead, marriage clinics and homemaking courses (such as one already in progress at Vassar College) were considered the keys to maintaining marital happiness, and were to be "sold" to the public by social hygiene groups, rather than legislated into law.

This view quickly changed, however, as the necessity for unemployed parents to travel far and wide in search of work came to be seen as a threat to the well-being of children and the family. Just ten months after claiming victory for the family, the American Social Hygiene Association abruptly reversed its thinking. "The stability of ordinarily normal persons is threatened; family relations are endangered as men or women leave homes and families to seek employment, and disease and vice increase, especially where massing large numbers of persons in employment camps or…a 'boom town' situation."[5] The Association named desertion of families by mothers or fathers as a particularly grave circumstance, as well as scenarios in which "the women in question" willingly entered or were coerced into prostitution. "The duty of every community is to see that there shall not be one girl who has to sell herself to keep her body and soul together."[6]

GOLDEN YEARS

As much as work, what people needed during the Depression was an escape from their day-to-day troubles. The easiest vehicle with which the working class could leave behind their miseries, at least for a few hours, were burlesque shows, which, along with motion pictures, would become the signature popular entertainment of the thirties. As a result, burlesque flourished as a growth industry, evolving artistically from simple chorus lines and broad comedy to extravagant spectacles with the caché of a Broadway production, with the striptease becoming the main enticement of the performance.

The origin of the first striptease is murky, though some legends attribute it to a chorus girl who had gone onstage without her starched collar and cuffs in what passed for public nudity in 1916. In another version, burlesque actress Hinda Wassau broke a strap on her chemise while singing her grand finale, and rather than awkwardly dash off stage in mid-song, bravely finished the number to enthusiastic applause. A third version credited an anonymous girl who purposefully shimmied out of her costume in 1927. In any case, the truth wasn't as striking as the speed at which burlesque theaters in Manhattan came to favor the striptease over the traditional comic skits and songs.

The appeal of the striptease depended on the audience's imagination and the performer's skill, since the routine was the same, no matter which theater featured it. The typical show in the early thirties saw the star of the company entering the spotlight for a solo bit as the house lights darkened so that all eyes could focus on the stage. With exaggerated gestures, the performer sang a sexually suggestive ditty in a gossamer slip or performed an erotic dance. During the applause, she would disappear into the wings for a few moments, before the encore. If the audience wanted more, as indicated by hooting and stomping, she took off her long gloves or stockings and returned to the spotlight. This cycle continued until her costume lay on the floor and she was wearing only a thick layer of pancake makeup. Cue the house lights.

The undisputed kings of New York burlesque were the Minsky brothers. The four sons of an immigrant theatrical producer were born on the Lower East Side—Abe, the oldest, in 1878; Billy in 1887; Herbert in 1892; and Morton, the baby, in 1902. By 1908, Billy Minsky, the most enterprising member of the family, was showing blue movies in his father's theater, the Winter Garden at Houston Street and Second Avenue. However, the Minskys independent operation couldn't compete with the larger movie theaters uptown, and after a foray into vaudeville failed spectacularly, Billy, Abe and Herbert tried burlesque as a last-ditch attempt to get people in the seats. Fortunately, the Lower East Side was teeming with poor Jewish and Italian immigrants, to whom the Minskys' brand of double-entendres, slapstick comedy and teasing chorus girls had great appeal. Abe also took a cue from the *Folies-Bergere* in Paris and installed a runway in the Winter Garden, which allowed the audience to get closer to the chorus girls.

By 1931, the Minsky brothers' reputation for providing crowd-pleasing escapism had outgrown the Winter Garden. The Lower East Side was no longer in the center of New York's entertainment orbit, and Billy Minsky, in particular, dreamed of becoming the next Florenz Ziegfeld, whose *Follies* at the New Amsterdam Theater on 42nd Street consisted of several song-and-dance routines, with young women decked out in enormous feathered headdresses, paste diamonds and skimpy flesh-colored costumes. With the profits generated by the striptease shows and the fourth brother, Morton, joining the company, the Minskys leased the Republic Theater on 42nd Street, to the horror of Broadway producers, who were aghast at the idea that burlesque, the poor man's theater, would appear on New York's glittery strip. If that wasn't enough, the Republic was the oldest of Broadway's venerable theaters, and many Broadway veterans felt that having its boards trod on by half-naked chorus girls and ribald clowns would both sully the theater's history and give the Minskys' burlesque the respectability it didn't deserve—which, of course, was exactly what the brothers craved.

Despite the enmity of the traditional producers, by the end of 1931, four burlesque houses had opened for business on Broadway. The Minskys took over the Apollo Theater on 42nd Street, which, with the Republic and Abe Minsky's Gotham Theatre on 125th Street, gave them control of half

the burlesque houses in Manhattan. Another house on 42nd Street, the Eltinge, was leased to a Brooklyn movie-theater owner named Max Rudnick,
who immediately started staging burlesque shows to challenge his rivals
across the street. Ironically, the theater already had a long history of girlie
shows, as it had been named for actor Julian Eltinge, the premier American
female impersonator of the 1910s.

If burlesque was booming, the rest of Times Square's bright lights were
fading fast. The *Works Progress Administration Guide to New York City* noted
that the Depression had brought out the worst side of Times Square's vivid
personality. "Theaters closed one after the other, and contract bridge games,
chess tournaments, and side shows occupied the vacant stores and restaurants...On 42nd Street west of Broadway, once the showplace of the district,
famous theaters have been converted into 'grind' houses devoted to con-
tinuous double feature programs or burlesque shows. Among the cut-rate
haberdasheries, cafeterias, and bus stations are tokens of a not-so-distant
past, [such as] the photographs of the Ziegfeld Follies in the lobby of the
New Amsterdam Theater."[7]

New York Times theater critic Brooks Atkinson also wrote a withering
review of the Broadway scene at the time. "The New Amsterdam [theater]
has strange neighbors now. Just across the street is a movie theater where
a film about the white slave traffic is on solemn display." (Could it have
been *A Traffic in Souls*, the blockbuster smash of 1913?) "At the Republic
Theater...Billy Minsky's burlesque academy entices the footloose male with
photographs of artful ladies and the hoarse ballyhoo of 'girls, gurls, gurls.'"
To further illustrate his opinion that 42nd Street was "fast becoming a sex
bazaar," Atkinson make note of a shooting gallery, Hubert's Flea Circus,
and the Eltinge's burlesque production on the opposite side of the street.[8]

Like many legitimate Broadway producers, Atkinson lamented the
lowbrow invasion of 42nd Street's storied ground, failing to see the important escapist role burlesque played in the Depression-era mindset. "The
burlesque grind is the most depressing entertainment that still holds the
stage," he sniffed. "It is ugly. It is obscene. It is monotonous. It is worse
than that—it is pitiful, for here is one form of entertainment that has lost

gayety and hope." But perhaps the audiences weren't looking for spiritual uplift; maybe they simply sought an hour away from their troubles with a reassuring routine of comedy and chorus girls. That very routine provided some hope of normalcy, just as the expected formula of tender redemption in a romance novel offered a sense of comfort to the reader.

Atkinson wasn't about to concede that point, however, and instead blamed the audiences for accepting and supporting such repetitive drivel. "When burlesque abandoned everything to the flimflam game of disrobing it gave up the ghost," he complained. "Every fifteen minutes the disrobing routine reappears, doomed to disappoint the audience yet maintaining a pretense of spontaneity. There is a mechanical flutter of applause. For the audience has resigned itself to frustration and charlatanry; the audience comprises of simpletons. On both sides of the footlights burlesque is the degradation of all the theater stands for." Atkinson refused to see the value in popular entertainment at a time when it was desperately needed. On this point, the Catholic Church could not have agreed more.

"A 'BOOM TOWN' SITUATION"

While performances on stage were becoming more and more risqué, outside the theaters, the freewheeling rebellion and coy sexual mores of the twenties were disappearing. With the future uncertain, people craved leadership, someone to tell them the truth, to explain the rules of survival, to provide security and hope. Religion offered conservatism, frugality, sobriety—in atmosphere and in alcoholic consumption—and therefore gained a degree of influence in public life not seen since Parkhurst's heyday.

After six decades as a Protestant-dominated movement, the Catholic clergy, led by Patrick Cardinal Hayes, the Archbishop of New York, took on the leadership of a new interfaith anti-vice faction. By turning New York's enormous Catholic population against commercialized vice, Hayes would eventually be able to alter the landscape of Times Square, with the help of his able sidekick, Monsignor Joseph McCaffrey, rector of the Holy Cross Church on 42nd Street.

Pugnacious and self-assured, McCaffrey preferred two-fisted moral combat to Hayes' arch pastoral concern. He embodied a new style of fighting vice, more volatile and populist than the high-minded paternalism of the Parkhurst tradition, by appealing to working people's sense of outrage and disenfranchisement—a feeling that brewed strong during the Depression years.

McCaffrey was also the Chaplain of the New York Police Department, a force dominated at the time by Irish Catholics. During this period, the department determined that loitering by out-of-work men outside of Times Square burlesque theaters encouraged crime and harassment of women on the street. At the same time, many civic groups were disgusted with the deterioration of New York's cultural focal point. Finally, real estate concerns and banks joined the protest for the first time, as it was in the financial institutions' best interests to clean up Manhattan's most famous street so increased tax revenues could be gained from property leases. To them, the moral aspect of Times Square's predicament was less of a concern than the millions of dollars lost because two-bit trades prevented better businesses from setting up shop. These factions' means may have been different, but their aims were the same: clean up the Square.

In April 1932, a hearing was held before the city's Commissioner of Licenses, James F. Geraghty, for the purpose of preventing the reissue of licenses for the Minskys' Republic and Max Rudnick's Eltinge.[9] Representatives from Holy Cross Church on 42nd Street, the Free Synagogue, Franklin Savings Bank, and the Bowery Savings Bank testified to the moral and financial degradation of the neighborhood, in the same spirit as when the Committee of Fourteen had banded together with brewers to prevent licensing of Raines Law hotels. John Sumner, executive secretary of the New York Society for the Suppression of Vice, revealed that he had visited the offending shows at the Republic and Eltinge "in connection with his duties," describing a striptease performance in great detail. Police Commissioner James P. Sinnott reported that the shows attracted an undesirable element of society—specifically men loitering about the lobbies and sidewalks—which "trade[s] on the shady side of night life."[10] In a change from previous decades, the Commissioner didn't emphasize the dangers to impressionable women and girls that burlesque houses represented; instead, he asserted that the theaters attracted impressionable men, creating a dangerously immoral environment for them. The focus had shifted from protecting innocent youth to saving unemployed men from their own sinful desires. And for that reason, Sinnott argued, the licenses for the theaters should not be renewed.

Cardinal Hayes weighed in on the matter with a letter that was read during the hearing. "New York City, I am ashamed to say, has a malodorous reputation throughout the country because it is said anything, no matter how foul or filthy, is tolerated and even licensed on the New York stage."[11] He decried the "moral menace" inherent in renewing the Republic's and Eltinge's licenses on behalf of New York's one million Catholics.

One of the few voices defending burlesque was Nathaniel Miller, manager of Silver's Cafeteria, which was next door to the Eltinge. Though not a critic, he insisted that the nudity he'd seen was "an exact portrayal of what I've seen at the art galleries." He also mentioned that his business had increased twelve percent—in the midst of the Depression—since the Eltinge started showing burlesque. The audience was made up of "hard-working men, like plumbers and carpenters, and, as far as I can see, they go there because they can't go to musical shows; all I can say is that it is simply a poor man's theater."[12]

The class disparity between those who enjoyed burlesque and those who wanted to shut it down as a public menace was not enough, however, to sway the acting mayor, Joseph V. Mckee. In what was probably the best-known decision of his four-month administration, McKee ordered the closing of the Republic and Eltinge while at the same time insisting that he was *not* a reformer.[13] "The worst thing that can be said about me is that I'm a reformer," the mayor announced.[14] Still, he and new Police Commissioner Edward Mulrooney were in agreement that burlesque was a bad influence on the city, and in combination with slot machines and speakeasies, was "responsible for homicides and other crimes. I don't think it's reforming to drive this sort of thing out of the city."[15]

Unsurprisingly, the Minsky brothers were not happy with Mckee's decision, as the Republic was their meal ticket. The final show at the theater was supposed to take place on September 20, 1932. Fifteen minutes before show time, however, the Minskys told the police sergeant and five officers posted outside that an injunction against the theater's closure had been obtained. The sergeant replied that he had to sign the injunction before the show could go on. A few minutes of confusion ensued, after which the officers conveniently disappeared, and the crowd of advance-ticket holders flooded into the lobby. (Across the street at the Eltinge, officers raided the night's performance and refunded 250 tickets while Max Rudnick accused the police of favoritism toward the Minskys.) It was later reported that no injunction existed, and that the Forty-Seventh Street police station had been instructed—by either the police commissioner or the mayor himself—not to interfere with the Minskys' show.

To add insult to injury for the anti-vice crowd, the Republic and the Eltinge both reopened one month later, with freshly minted licenses, though technically, the theaters did not receive licenses for "burlesque" performances, but for "revue," productions called "frolics" and "follies" respectively. "It is to be burlesque in the classical sense," insisted the Minskys' lawyer, meaning that film screenings and gentle musical comedy were in, while striptease and double-entendres were definitely out. In conjunction with the licenses, a burlesque czar was appointed to censor the shows as needed.[16]

Was the whole burlesque brouhaha just an act to gain public approval for a crooked city administration? It all came down to semantics. At a press conference following the licensing announcements, Mayor McKee again reiterated that he was most assuredly *not* a reformer, and "that he had nothing against burlesque as such."[17] McKee's reluctance toward proper reform was in marked contrast to his anti-vice predecessors like Parkhurst and the Lexow Committee, who made institutional reform their explicit goal. Perhaps McKee, who was sworn into office after the still-popular mayor Jimmy Walker had resigned in scandal, was afraid of alarming New Yorkers accustomed to an anything-goes city?

"LOOK AT THEM—AND BLUSH!"

While the Church was occupied with the perpetrators of prurience, the repeal of the Eighteenth Amendment on December 5, 1933 eliminated much of the violence and mob activity from the city's nightlife. Though alcohol was again legalized, the celebration was decidedly low key, as just a handful of restaurants and clubs received their liquor licenses the afternoon of December 5, and only two liquor stores in the city were able to have alcohol trucked in from warehouses. Speakeasies and bootleggers, sensing their impending obsolescence, provided drinks for the last time, while Bloomingdale's proudly claimed to have made the first legal sale of liquor in fourteen years. Fred A. Victor of the Anti-Saloon League saw his life's work flash before his eyes as he called the drinkers immoral, "if not plain yellow."[18]

The repeal did not go over well with Cardinal Hayes or his attaché Monsignor Joseph McCaffrey. Both men feared that the end of Prohibition would bring the return of vice and depravity to the city. However, unlike the forces that had struggled against vice during the 1920s, Hayes and McCaffrey had an ally in their fight in the person of Fiorello H. LaGuardia, the newly elected mayor.

The son of an Italian father and a Jewish mother, LaGuardia was born in Greenwich Village, though he was raised in Arizona and Italy.[19] Always feisty and independent, LaGuardia was an avowed enemy of Tammany-style machine politics, institutional graft and moral exploitation. As promised during his campaign, LaGuardia cleaned house of Tammany parasites upon his election, appointing a group of commissioners who shared his disgust with Tammany-approved gambling rackets, mob-owned nightclubs and the black market. Famously, LaGuardia was fond of smashing slot machines with hammers while the cameras flashed.[20]

While Hayes' fight against the Minskys had failed due to McKee's obvious disdain for moral reform, a new opportunity now presented itself with the LaGuardia administration. Setting aside his attack on burlesque for the moment, Hayes announced a new drive against "evil" films, coinciding with the establishment of the Legion of Decency, a Catholic Church-backed interfaith watchdog organization whose job would be to monitor movies for sexual immorality. The Legion was to work closely with the movie industry's own censors, Joseph Breen and Will Hays, originators of the infamous Hays Code. "It is most heartening…to observe the widespread awakening throughout the country to the evil character and shocking debasement of many motion pictures," Cardinal Hayes wrote in a pastoral letter announcing the group. "The American public—Protestant, Jewish and Catholic—is rising ... [to] stop productions that, for the sake of monetary greed, debauch the sense of America's moral decency." The group's informal spokesman, Sidney Goldstein of the Central Conference of American Rabbis, remarked defensively, "As Jews, we are more interested than others in the endeavor to make sure that only wholesome pictures are shown in American theaters, since, as it is generally known, so large a part of the persons in the motion picture industry are Jewish."[21]

The Legion devised a coding system for motion pictures, similar to the movie industry's own rating system. But whereas the industry measured films' levels of violence, profanity, and drug use, the Legion of Decency focused exclusively on sexual expression in opposition to Catholic teachings. According to the Legion's rating system, "A" films were acceptable for Catholics and non-Catholics to view; "B" films were "morally objectionable in part for all;" and "C" films were condemned outright.[22] The Church had no qualms with "normal, reasonable and wholesome amusement," Hayes wrote, but was responsible for shielding its flock from "the moral defilement that lurks in every depraved motion picture."[23] (The Cardinal did not mention any such films by name, perhaps to avoid a public rush to the movie theater for an informed viewing.) In the last major movement against "moving-picture evils" back in 1913, children's inquisitive souls had been at stake, as protecting the young from celluloid crimes of passion was deemed necessary to allow them to grow into model, moral citizens. Twenty years later, with the advent of the Legion of Decency, the focus had broadened from simply protecting youthful innocence to regulating *adult* morality. If a Catholic man and woman went to see a "C" film, for example, were they immoral? If the same couple only saw "A" movies, were their souls free of sin? Ultimately, the Legion's rating system was as much a tool of control over the actions of its followers as it was an attack against the movie industry.

Hayes also declared that he was extending the Legion of Decency's censorial reach to stage shows, salacious magazines and dance halls, with the bulls-eye painted squarely on 42nd Street. Cue Monsignor McCaffrey, whose own plan to clean up the street dovetailed with the Cardinal's announcement. Assailing magazine stands, theaters, clubs, and a "nudist gymnasium," McCaffrey decried Times Square as the "filth centre of the world." Much less timid than he had been during the 1932 burlesque fight, the Reverend now vowed that his pulpit "will not be silent until these conditions are corrected."[24] Times Square, he declared, was the ugly eye of a sinful hurricane. "The most salacious, the most lewd, the most vile literature that can be found anywhere in the world is put on display and sold openly on the news stands in Times Square…Books on sexuality, on the vagaries of sex, books that cater and pander to the lowest forms of vice, openly sold!" he cried. "Look at them—and blush!"

Like Charles Parkhurst, McCaffrey assumed that the wild proliferation of vice was abetted by some sort of official protection. Unlike Parkhurst, however, McCaffrey immediately dismissed any notion that the police were to blame—most likely because he was also Police Chaplain—and claimed that many high-ranking officers had complained that it was not lack of initiative that aided vice, but the cumbersome details of court trials that tied their hands. "Who has licensed 42nd Street as a sanctuary for indecency?" McCaffrey asked, deploring the perceived flimsiness of laws that freed people accused of indecent performances on legal technicalities. "Who speaks the word that encourages undesirables to locate in this vicinity and locate here with impunity? Who is responsible for this? We have a right to know!"[25]

Shortly thereafter, McCaffrey gave a radio talk in which he demanded that bookstores selling offensive literature be stripped of their licenses and the proprietors blacklisted so that they could not open another store or any other business.[26] At the same time, Police Commissioner John O'Ryan promised to cooperate with the Department of Licenses in launching a clean up of Times Square's burlesque scene. Two weeks later, Commissioner of Licenses Paul Moss launched an offensive against the newsstands. (Ironically, Moss was the brother of prominent vaudeville producer Benjamin S. Moss, owner of B.S. Moss' Colony Theatre on Broadway.) On the very same day, a "crusade for Christian decency in regard to reading" was announced by Cardinal Hayes under the auspices of the New York archdiocese. The timing of all these actions made it difficult to believe that both sides—

Hayes and McCaffrey of the Catholic Church, and Moss and O'Ryan of the city government—were acting independently.

"STRENGTHEN MARRIAGE AND PROTECT THE FAMILY"

Ironically, while the Church and its municipal sympathizers were focused on the soul-corrupting influence of burlesque and naughty magazines, a city-wide, mafia-run prostitution racket was flourishing directly in their sights. Upon taking office, Mayor LaGuardia had vowed to obliterate organized crime in New York, which, as an Italian-American, he took as a personal insult. In the early thirties, the gangster Charles "Lucky" Luciano was the acknowledged capo of New York's prostitution industry, having pioneered the "combination" business model. In a combination scheme, henchmen known as bookers coerced unaffiliated prostitutes to work under a madam who was already part of the scheme. Most madams had been strong-armed into participating themselves, and were forced to pay five dollars out of their own pocket, plus ten dollars from each of their girls, to the combination. In return, the bookers took ten percent off the top and used the remaining funds to bail girls who got arrested out of jail.[27] Though a brutal system, it apparently worked; in 1935, 147 of Luciano's combination girls were arrested, but none received a jail sentence.[28]

Luciano's gang also controlled the ubiquitous nickel slots, the gambling machines found in most of the saloons and arcades where young men congregated. In a good location like 42nd Street, one machine could generate twenty dollars a day in revenue. At the nadir of the Depression, there were twenty five thousand to thirty thousand nickel slots in New York—an ever-present temptation to a man down on his luck.[29] Recognizing that the slots were operated by underworld cabals, La Guardia ordered police to confiscate the machines; however, they were immediately replaced by pinball machines, which may have looked comparatively innocuous, but averaged thirty to forty dollars each per week, solely on nickels from the poor. La Guardia ordered a report from the city's Commissioner of Investigations, who surmised that the "machines exerted a demoralizing influence on youth."[30]

In 1936, La Guardia and federal District Attorney Thomas E. Dewey succeeded in convicting Luciano on charges of compulsory prostitution, after a trial that brought out the underworld's most vicious and tragicomic characters. The female victims of Luciano's combination were especially eager to speak out. One vengeful madam, "whose screaming intonations and gestures enlivened the trial," fingered two bookers named "Spike" Green and Charles Spinach, who had ransacked her disorderly house when she refused to pay tribute money to the combination.[31] Another witness, a drug addict named Cokey Flo, did a "thoroughgoing job and enjoyed herself," accusing Luciano of planning to go corporate with his ten million dollar vice ring by opening franchises with female house managers on commissions and salaries.[32] Luciano's alleged plans for a vice empire supported Dewey's statement after the guilty verdict: "This, of course, was not a vice trial…the control of all organized prostitution in New York by the defendants was one of their lesser rackets….the top-ranking defendants in this case, together with the other criminals under [Luciano], have gradually absorbed control of the narcotic, policy, loan shark and Italian lottery syndicates, the receipt of stolen goods and certain industrial rackets."[33]

The sensational trial and revelations of underworld power led to the perception of a total breakdown of the social order in the city. To add to this view, the New York Society for the Suppression of Vice noted in its annual report for 1934 that public morals had improved little since 1873. "The activities of evil-minded people are certainly as great as they were then," William Parsons, NYSSV executive president, stated resignedly.[34]

Reform groups, sensing their relevance once again, evaluated the host of fears and threats against the stability of the family, the cornerstone of the social order, focusing this time on the issue of divorce. A report compiled by several clergy and social service groups and presented to New York Governor Herbert Lehman in 1935 by Sidney Goldstein of Legion of Decency fame showed that while the number of marriages had increased 400 percent since the relatively idyllic 1870's, divorces had increased 2,000 percent—to one per every six marriages.[35] Everyone in society suffered from so many broken families, the report claimed. State relief funds were stretched, more people went hungry, children missed school due to a lack of parental supervision, and the moral rectitude implicit in a strong family life was destroyed.

Since marriage had been removed from the domain of religious law and absorbed by the civil law of the state—which was responsible for enforcing its regulations with regards to granting marriage licenses—the report proposed the establishment of a state department to "protect marriage and strengthen the family." Among its recommendations, the writers suggested the "organization of courses in preparation for marriage [and] the establishment of consultation centers" for young couples.

Another perceived threat to the institution of marriage was the increased rate of venereal disease among New Yorkers. New syphilis and gonorrhea cases made up 37 percent of all reported diseases in the city in 1935, though physicians estimated that the number of cases to be as high as 118,000.[36] As social hygiene leaders launched a Progressive-like public education campaign with $100,000 of Works Progress Administration funds, public squeamishness was apparent in newspaper reports that reused the World War I term "social disease." As it had been since the nineteenth century, one's contraction of syphilis was still considered a personal moral failure because of its assumed link to prostitutes and faithless marriages. It was therefore of paramount importance to the city's leaders to promote sensible moral hygiene as a means of both maintaining the social order and protecting the institution of marriage.

PANSIES ON PARADE

As the Depression dragged on into the mid and late thirties, gay-themed culture rapidly faded from public view in New York City. The repeal of Prohibition had killed the clandestine clubs and speakeasies where gay-orientated entertainment had flourished during the Roaring Twenties, while the economic hardships of the Depression had led Bessie Smith and other divas to take their shows on the road. In addition, the socially conservative atmosphere that followed the crash was enforced by police and municipal authorities to negate the very existence of gay men and lesbians from the public consciousness.

Gay and drag acts had been a popular part of Times Square's entertainment milieu in the early thirties (the naming of the Eltinge Theater was proof of gender-bending allure), a trend which historian George Chauncey has termed the "pansy craze."[37] The appearance of effeminate, lisping actors in "pansy" shows was an extension of the twenties' idiosyncratic convention-bucking, tamed for a mass audience. Like the burlesque shows on Broadway, the black jazz performers in Harlem and the free-loving bohemians of pre-war Greenwich Village, the Times Square pansy shows became something of a tourist attraction.

Unfortunately, the pansies would become a victim of the conformity-obsessed, Depression-era city. As early as 1931, Police Commissioner Mulrooney declared, "There will be a shake-up in the nightclubs, especially those which feature female impersonators."[38] Like Minsky's Burlesque elbowing its way onto the Great White Way, the presence of the pansy shows was considered a symbol of the invasion of working-class entertainment into respectable, middle-class territory. Mulrooney's objective could be interpreted as not only banishing unconventional sexuality, but all elements attributed to the working class, from Times Square. But as the Depression added more and more people to the ranks of the working class, it became more difficult for the anti-vice forces to push out the sexual non-conformers. A wave of police roundups for "painted queens" in Times Square that began in 1931 and ran until 1935 was modestly successful, but it left the average-looking gay men alone.[39] They, together with the working class, simply outnumbered everyone else.

Beginning with Repeal in 1933, law enforcement employed another angle to persecute "sex degenerates," a euphemism for homosexuals. With alcohol again legalized, the many bars on the side streets of Times Square and neighboring Hell's Kitchen grew very popular with the remaining painted queens and the soldiers, sailors and hustlers who admired them, providing virtually the only venue where gay men of all classes could mingle. However, once gathered together, gay men became easy scapegoats for the regulation of public morality in Times Square.

The Committee of Fourteen had learned long ago that joining forces with the body that licensed saloons was the most effective way of regulating them. By the mid-thirties, however, the Committee was out of money and basically defunct; in its wake, a new regulatory board—the New York State Liquor Authority (SLA)—took on the roles of both social reformer and industry-monitoring organization, with the approval and legitimacy of a state entity rather than a group of volunteer vigilantes.

As in the beginning of the century, alcohol laws enacted in the thirties were meant to regulate public socializing, and in this case, marginalize gay men out of the public sphere. Bars and clubs were required to be "orderly," and serving drinks to or tolerating prostitutes, criminals, gamblers, hustlers, or known homosexuals on the premises made an establishment "disorderly," which could result in closure. In the case of gay bars, while extreme discretion on the part of the patrons and the bar owner was necessary, many were still raided by SLA agents on suspicion of "degenerate disorderly conduct," the special designation for homosexual expression. Though agents employed the time-honored tradition of undercover infiltration, it was often difficult to make arrests. Upon entering an establishment, agents had to recognize gay men by sight, which was an extremely arbitrary exercise in a smoky and dimly-lit bar. Simply suspecting the presence of gay men wasn't enough, however; agents had to catch suspects in homosexual acts, even as innocent as putting one's arm around another's shoulder or touching a friend's leg under the table. Then, having witnessed the offending behavior, the agent was burdened with proving that the bartender was fully aware that he was serving and tolerating known degenerates.[40]

As all three points were difficult to observe in one setting, inspectors often resorted to another time-honored tradition: entrapment. In the SLA's eyes, arresting homosexuals by any means necessary was simply a means to the end, which was to scrutinize its licensed bars and owners for violations of a moral code. The mere presence of suspected homosexuals—even a single person—on the premises was enough to put a bar under SLA surveillance for disorderliness, and the owner under arrest for disorderly conduct. Most owners pledged to ban homosexuals to avoid a disorderly premises violation. In this context, simply *being* homosexual was a crime.[41]

Not that police scrutiny dissuaded homosexuals from camping it up. "We didn't slink about and we certainly didn't whisper about ourselves," wrote memoirist Donald Vining in the 1980s. "We conceived of ourselves as far superior beings—wittier, quicker to appreciate everything cultural, more sensitive, and if nature gave us the slightest assist, more stunning to look at." For gay men to recognize one another in public, a distinct code of dress, language and mannerisms was employed. "[They] generally made sure to wear a bit more jewelry than was then considered proper for males, and to wear a fairly noticeable cologne, which John Breadwinner didn't deem masculine. This identified one as gay without in any way getting one in trouble with the law."[42]

"THE COURAGE TO STEM THE TIDE OF FILTH"

With an ally in City Hall in the person of Mayor LaGuardia, Cardinal Hayes and Monsignor McCaffrey were again able to gather together a co-alition of Catholic groups to go on the offense against burlesque theaters. As a result, on April 8, 1937, the manager of Abe Minsky's Gotham Theatre was found guilty of having featured an indecent striptease performance the previous August. The plaintiff in the case was none other than John Sumner of the New York Society for the Suppression of Vice, who triumphantly proclaimed, "at last we have a check on the strip-tease situation."[43]

License Commissioner Paul Moss was asked if he planned to pursue a ban on the striptease, and by extension burlesque, once and for all. "We have been gathering evidence…against theaters putting on these acts, which may result in other prosecutions," Moss replied ominously, adding that the po-lice, with the conviction against Minsky's theater, had been handed their first victory in the all-but-imminent cleanup of Time Square. Indeed, a week later, the Gotham Theater was fined five hundred dollars and its li-cense revoked, with the protests of Catholic organizations and the NYSSV read into the court record. At one point in the proceedings, the judge de-manded that Abe Minsky, who was present in the audience, take the stand; he refused and stormed out.[44]

This was all the encouragement that Paul Moss, Cardinal Hayes, and the interfaith crusade needed. Persuaded by the Catholic lay group Knights of Columbus, Moss called a hearing on the burlesque houses' licenses at the end of April 1937. At that time, theaters in New York City were granted annual exhibition licenses, which expired on May 1; the Commissioner of Licenses had the option of not renewing a theater's license, thereby putting it out of business.

On the first day of the hearing, the Knights of Columbus reported that several of its members had personally visited burlesque shows and singled out the striptease as a particularly degenerate act. The Catholic Club, "having been called upon through direct information from Cardinal Hayes," sent amateur sleuths into the theaters to collect evidence amounting to "more than a general protest."[45] Burlesque inspector Mrs. D. Leigh Colvin of the Women's Christian Temperance Union—back in action after Repeal—was too overcome with shock to describe what she had seen.[46] The ever-present Monsignor McCaffrey of Holy Cross Church opined that burlesque incited "not only immorality but bestiality and degeneracy." A slew of other witnesses spoke out against the Apollo, Eltinge and Republic on 42nd Street, insisting that those theaters bred "sex crime" and undermined social reform in Times Square.[47]

The second day brought a personal letter from Cardinal Hayes to Paul Moss. "Information that has come to me of the spread, evil influence and destructive results from these disgraceful and pernicious performances is the cause of much concern to me…I heartily approve the actions of the Catholic laymen."[48] Rabbi Samuel H. Goldenson, chairman of the Board of Jewish Ministers, concurred. "These houses cater to the lowest appetites and passions of men and women and altogether are a menace to the moral life of the community."[49]

Conveniently, the annual report of the New York Society for the Suppression of Vice was released at precisely this time, with predictable results. "Decent adult persons having the good name of the city at heart should recognize that the so-called burlesque of today is not in reality a burlesque—certainly nothing like the sprightly and amusing music hall entertainment of an older generation." Dismissing burlesque as fit only for the weak-willed and depraved—who, presumably, were beyond salvation—the NYSSV declared, "it is our duty…in the case of [material] which we believe to be frankly filthy and gratuitously indecent in the name of realism, to try to keep it out of public sale and circulation as a measure of protection to minors."[50]

A small group of burlesque producers and two actors took the stand in favor of their profession. Thomas J. Phillips of the Burlesque Artists Association of the United States described how an Assistant District Attorney and a male stenographer had parked themselves in the front row of several performances, accompanied by detectives, and arrested performers after the show's conclusion. Phillips, however, indicated he would rather compromise with the Commissioner than see people unemployed during the Depression. "What is going to happen to thousands of people in burlesque if the theaters are closed? Should they, perhaps, go out and commit crimes so that they may have sustenance?"[51]

Phillips' plea was drowned out by the chorus of moral indignation. Bowing to anti-vice pressure, Moss surprised the producers and the public by refusing to renew the licenses of fourteen burlesque theaters. "I am satisfied that the proof before me clearly indicates that the type of performance, the language used, the display of nudity are coarse, vulgar and lewd and endanger public morality in the welfare of the community." Cardinal Hayes commended Moss for his "courage to stem the tide of filth," even after a court order temporarily allowed the Eltinge and Gaiety Theater at Broadway and 46th Street to remain open.[52] At the other twelve theaters, only the posters promising such delights as "gorgeous glorified maids and models in a landslide of loveliness" remained.[53] Mayor LaGuardia, content until now to let Moss handle the case, boasted, "this is the beginning of the end of incorporated filth."[54]

Following the burlesque ban, a massive municipal cleanup campaign was launched in1938, using the resources of nearly every government agency and civic organization, to beautify the city and restore its luster in time for the World's Fair of 1939. While mothers scrubbed Times Square sidewalks with mops and schoolchildren picked up garbage in Central Park, police sweeps were launched to clear out the morally-questionable "riffraff." In a typical raid, plainclothes policemen busted a basement restaurant "of dubious repute" in Times Square and arrested the proprietors and thirty male patrons. Whether this was an ordinary clip-joint (unlicensed bar) or one of Donald Vining's gay haunts was not clear in the *New York Times* report, but the roundup of patrons and seizure of the property by police was all part of the plan to make New York City safe for tourists.[55]

The purpose of the World's Fair, arriving at the tail-end of the Depression and the flashpoint of war in Europe, was to unify the nations of the world and illustrate their interdependence. Planners hoped to showcase New York City and "lose some of its bad reputation for aloofness and remoteness from the rest of the country."[56] Interestingly, the president of the Fair's board was Grover Whalen, the former Police Commissioner who had ineffectively raided Harlem speakeasies in search of hostess racketeers a decade before. Whalen would prove more adept at convincing European nations to peacefully co-exist in their respective Fair pavilions.

The planners organized sixty foreign nations and organizations, thirty-three U.S. states, numerous American corporations and hundreds of smaller exhibitors into seven thematic zones covering 1,216 acres of Flushing, Queens. The Amusement Area was one of those zones, which circled a lake with Coney Island-style games and exhibits. One critic, describing the Amusement Area, said dismissively, "there is no need to show one more roller coaster, sky ride, auto dodgem, freak show, striptease act, penny arcade, shooting gallery or archery range."[57] One could assume that the same crowds of young people and working-class folks that populated the amusement parlors of Coney Island and Times Square also flocked to the World's Fair to see, among other novelties, the Arctic Girl's Tomb of Ice, where "self-hypnotized" girls appeared frozen in blocks of ice—which somehow necessitated wearing only skimpy leotards.[58]

Despite the perceived wholesomeness of the activities, in its annual report of 1939, the New York Society for the Suppression of Vice offered a tantalizing peek into this "dark side" of the World's Fair. The NYSSV commended the city on its return to morality, though one or two "girl shows" did prompt a few complaints from fairgoers, and the NYSSV's John Sumner noted an "underworld element" that tried to exploit the Fair by selling obscene articles. During the five months of festivities, nine people were arrested and incarcerated on vice charges. NYSSV president Francis Bertram Elgas also detailed the NYSSV's next target, "a type of magazine publication containing fiction based almost entirely upon sex crimes and the vileness of perversion."[59] Such "pulp" magazines notwithstanding, the city's overall effort to wipe its face clean of filth was, Elgas wrote, "noticeable, as we hope for a successful conclusion of our campaign."

The Reverend Charles H. Parkhurst,
looking authoritative. (*Library of Congress*)

Anthony Comstock in all his glory.
(*New York Public Library*)

The original 1913 movie poster
for *The Inside of the White Slave Traffic*. (*Advertising Archives*)

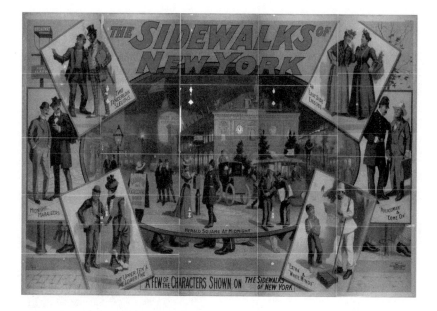

An 1899 lithograph illustrates the dangers of the Tenderloin night, picturing vagrants, prostitutes and newsboys interacting with police. (*Library of Congress*)

An 1898 lithograph shows the "latest New York craze," slumming—that is, upper-class citizens going down to the Bowery to see the sordid sights (like the cheap playhouse, left). (*Library of Congress*)

A 1936 portrait of blues singer, Bessie Smith by her friend Carl Van Vechten. *(Library of Congress)*

A demure portrait of Anthony Comstock's sworn enemy, birth control pioneer, Margaret Sanger. *(Library of Congress)*

Billy Minsky's Burlesque at the Republic Theater (209 W. 42nd St.) in 1936, one year prior to being closed down by Mayor La Guardia. *(Daily News)*

4.

THE UNDESIRABLES
1941-1955

The moral agenda promoted by church and civic groups during the Depression, which had been widely supported by citizens weary of Prohibition's lawlessness, was waylaid by America's declaration of war against the Axis powers in December 1941. The economic depression evaporated as a large portion of the male population was drafted into battle, millions of jobs were created in America's defense industry, and women joined the work force. Taken together, these events disrupted the social order more completely than any cultural force during the first part of the century.

War transformed New York City into a metropolis devoted to facilitating sex and fostering sexual identities. With the gloom of the Depression lifted, the city was reanimated as a vibrant, exciting capitol of the world, dedicated to servicing young men with all the attendant amusements and sexual gratification they could dream up. As the military's port of embarkation to the European theater of war, young men flooded the city on their way to uncertain fates abroad, determined to get the most out of what could be their last glimpse of home. For its part, the city offered this virile population all types of amenities, including hotels, bars, nightclubs hosting entertainers like Benny Goodman, Glenn Miller, and Tommy Dorsey; dime-a-dance halls, movie houses, all-night restaurants and unlimited opportunities for meeting the objects of their desires.

AMATEUR HOUR

One of the initial effects of the war on New York's sexual personality was a change in the definition of what it meant to be a prostitute. As soldiers flooded the city, it became difficult to distinguish professional prostitutes from the new "amateurs"—younger girls, mostly teenagers— who were smitten with the allure of military men. Called by various names—khaki-wackies, victory-girls (v-girls), charity girls, and good-time Charlottes— these girls availed themselves for dates, dances, and sex, defying the Depression-era conservatism. New York City was a magnet for these girls in the same way it was a lure for anyone looking to follow a dream or improve his or her fortunes. However, to the military, the encroach of the "v-girl" into the city came with a steep price: venereal disease. Lieutenant Commander Michael Wishengrad, the Navy's venereal disease control officer stationed in New York, called v-girls a growing moral and physical threat to servicemen, as an Armed Forces study showed that they outnumbered professional prostitutes four to one as carriers of venereal diseases. (Ironically, one public health official attributed the rise of the v-girl to the efforts to make it difficult for professional prostitutes to operate through the systematic crackdowns by social reformers and law enforcement in the previous decade.) Wishengrad calculated that in the Third Naval District, encompassing New York City, only 20 percent of venereal disease cases were spread by professional prostitutes, with the remaining 80 percent by teenage pick-ups. "Go to the Mall in Central Park and see for yourself," he stated grimly.[1] Similarly, a doctor in the *Journal of the American Medical Association* wrote that, "The oldtime prostitute in a house or the formal prostitute on the street is sinking into second place. The new type is the young girl in her late teens and early twenties...who is determined to have one fling or better...The carrier and disseminator of venereal disease today is just one of us, so to speak."[2] Thus, the line between corruption (inherent in prostitution) and middle-class morality had been erased, as there was no longer a distinct moral difference between amateurs and professionals.[3]

The VD rate was likely to climb if the Army and Navy did not take action against the khaki-wacky menace. As a result, the New York City Police Department and the D.A.'s office instigated a sweep against "vice promoters" and prostitutes beginning in May 1942.[4] Eight hundred people had been arrested by July, but the arrests were not an immediate deterrent, as the Army and Navy formally complained to NYPD Commissioner Lewis J. Valentine that the prostitutes and v-girls still operated unchecked wherever servicemen were concentrated, and that VD cases increased proportionately. Valentine thus called for more sweeps, especially in the "Broadway theatrical zone and Harlem" and in the sprawling Brooklyn Navy Yard across the East River from Lower Manhattan. If that weren't enough, Valentine also allowed his officers to "invoke the laws against loitering and vagrancy if it was too difficult to get conclusive evidence of prostitution."[5] This last suggestion was directed at the v-girls, who could not be arrested on prostitution if no money was observed changing hands. Valentine also ordered his officers to repeatedly investigate bars and restaurants for "lone women," and report said women to the authorities. This recalled the Committee of Fourteen's conviction that a solo woman in a saloon was indubitably a prostitute.

However, bars were not the only haunts of v-girls and their quarry. In 1943, police reported the arrests of three proprietors of rundown men's hotels in Times Square for allowing prostitutes to meet with servicemen on the premises. Officers were also recommended to patrol "taverns, beer joints, hotels, auto courts, [train] stations, public parks" and secluded lovers' lanes, indicating the pervasiveness of the v-girl problem.[6] Unfortunately for the NYPD, the Welfare Council of New York City released a study at this time detailing the arbitrary rehabilitation of prostitutes arrested in these kinds of sweeps. "The treatment of the prostitute is rightly regarded as one of the major elements in the entire fight against the present incidence and future spread of venereal disease," the study revealed. "Unless ways and means are found for securing maintenance, including medical care and personal guidance and training, for infected women…they will continue in their destructive practices and constitute a more serious menace to the health of the community than the Typhoid Marys."[7]

"ONE BIG CRUISING GROUND"

While the prostitution problem occupied law enforcement, another group used to being under the social microscope was gaining strength in numbers. The harsh liquor regulation laws of the thirties had for the most part eliminated public homosexuality, forcing most openly gay bars to close. Gay men adapted to the new climate by establishing their own innovative ways of gathering and fostering community. The key was the gradual appropriation of existing public and private spaces, and the construction of a verbal network that informed men of which places had been thus appropriated. As a result, the gay social scene during World War II far surpassed that of the previous decade. "From the 'gay' side of the Astor Hotel bar to the bushes behind the 42nd Street library…to the public tearoom right outside of Fordham University… to the eighth-floor restroom in the RCA building to the restroom across the street in the parking garage," one New Yorker wistfully recalled, "New York seemed to be one big cruising ground."[8] For the first time, gay men born elsewhere came to the city en masse, for a dual purpose: to serve their country, and to find others like themselves. Gay soldiers and sailors found an open-secret society with an established network of goods and services specifically for them (lesbian members of the Women's Army Corps, who were not drafted, had better luck at military bases elsewhere in the country). The homosexual community forged in New York during the war, even with a transient population of GIs, would be instrumental in creating a visible political movement later in the century.

Times Square was the epicenter of the gay network, where people met, made plans, and picked up dates. "I always associate New York with homosexuality," reported one gay soldier.[9] Asking for a match or the time became so familiar as a gay pick-up line that straight people ceased to ask those questions to strangers. The need for discretion also fostered a unique language of eye contact that other gay men would recognize, but that straight men wouldn't notice. A gay man would return another man's gaze; a straight man would look away immediately.

Not surprisingly, Times Square was also the headquarters of New York's hustlers, who waited for other men under the brightly-lit marquees of the movie theaters or in shadowed doorways. Author John Rechy, drafted into the Army and sent to New York, found himself drawn to Times Square, where he discovered hustling for money and aloof companionship, and business conducted "from 42nd Street to about 45th Street, from grimy

Eighth Avenue to Bryant Park—where, nightly, shadows cling to the ledges: male-hungry looks hidden by the darkness of the night; and occasionally, shadowy figures, first speaking briefly, disappear in pairs behind the statue with its back to the library and come out after a few frantic moments, from opposite directions: intimate nameless strangers joined for one gasping brief space of time."[10]

In addition to Bryant Park (which Mayor La Guardia had gated and padlocked in 1944 to cut down on male prostitution), Manhattan's main gay cruising ground was the wild, overgrown Ramble in Central Park, a hilly, wooded area with heavy foliage and few streetlamps. The language of the cruise was also spoken in Riverside Park, Battery Park and Bowling Green, all near the seaport; and in the heart of Brooklyn at Prospect Park, not far from the Brooklyn Navy Yard, home to numerous visiting ships, sailors and shipyard workers.

For a modicum of privacy in a public space, public toilets were convenient—many were located in public parks and subway stations—and reliable. (The Times Square subway station restroom in particular was synonymous with gay sexual activity.) Dubbed T-rooms, shorthand for toilet-rooms, the term eventually evolved into tearoom; in these places, men of all classes could find a casual partner on the commute home from work, communicating by eye contact.[11] Their ubiquity, however, made tearooms especially vulnerable to police surveillance. In many cases, officers hid behind grilles in the walls to observe men having sex in the stalls; others cut holes in the ceilings and watched from above.[12] Military police would sometimes tail servicemen they suspected might be searching for sex partners. These "comfort stations" had originally been erected as a social hygiene measure when private indoor plumbing was rare, ostensibly to give working-class men a place to relieve themselves other than a saloon; ironically, facilities that had been meant to prevent morally-suspect behavior were now providing the prefect place for it.

If the scene on the streets became dangerous, gay men could resort to private spaces for networking and sex. There had long been a tradition of housing in New York for single men, whether they were unmarried immigrants in Bowery flophouses, Depression-era workers in Hell's Kitchen's single-room occupancy hotels, or soldiers crashing in the rooming houses near the action of Times Square. There was no cause for suspicion, then, when certain accommodations for GIs seemed to attract only men.

With delicious irony, the two main facilities of the Young Men's Christian Association became known around the gay world as the places to go for sex. Having been founded in the 1850s by Morris K. Jesup, a close friend of Anthony Comstock, as a refuge from the immorality and deviance of the city's streets, it was particularly paradoxical that the Y often turned a blind eye to the goings-on among its bunks and showers. The massive Sloane House YMCA, at West 34th Street and 9th Avenue, was built in 1930 as a shelter for working-class men; by the middle of that decade it was notorious for the sexual activity that occurred among its twelve hundred nightly residents. John Rechy recalled staying there: "In the incessantly running showers of the Sloane House YMCA the day I arrived in New York, the big hairy man made conversation with me; where am I from and what am I doing?" Rechy, of course, had come to the Y on purpose. "Even before the man speaks it, I know that something of what I've come to find in this city will soon be revealed in this room…they don't call this Y the 'French Embassy' for nothing."[13] The West Side YMCA, at 63rd Street and Central Park West, was smaller and reputedly more exclusive than the Sloane House. "If you go to a shower there is always someone waiting to have an affair. It doesn't take long," reported one enthusiast.[14] For some men, the Y's showers were their first chance at seduction, while for others, it was a reliable social club—so reliable, in fact, that civilian New Yorkers were known to borrow military uniforms or sign in with a false name to hit the scene inside.[15]

The Y's showers should not be confused with the baths, the *ne plus ultra* of gay cultural life, which were hugely popular with GIs. Many baths had originated as municipal bathing facilities for the poor in tenement neighborhoods, but had been made obsolete by modern plumbing in the 1920's, thus allowing them to be appropriated by gay men in the 1930's and 1940's. The baths provided tiny cubicles with cots for men on leave, but those accommodations were often not used for sleeping. The popular Everard Baths at 28 West 28th Street (dubbed "Ever-hard" by its fans) was typical.[16] A patron paid a daily fee (usually one dollar) to the desk attendant and received a towel and the key to a cubicle. Walking through dim hallways, he passed a tiled shower room, a wood-lined sauna, and a dressing room with rows of lockers. Groups of men socialized in the steam room. Upstairs, on either side of the narrow passageway, were numbered doors. Some were ajar, others closed. The cubicles' walls did not reach the ceiling, leaving a gap of a few feet, through which the muffled sounds of moaning and low voices could often be heard.

PROSPERITY AND PERIL

New York underwent a crucial shift in atmosphere when the war ended in 1945. The massive, spontaneous celebration that occurred on V-J Day in Times Square, at which Alfred Eisenstaedt's famous photo of an anonymous GI kissing a nurse was taken, marked the close of another chapter in the city's fortunes. The constant stream of enlistees on their way to Europe stopped, and as a consequence, businesses that had catered to GI's suffered. The v-girls also faded from the front pages, having done their part for the war effort, and the spread of venereal disease resumed its role as a public health and moral issue rather than a matter of national security.

The postwar era presented its own developments in the city's social fabric. Veterans took advantage of the federal government's generous GI Bill, which provided money for college education, a year of unemployment compensation, and low interest, no-down-payment loans for home mortgages and start-up businesses. As a result of the government's largesse, many vets found themselves financially stable, and those who previously could not have afforded homes outside of urban areas were able to buy property in the fast-developing suburbs. Levittown, the planned suburban community on Long Island, was emblematic of the shift from urban to suburban living; the town provided inexpensive homes for young GIs and their families, but expressly excluded non-whites from buying property. This systematic racism created a scenario in which suburban communities became overwhelmingly white while minorities made up an ever-larger percentage of the urban population.

United States Census figures illustrate the "white flight" phenomenon. In 1940, the white and "foreign-born white" population of New York numbered nearly seven million, while the "Negro" and "other races" (which included Chinese, Japanese, and Indian) population was 477,000. [17] In 1950, while the white and "foreign-born white" categories numbered 7,116,000, an increase of only about 139,000, or 2 percent, the total for "Negros" and "other races" was 776,000, an increase of almost 300,000, or 39 percent.[18] This pattern continued with the 1960 Census, in which the white and "foreign-born white" categories were combined, totaling 6,641,000—a decrease of 7 percent. In contrast, the "Negro," Chinese, Japanese, Indian, Filipino, and "other races" categories combined for 1,141,000, an increase of 32 percent.[19]

By far, the group with the greatest increase in population in New York City during the 1940s and '50s were migrants from Puerto Rico. (The term "migrant" is used rather than "immigrant" because Puerto Rico is a United States Commonwealth, and movement from Puerto Rico to the U.S. mainland is considered internal migration.) Several economic and social factors made New York City an attractive destination for Puerto Ricans. First, at the outbreak of World War II, the United States economy was booming, while Puerto Rico was still suffering the effects of the Depression. Consequently, the war effort offered military opportunities for men and homefront jobs for women, which were scarce in Puerto Rico. Secondly, beginning in the 1950s, commercial air travel from Puerto Rico to the mainland, primarily to New York City, greatly eased the time, distance and cost of migration. By then, *barrios* (concentrated populations of Puerto Rican New Yorkers) in East Harlem and other parts of the city had become established, providing a transition between the mostly agricultural, Caribbean culture and industrialized America.

The tidal wave of Puerto Rican migration was noted in a special report by the U.S. Census in 1950. At the start of the Great Depression in 1930, roughly 53,000 people of Puerto Rican descent lived in the United States. By 1940, that number had increased 32 percent to almost 70,000, with 87 percent living in New York City. By 1950, the population had exploded, as approximately 226,000 Puerto Ricans lived in the U.S., a staggering increase of 223 percent in just ten years. Eighty-two percent of them lived in New York: from 1940 to 1950, the number of Puerto Ricans in the city jumped 205 percent.[20]

The majority of migrants were poor, and finding suitable housing was difficult, as supply lagged far behind demand. Overcrowding, hunger, malnutrition, a lack of education and knowledge of English were additional barriers to adjustment. Beyond the assistance of friends and family, there was little infrastructure set up to help migrants adjust to city life.

At the same time that Puerto Rican migration was growing, the cityscape itself was being torn down and built up again on a grand scale by Robert Moses, the omnipotent urban planner who worked officially or unofficially under five New York City mayors and six governors, and whose official title, Parks Commissioner, barely hinted at his unmitigated influence over city projects and politics. While Moses had despised Tammany's waste and cronyism, he ended up building a power structure so irrefutable that he alone signed off on city business. The suburbs of Long Island and Westchester County could not have been built or populated without his expressways, parkways and bridges; New York's electricity supply would have been a fraction of what it was without Robert Moses' Hydro-Electric Dam at Niagara Falls. He built 658 playgrounds for slum children, who had no other place for exercise. During the Depression, when city coffers for helping the destitute and hungry had been drained by Tammany backslappers, Moses was accumulating federal public-works money to revolutionize transportation in, out, and around the city. He linked Manhattan, Staten Island and Long Island to the mainland United States by the Henry Hudson, Triborough, Bronx-Whitestone, Throg's Neck, Cross-Bay, Marine, and Verrazano Bridges. He made it possible for drivers to completely circumvent the tangle of local streets by building expressways around and through the boroughs and connecting them to highways outside of town. The best-known included the Van Wyck, Bruckner, Major Deegan, Gowanus, Cross-Bronx, Brooklyn-Queens, Staten Island and Long Island Expressways. Moses wanted to beautify the trip for the motorists, so he created parkways—highways flanked by "ribbon parks" along the routes and surrounded by open spaces—

like the Grand Central, Belt, Northern and Southern State, Henry Hudson, Cross-Island, Cross-County and Saw Mill River, to name but a few. Some of these parkways went through state parks created by Moses, such as Jones Beach State Park, Valley Stream and Hempstead Lake.

Underlying Moses' zeal for public works, however, was his disdain, and occasional contempt, for the working-class and for racial minorities. While his state park projects were conceived as beautiful, open spaces to be en-joyed by the public, especially residents from the city who craved fresh air, in practice, Moses was not as altruistic as he appeared. Jones Beach on the south shore of Long Island, for example, was created specifically as a seaside oasis for city residents, but poor and minority New Yorkers found it almost impossible to get to the park, per Moses' design, as working class people who didn't own a car were forced to take several forms of public transporta-tion (the subway, a train and a bus) to get there. African-Americans who chartered their own buses had to obtain a permit to park, which Moses rarely granted; they were also forced to park in the most remote lots and be satisfied with using the most remote beaches. They were kept from setting foot on the "white" (i.e., best) beaches by lifeguards.[21]

As the city's master planner, Moses gained an admirable record of imagining public works and actually getting them built. But his success was dependent on ordering the wholesale demolition of working-class neigh-borhoods to make way for his gargantuan projects; it was very convenient, in that case, that Moses was also Slum Clearance Committee chairman, in charge of demolishing large swaths of private apartment buildings. More-over, the resulting highways, suburban parks and cultural pavilions he built seemed more suited for use by the middle class, not the disproportionately poor and non-white people who were being displaced by them. One of his crowning achievements, Lincoln Center, necessitated demolition of sixteen acres of homes and the displacement of seven thousand low-income fami-lies.[22] Moses responded by building public housing projects, but the small apartments in identical clusters of tan-brick high-rises, situated on the pe-rimeters of the boroughs, were too expensive for many relocated families to afford.

THE MIRACLE MESS

By the middle of the 1950s, the growing minority communities in the city, the shifting of white city-dwellers to the suburbs, and the destruction of established working-class communities had frayed the social fabric of New York. This imbalance encouraged the sense that the city was a predatory, dangerous, and immoral place. Seizing upon the people's feeling of dread were two moral leaders who offered security and comfort against the cruelty and degradation around them: our old friend Joseph McCaffrey and his new boss, Francis Cardinal Spellman.

In terms of powerful friends and associates, Spellman was the most influential clergyman in New York. His kind, doughy face masked a ferocious ambition to rid America of subversives and undesirables, who, he was convinced, had infiltrated all levels of government and civic life. Spellman set the moral standard for New York City in the late forties and fifties according to Catholic doctrine, and that included vociferous opposition to public immorality.

The *Miracle* controversy of 1950 set the tone of his arguments for the remainder of the decade. In December 1950, in cahoots with the Legion of Decency, Spellman charged the Roberto Rossellini film *Il Miracolo (The Miracle)* with sacrilege upon its New York premiere at the Paris Theater. *The Miracle* tells the story of a naïve village woman who, while drunk, is seduced by an itinerant ne'er-do-well, who she mistakes for St. Joseph. When the woman discovers that she is pregnant, she believes it is the result of immaculate conception. The villagers mock and hound her, until she escapes to a mountaintop church, where she gives birth and experiences a religious epiphany.

Despite refusing to see the film ("Must you have an illness to know what it is?" he remarked[23]), Spellman issued a pastoral letter denouncing *The Miracle*, purporting, as he did with anything he found indecent or immoral, that it was all part of a Communist design to take over the hearts and minds of the nation. "To those who perpetrate such a crime as *The Miracle* within the law all that we can say is this: How long will the enemies of decency tear at the heart of America?...Divide and conquer is the technique of the greatest enemy of civilization, atheistic communism…[this film] should divide and demoralize Americans, so that the minions of Moscow might enslave this land of liberty."[24]

The Cardinal's influence among the two million Catholics in New York was apparent in the daily protests outside the Paris Theater on 59th Street and Fifth Avenue, where thousands of men and women from the Catholic War Veterans, Knights of Columbus, and Catholic lay organizations carried placards excoriating the film. "This Film is an Insult to Every Woman and Her Mother," read one sign, while another shouted "Don't be a Communist—All the Communists are inside." [25]

The conflict came to head when Edward T. McCaffrey, the city's Commissioner of Licenses, entered the fray. Prompted by the Catholic War Veterans—of which he was the former state commander—McCaffrey yanked the Paris Theater's license after coming to the conclusion that *The Miracle* was "officially and personally blasphemous."[26] The film's distributor, Joseph Burstyn, sued the city all the way to the Supreme Court, saying that it had violated the First Amendment ban on state-sanctioned religion by censoring the film. The Court eventually ruled in Burstyn's favor, unanimously deciding in May 1952 that "New York cannot vest in a censor such unlimited restraining control over motion pictures as that involved in the broad requirement that they not be 'sacrilegious'."[27]

Despite this defeat, Spellman's protest against the film increased his influence in politics, and he used this increased power to position sex as a Communist tool designed to dull the people's natural moral defenses. At the time, it seemed as if most of society agreed with him. Beginning in 1950, a constant stream of frightening reports from Washington supposedly confirmed the moral dangers posed by Communists and "sex perverts," a euphemism for homosexuals. On April 19, 1950, Republican national chairman Guy George Gabrielson officially linked Communist infiltrators and homosexual employees as twin security risks within the U.S. State Department. "Perhaps as dangerous as the actual Communists are the sexual perverts who have infiltrated our Government in recent years. The State Department has confessed that it has had to fire ninety-one of these," he told a gathering of Republican Party workers. Gabrielson implied that the danger was graver than anyone knew: "the country would be more aroused over this tragic angle of the situation were it not for the difficulties of the newspapers and radio commentators in adequately presenting the facts while respecting the decency of their American audiences."[28] New York Governor Thomas Dewey jumped on the bandwagon by accusing the Truman administration of harboring "spies…and sex offenders in the Government service."[29]

Soon after, a Washington D.C. police officer suggested, without evidence, that 3,500 homosexuals were employed by the federal government. In June 1950, the Senate ordered an investigation into this claim. Senator Kenneth S. Wherry (R-NE), a tireless anti-homosexual proselytizer, spoke to *New York Post* columnist Max Lerner about the proceedings. Lerner asked whether the issue was political or moral, and Wherry answered that "it was both, but security was uppermost in his mind. I asked whether he made the connection between homosexuals and Communists. 'You can't hardly separate homosexuals from subversives,' the Senator told me. 'Mind you, I don't say every homosexual is a subversive, and I don't say every subversive is a homosexual. But a man of low morality is a menace in the government, whatever he is, and they are all tied up together.'"[30] In its final report, "Employment of Homosexuals and Other Sex Perverts in Government," the Senate committee recommended that all federal employees be screened for deviance and concluded that, in the words of the *New York Times*, "Communist and Nazi agents sought to get secret Government data from Federal employees 'by threatening to expose their abnormal sex activities.'"[31]

"HOODLUMS AND PERVERTS"

The fervor in Washington intensified the fears of many New Yorkers. The common meme now held that they were out to get us—"they" meaning the Reds and their covert agents, "us" meaning God-fearing, law-abiding middle-class Americans. People felt under siege by "undesirables," a heterogeneous group that included Communists and "perverts" as well as petty criminals, juvenile delinquents, vagrants and prostitutes. To many, the sidewalks of Midtown Manhattan literally teemed with "hoodlums and perverts"—the former referring to gangs of teenagers and petty criminals, the latter meaning hustlers and their male customers.

Backing up many people's feelings of a society spiraling out of control, the police announced a staggering increase in crimes between 1952 and 1953. Murders rose 22 percent, manslaughter increased 42.5 percent, and "felonious assault" went up 10.7 percent. (There were, however, modest decreases in rape, robbery, burglary and drug arrests.[32]) "Attacks on women in subways and elsewhere startle and terrify the city; hold-ups, muggings and other crimes arrive in such numbers daily that they arouse comment everywhere," the *New York Times* wrote in a 1952 editorial lamenting the Mayor's refusal to add additional cops to the NYPD beyond the normal quota.[33]

As a result of this atmosphere of fear, juvenile delinquency became a major concern of law enforcement in the fifties. As stable, middle-class families moved to the suburbs, the remaining inner city population was becoming increasingly poor and thus susceptible to the social problems associated with economic want. Teenagers, growing up in a city that was itself undergoing massive change, and feeling the absence of anything solid to rely on for emotional and professional support, became rebels without cause, tough and swaggering on the outside to mask an existential crisis of purpose on the inside. Law enforcement, which did not usually care to examine young people's psychological needs, viewed the growing groups of teenage girls and boys as a menace to the ever-lessening group of upstanding New Yorkers.

The New York State Youth Commission, in a 1953 report "Blueprint for Delinquency Prevention," cited "culture conflict in American communities" as the primary cause of juvenile delinquency, adding that "section, regional, and rural-urban migrations"—referring in part, no doubt, to the explosive growth of the Puerto Rican community in New York City—further disrupted social stability.[34] The 1955 Report of the Temporary State Commission on Youth and Delinquency concurred: "Overcrowding, poverty, transiency, and minority status create special problems for young people [and] tend to have a higher rate of youthful delinquency." The report added, "The Commission also wishes to emphasize its belief that moral and religious values should be stressed in all rehabilitative treatment of young delinquents."[35]

The consequences of not helping these "vulnerable" children was made clear on August 30, 1959. On that late summer night, fifteen Puerto Rican youths attacked six "gringo" youths in a playground in Hell's Kitchen. The rumble was meant to avenge the earlier beating of a Puerto Rican boy, but the situation got out of hand, and Salvador Agron, a fifteen-year-old Puerto Rican migrant, allegedly stabbed two sixteen-year-old boys to death. (Strangely, he was wearing a black and red cape at the time.) Agron was convicted of first-degree murder and sentenced to the death penalty, but the sentence was commuted by Governor Nelson Rockefeller based on the evidence that Agron had been "grotesquely deprived" of needed social assistance. The case of "the Capeman," as it was dubbed in the press, plainly illustrated the pitfalls for Puerto Ricans, and teenagers in general, in New York.[36]

Hell's Kitchen, where the Agron murders occurred, was a west-side slum that had been torn up in the late forties to make way for the building of Robert Moses' Lincoln Tunnel and Port Authority Bus Terminal at the intersection of 42nd Street and Eighth Avenue. The mammoth transportation complex was designed to simplify and smooth vehicle traffic into midtown Manhattan from New Jersey, but an unintended effect of its convenience was a flood of flim-flam artists and young runaways from more distant points coming to seek their fortunes in the city. To meet their needs, all-night cafeterias, drugstores, and transient hotels popped up around the terminal and nearby side-streets. With these services in the immediate area, the new arrivals stayed put where they landed, increasing the number of poor, young and tenuously-employed people in the neighborhood, who often resorted to prostitution, hustling, drug-dealing and begging where their initial plans failed.[37] "The so-called teenagers, both boys and girls...throng Times Square after dark until all hours. Some of the latter, rouged to kill, look no more than fourteen or fifteen years old," wrote an outraged citizen in a letter to the *New York Times* in 1954. "If the Police Department is now powerless to act, not only for the good of the children themselves but also to prevent them from possibly becoming some day a charge upon the community via the juvenile courts, cannot a city ordinance be passed to keep minors under eighteen from loitering in such a moral cesspool?"[38] Despite this citizen's outcry, no ordinance was passed, and the streets remained chaotic.

In contrast to the fear and anger of many citizens, the Beat writers of the mid-fifties—William S. Burroughs, Jack Kerouac, Allen Ginsberg, John Clellon Holmes—absorbed inspiration from the mad rush. The Beats embraced the purity and utter validity of experience—kicks for kicks' sake— and had little interest in political agitation (even if some of their writings, like Ginsberg's poem *Howl*, were awash in disappointment with postwar politics). Beat thought was directed inward, to find the soul of one's experience, in direct contrast to the conformity, social ladder-climbing, and achievement of middle-class respectability then valued by much of society.

The Beat writers were analogous to the post-WWI generation of disaffected young artists who had opted out of a society they didn't believe in. But as John Clellon Holmes wrote in his definitive 1952 article "This is the Beat Generation," the Beats were searching for something more than mere rebellion and escape. "They drink to 'come down' or to 'get high,' not to illustrate anything. Their excursions into drugs or promiscuity come out of curiosity, not disillusionment," Holmes wrote. "Unlike the Lost Generation, which was occupied with the loss of faith, the Beat Generation is becoming more and more occupied with the need for it."[39] That search for faith brought the Beats down to the gutter instead of heavenward, and specifically to Times Square. The hustlers, prostitutes, drunks, junkies, and lowlifes, whom the "squares" saw as a nuisance, were examples for the Beats to follow in the search for unconventional nirvana. Times Square supplied the highs, in both divine experience and in drugs. Bickford's Cafeteria on West 42nd Street was appropriated by Burroughs, Kerouac et al. as the headquarters for their nocturnal lifestyle, in which they observed the naked city, under cover of darkness, and the saints that emerged from the shadows to impart their wisdom.

Such a spiritual figure was Herbert Huncke, a hustler and junkie, who served the Beats as literary inspiration, symbol of sexual otherness and drug connection. It was Huncke who famously turned Burroughs on to heroin and the sexual underground around Times Square. Huncke's position as a gay hustler gave the Beat writers their starting point in describing sexual variance and introduced American readers to the intersection of male homosexuality and drug culture.

Hustlers like Huncke were, by now, a fixture of the post-war city, inviting scrutiny and study by an interested medical establishment. "It has been estimated that there are one hundred thousand such men in greater New York. They may be found in Times Square, in Harlem, on Fifth Avenue, on Riverside Drive, in parks, in public toilets, on beaches, in baths, and in numerous bars, restaurants, night clubs and hotels," reported George Henry in *All the Sexes: A Study in Masculinity and Femininity*, a socio-medical study of the "sex variant" (as homosexuals were often called) in the mid-fifties.[40] A heterosexual physician, Henry tended to pathologize his subjects, but his work offers numerous snapshots of hustling culture in nineteen-fifties New York. One man, describing his night out on the town, recalled, "We got to a movie house just in time to be greeted by a general exodus of [hustlers] being ushered out by policemen. It was obvious that he knew what the boys and queens were doing, but he could do little more than tell them to move on."[41]

Henry wrote that, in his experience, nearly all hustlers were "clip artists," pickpockets or blackmailers who wouldn't hesitate to get their clients drunk and slash their pockets for the goods.[42] Though these particular crimes were practiced by and on hustlers and their male customers, in the eyes of the law, it was analogous to the non-sexual thievery committed by teenage hoodlums—all of it the work of "undesirables."

RIDE THE MIDWAY

The impression that the situation in Times Square's was getting out of hand had gained enough ground by 1954 to prompt action by the city's morality police. On the sweltering night of July 30, 1954, the NYPD launched a massive sweep of undesirables in Times Square, in response to numerous complaints by individuals, civic organizations, churches, and tourists. Plainclothes officers poked around the rowdy bars along Eighth Avenue known to be popular with gangs and hustlers, peering through the haze of cigarette smoke for tell-tale youths. One-hundred twenty-five prostitutes, juvenile delinquents, hoodlums, "sex perverts" and miscellaneous riff-raff were arrested on charges of "vagrancy, disorderly conduct, loitering, using loud and abusive language, annoying passers-by and blocking sidewalks."[43] Most of the teenage boys arrested were dressed in identical tee-shirts and dungarees, prompting some police officers to go undercover in the same costume. The next day, twenty-three more "undesirables" were taken into custody as part of the campaign, this time apprehended in bars, grills, and dance halls.

Police officers reported satisfaction at the weekend's arrests, saying that the sweeps were the first step in pushing out the ruffians and "perverts" from Times Square. Deputy Chief Inspector James B. Leggett stated that "the rise of organized young hoodlums and the patent increase of homosexuals on the city's streets had brought a wave of rape, muggings, and other crimes of violence often culminating in murder."[44] There was, of course, no proof that any homosexuals had committed said crimes—it was their mere presence, supposedly, that had caused the rowdy, unwholesome atmosphere.

Monsignor Joseph McCaffrey also rejoined the action as the raids began, claiming through a spokesperson, "we hope that this drive will be the gradual start of the successful reformation of the Times Square area and that it will be the start of the clean-up of the honky-tonk area and the undesirables in this neighborhood."[45] Such words were uncharacteristically mild for the Monsignor, but perhaps he was simply waiting to unveil his own anti-vice campaign.

Concurrent with the sweeps, Police Commissioner Francis W. H. Adams lobbied Mayor Robert Wagner's administration for more money and nearly two thousand additional cops to "[step] up the control of juvenile delinquents…and…the round-up of undesirables in midtown." To press his case for additional funding, Adams calculated the number of crimes that he believed would be committed during the upcoming twenty-four hours, basing his figures on the sweeps of the previous weekend. Among his predictions: thirty-one robberies, one-hundred-forty burglaries, forty automobile thefts and one murder. In actuality, he overestimated the numbers for all crimes except rape (seven), felonious assaults (forty-three) and narcotic cases (three).[46]

As the initial campaign started to wind down during the last weekend of August, the police began a sweep based on a new charge—violation of parking regulations. Seventy men were picked up for parking near Central

Park, Bryant Park, and Battery Park between the hours of midnight and sunrise, and nine were arrested in the same vicinities explicitly for "degeneracy." One can assume that, knowing those parks to be prime cruising spots, most if not all of those arrested were gay men looking for sex. The *New York Times*, which reported the arrests, evidently felt the details too depraved to publish.[47]

The crowds of hoodlums thronging Times Square's sidewalks only exacerbated its decline, to the dismay of the businesses that depended on theatergoers and tourists for their income. The Broadway Association, a group of Times Square business leaders, called for special regulations in a new zoning plan to prohibit the types of fly-by-night enterprises that "contribute to the deterioration of property values." Those included open-front shops selling cheap electronics, record shops that blared music outside their doors, shooting galleries and arcades. Times Square, the group protested to the City Planning Commission, which ruled on zoning changes, was in danger of becoming a "midway" like that of Coney Island—while City License Commissioner Edward McCaffrey, who had tried to ban *The Miracle* two years earlier, had done nothing.[48]

That was all the encouragement Monsignor Joseph McCaffrey—no blood relation, but definitely kindred, in his moralistic worldview, to the License Commissioner—needed to strike up the protest band. Undaunted by his ignoble defeat in *The Miracle* case, Monsignor McCaffrey struck anew at the "shocking" billboards and theater advertisements that blanketed the area in vicinity of his church in Times Square. The movie theaters—which had a combined capacity for more than ten thousand patrons—displayed garish ads for second-run action movies, crime capers, and low-budget sex farces. In a move worthy of Charles Parkhurst, McCaffrey lambasted the films full of nude bodies and, ironically, wistfully recalled a time when vaudeville comics drew audiences to Times Square. These current spectacles, he swore, "were a disgrace to any city anywhere."[49] In addition to the "filth" of the theaters, "flea circuses, shooting galleries, penny arcades, wax museums and bagatelle games" made up the street-level dreck, while underground, in the IRT arcade, commuters could kill time with hand-cranked peep show machines and carnival games.[50] Men's bookstores also began to proliferate, with the pulp detective stories and humorous paperbacks increasingly being replaced by nude playing cards, posters, pin-up postcards, and cheap sex novels. "Bookstores display pornographic literature and openly sell magazines displaying nudes...these have all driven away the better element," McCaffrey testified during a hearing on the new zoning regulations.[51]

One would have assumed that the Monsignor would have blamed the police for not doing enough to curb the grotesquerie in their midst. But McCaffrey, as he done during the burlesque battle two decades earlier, absolved law enforcement of any responsibility for the sorry state of things—he was, after all, still the NYPD chaplain. Rather, he considered Times Square as representative of the disintegrating morals of the city itself, and declared that the area would recover only if public morality was drastically improved.

Morality would return in a form than no one expected: burlesque.

"UNVARNISHED SALACIOUSNESS"

In February 1955, Thomas J. Phillips applied for an exhibition license for the Orpheum Theater at 574-578 Fulton Street in downtown Brooklyn. The now sixty-eight-year-old executive director and only officer of the Burlesque Artists Association, who had bravely stood up to LaGuardia and former License Commissioner Paul Moss in 1937, told a reporter, "I felt a great wrong had been done to the theater as a whole" when burlesque was banned. "I felt the punishment didn't fit the crime."[52] Sensing that burlesque of a moral character might be the antidote to the grindhouse movies and cheap amusements of the current era, Phillips proposed "clean" burlesque to be enjoyed by families and the middle class, as opposed to burlesque's customary audience of working-class men.

Edward McCaffrey promptly called a public hearing on Phillips' application at the License Commission's headquarters at 137 Centre Street. All the usual suspects were front and center: the Catholic War Veterans, the Brooklyn Jewish Community Council, the Protestant Councils of New York and Brooklyn, even the Girl Scouts. T.J. McInerney of the Broadway

Association claimed, "as far as the public is concerned, there can be no such thing as clean burlesque."[53] Phillips' lawyer countered by promising that his client's show would have no strip acts and no runway, and none of the scandalous trappings of the Depression-era style. Phillips described his planned opening-night tour-de-force to a reporter outside the hearing: "A mythical character known as Burlesque has been exiled from his favorite haunts...we have brought this exile back—putty nose, baggy pants, big shoes, red hat— and he wants to go before the jury, which shall be the audience." Continuing with his imaginative description, Phillips went on to talk about how in the "second act," a chorus girl is on trial for killing the "inventors of movies, radio and television, who were driving her brothers and sisters off the stage in favor of mechanical entertainment." When asked to present evidence of her case, the actors, according to Phillips, launch a series of vintage specialty skits to show how unique and amazing an art form is burlesque. At the conclusion of the trial the audience is asked for its verdict in the form of applause.[54]

The ubiquitous Joseph McCaffrey countered by saying that, "no one could ever claim that he was elevated in mind or thought by attending burlesque."[55] It was, he insisted, "indecent, obscene, salacious and shocking."[56] On April 20, 1955, Phillips' license application was denied by Commissioner McCaffrey in a statement expressing high moral dudgeon. "The history of burlesque shows plainly that...[it] has followed closely and to a great extent slavishly the dictates of its public...the current meaning of the word burlesque is synonymous with the strip and the tease, the bump and the grind, and the dialogue of double meaning or unvarnished salaciousness." It was the Commissioner's duty, he wrote, to protect both upstanding citizens and the "panting, womanless hordes" from misrepresentation and moral peril.[57]

Feeling that city officials only remembered the worst of burlesque, Phillips took his appeal to the State Supreme Court, where he argued that his wholesome show, "without the strip-tease, the bumps and grinds and runway gyrations that brought the 'take it off' huzzahs from the patrons," wouldn't offend the delicate sensibilities of a 1950s audience.[58] One month later, the State Supreme Court ruled in Phillips' favor. Tersely, the judge condemned Commissioner McCaffrey for taking liberties as the public's moral guardian. Stung by the judge's remark, McCaffrey relented, and the license was granted—though Phillips wasn't allowed to put the word "burlesque" on his marquee. Defiantly, he ignored the Commissioner's threats ("I'll send a policeman in for every performance")[59] and vowed that burlesque would once again grace New York City. Harold Minsky, of New York's most famous and long-lived burlesque family, immediately began scouting Manhattan locations for his next theater.

Phillips was finally vindicated in December 1956, when his debut burlesque performance, *Welcome Exile* (the script he had described to the reporter eighteen months before) opened in a triumphant blaze of klieg lights at the Columbia Theater at 66 Second Avenue. Sadly, it only lasted seven performances. But the damage had been done.

5.

PRURIENT INTERESTS
1956-1968

While the public was perceiving juvenile delinquency as a symptom of the breakdown of family-oriented values, a much larger and subtle shift was already underway that would alter the character of the American family, particularly with regards to the way men and women dealt with another in both the workplace and in the bedroom.

Between 1940 and 1960, the number of working women doubled, while the number of working mothers quadrupled. Overall, about one-third of married women now worked outside the home. For these women, work provided a distraction and a degree of financial empowerment, as well as relief from domestic monotony—"the problem with no name," as cited by Betty Friedan in her landmark book *The Feminine Mystique*.[1]

Critics—many of who were, unfortunately, male employers—saw women's increasing role in the workforce as the chief cause of the breakdown of the family, a result of women's abdication of their traditional duties as wives and mothers. As a consequence of these attitudes, despite their gains, middle-class working women who were married were still expected to quit their jobs to keep house for their husbands. Similarly, a woman who continued to work after marriage but then became pregnant was expected to quit her job to be a stay-at-home mother. To avoid unwanted complications, many companies hired only unmarried women.

Others went even further in their attitudes and considered working women a *result* of the family breakdown, a situation wherein the husband mistakenly allowed his wife to work, thereby assuming what should be the male role. In this scenario, a wife's ambitions outside the home supposedly masked a power imbalance within the marriage that, if left unexamined, would devolve into a torrent of resentment, leading to "wives are not feminine enough and husbands not truly male."[2] One New York City psychiatrist warned that "One of the worst aspects of this…is that it tends to repeat itself in magnified form with each new generation. The masculinized mothers and the feminized fathers produce girls who are even more masculine, boys who are even more feminine…[I] have been struck by the increase in male homosexuality." A 1956 *Life* magazine article opined that "In New York City, the 'career woman' can be seen in fullest bloom and it is not irrelevant that New York City also has the greatest concentration of psychiatrists."

The limits of women's independence were dictated by the liberation of female sexuality, and until the late fifties, fertility and pregnancy were the extent of that liberation. The same contraceptive devices that Margaret Sanger found so difficult to distribute in the beginning of the twentieth century—diaphragms and related barrier devices like condoms—were still the primary types of birth control used more than fifty years later. The rhythm method, which was the only form of birth control approved by the Catholic Church, was unreliable and impractical for all but the most devout. Development of more effective (or less stigmatized) methods of birth control was not on the radar at research laboratories. Perhaps one reason for the lack of interest in birth control development was that so many women were already mothers: the post-World War II baby boom had reoriented social expectations of women, and family life focused on the children.

Sanger, however, had not given up her decades-old dream. She still believed that women would benefit from a simple oral birth control pill. "I consider that the world and almost our civilization for the next twenty-five years is going to depend on a simple, cheap, safe contraceptive," she wrote in 1951.[3] To help achieve this goal, Sanger enlisted the financial assistance of spice heiress and feminist Katharine Dexter McCormick, an old friend from their days as suffragist agitators. Together, they hired two Massachusetts doctors, Gregory Pincus and John Rock, to develop a prototype pill.

The pill the two eventually formulated was able to trick a woman's body into believing it was already pregnant, thereby preventing her ovary from releasing an egg, making fertilization impossible. If the dosage was halted, menstruation would result.[4] After several years and a series of successful field trials, the Food and Drug Administration finally approved Enovid— the Pill—as an oral contraceptive on May 11, 1960.[5]

The Pill's reliability, safety, and convenience distinguished it from all other birth control methods, allowing women (and men) to have sex whenever they wanted. For the first time in human history, the sex act was separated from procreation. Five years after its release on the market, five and a half million women were on the Pill (most of them white and middle-class).[6] A study in 1965 revealed that married women on the Pill had sex 39 percent more often than those who used other means of contraception. Less than a decade later, another study found that married couples were still having more sex than unmarried couples, and that couples who used the Pill had sex most frequently.[7]

By 1964, *Time* was marveling at the new "sexual democracy" in America, under which men and women practiced "serial polygamy."[8] The Pill allowed women to claim sexual pleasure as a right. Women's presence in the workplace, rather than threatening male superiority, now provided opportunities for affairs "with the office girl, from head buyer to perky file clerk." The concept of sin—in premarital sex, adultery, divorce—lost meaning and influence in secularized society.

As in previous decades, the seemingly rash turn from conservative values to liberal experimentation prompted tradition-minded parties to try and identify the source of immorality, so as to stamp it out post-haste. During the late fifties and throughout the sixties, these forces would have a wealth of sources to blame, as the commercialization of sex reached greater levels of organization, diversification and profit than ever before. Landmark Supreme Court decisions, on cases that originated between New York City merchants and the anti-vice brigade, would legalize the rapid expansion of commercial sex in America, which would come to be seen in the meteoric growth of three distinctly New York industries: radical publishing, sexploitation films and peepshows.

A SCAPEGOAT EMERGES

Lawmakers and social reformers were so concerned about preventing juvenile delinquency and family breakdown in the mid-fifties that Congress
launched a federal investigation into the myriad comic books, adventure
movies and sexy pulp novels that were supposedly influencing impressionable youth. Senator Estes Kefauver, Republican of Tennessee, and head
of the Special Subcommittee on Juvenile Delinquency, held three days of
hearings in New York City in May 1955 in the hope of ridding newsstands of such allegedly harmful, sexually themed publications. During the
hearings—which were televised to Times Square movie theaters—a parade of witnesses testified that such pornography was a social menace that
caused delinquency, or, on the contrary, that it was merely an example of
Constitutionally-protected free speech. Of the former, Dr. George Henry
(of *Sex Variants* fame) insisted on an inescapable correlation between the
suggestive pictures and stories available and the rise of juvenile delinquency.
Henry testified that young people are "more susceptible that adults to the
perverted ideas in which pornography traffics."[9]

A witness for the cause of free speech by the name of Samuel Roth
defiantly claimed that "no one under twenty-five could be influenced for the
bad" by such products. Born in Austria on November 17, 1894, Roth im-
migrated to New York City with his parents in 1903, settling on the Lower
East Side. A well-read child, Roth contributed articles to the Yiddish dai-
lies in his neighborhood, and developed an idiosyncratic set of principles
regarding the free dissemination of ideas. He eventually fell in with Emma
Goldman and other Lower East Side Socialists, but he was ultimately too
much a follower of his own ethics to remain unified with any group, no
matter how radical.

While at Columbia University, Roth started a student magazine called
Lyric, publishing excerpts from the works of D.H. Lawrence, Stephen Vincent Benét, and others. It was Roth's first taste of publishing real works of
literature, and he was hooked. After World War I, he opened a bookshop
at 49 East 8th Street in Greenwich Village and began publishing another
magazine called *Two Worlds Monthly* with his wife Pauline.[10] Like *Lyric*,

Roth's new venture published "lightly libidinous" short works from European novelists.[11] Unfortunately for Roth, in a 1927 issue he published extensive passages of James Joyce's *Ulysses*, a novel that was banned in the United States at the time. Joyce himself was not at all pleased about this because he had not given Roth permission to reprint any of his work. Roth countered by claiming that Ezra Pound, whom Roth assumed was acting as Joyce's agent, had given him permission to run the excerpts, although it was unclear whether Joyce had actually given Pound that authority.[12] A bizarre international feud ensued between the novelist, the poet, and the small-time publisher.[13]

At the same time that he was battling Joyce, Roth was being targeted by agents from the New York Society for the Suppression of Vice. In October 1929, Charles Bamberger—the same man who had tricked Margaret Sanger's husband into giving him a copy of *Family Limitation* in 1915—informed the police of the kind of materials Roth was publishing, resulting in Roth's arrest on suspicion of distributing obscene material through the mail—in violation of the Comstock Act—and the seizure of more than three thousand books.[14] Roth eventually served three months in prison at hard labor.

Except for another obscenity arrest and imprisonment in 1936, Roth remained relatively clean until 1955, when he was arrested and charged with twenty-six counts of printing and mailing obscene materials. The offending publications were several advertising circulars, a magazine called *Good Times: A Review of the World of Pleasure*, and Volume 1, Number 3 of a journal called *American Aphrodite*, in which Roth had published excerpts of the artist Aubrey Beardsley's decadent novel *Venus and Tannhäuser*, an erotic story of the goddess of love, her suitor, and her unusually ardent unicorn Adolphe. During Roth's trial, the "filthiest" passages of the book were read out loud by the federal prosecutor, George H. Leisure. One segment described Venus' manual manipulation of her pet's manhood: "The Queen bared her left elbow, and with the soft underneath of it made amazing movements horizontally upon the tightly strung instrument. When the melody began to flow, the unicorn offered up an astonishing vocal accompaniment...Adolphe had been quite profuse that morning. Venus knelt where it had fallen, and lapped her little aperitif!"[15]

Roth's lawyer, Nicholas Atlas, countered by offering copies of *American Aphrodite* to the jury and encouraging them to admire its hard-bound craftsmanship and high-quality artistic reproductions. The move had little effect. After a nine-day trial, the jury returned with a verdict of guilty on the count of sending obscene matter through the mail. Roth was sentenced to five years in prison and fined five thousand dollars.

Roth's lawyers immediately filed an appeal. In April 1957, the Supreme Court heard the case, now known loftily as *Samuel Roth vs. the United States of America*. In its case, the defense used an unusual tactic: rather than arguing that Roth was innocent of violating the Comstock Act, it strove to have the Act itself declared an unconstitutional abridgment of free speech. For its part, the prosecution had to prove that the Comstock Act was still necessary. While the United States Post Office had officially censored sexually explicit mail for nearly a century, Roth's case called into question the Comstock Act's relevance in a period of radically shifting social values. During the trial arguments, it became clear that Roth was but a front for this larger debate: for the first time, the Supreme Court was being forced to consider the legal definition of obscenity

In June 1957, in a surprising six to three decision, the Court upheld the criminal conviction of Samuel Roth on obscenity charges while at the same time setting a legal precedent for obscenity. While it was not an area of speech protected by the First Amendment, the Court defined obscenity so narrowly that sexual material with even a modicum of redeeming social value would be protected. The *Roth* case marked the first time the Supreme Court had drawn a distinction between sex and obscenity. Justice William Brennan, writing for the majority, concluded, "The standard for judging obscenity…is whether, to the average person, applying contemporary community standards, the dominant theme of the material, taken as a whole, appeals to prurient interests."[16] While the "Roth Test," as it became known, set the bar for all future cases, the vague terminology of the statute left the door wide open for legal challenges. "The question was how could a publisher, a bookstore owner, a librarian, or an author tell the difference between a protectable discussion or depiction of sex and an unprotectable obscenity? How could a painter or a photographer or the curator of an art gallery or museum tell? How could a policeman, a prosecutor, or even a judge tell if the Supreme Court did not tell?" wrote the First Amendment lawyer Edward De Grazia about the decision.[17]

Samuel Roth, after serving as the dubious symbol of this intellectual and moral debate, was devastated by the loss of his appeal. He went on to serve his entire five-year sentence and paid his fine of five thousand dollars. But his imprisonment had no deterrent effect on the production of pornography in the New York publishing world; in fact, though the case resulted in Roth's conviction, it protected ever more sexually explicit material from the same kind of prosecution.

THE TROPIC CASE

Nearly concurrent with the *Roth* case, Barney Rosset was fighting a similar battle on behalf of literature of a somewhat higher pedigree. When Rosset bought the struggling publishing company Grove Press in 1952 for three thousand dollars, New York's publishing houses produced either "respectable" literature in handsome hardcovers, or lesser-quality "pulp" paperbacks. With Grove, Rosset wanted to combine the two opposing classes of literature by promoting ultramodern, radical writers—who often wrote of sexual taboo, the subject of the pulps—to the forefront of highly regarded arts and letters. In doing so, he would, as Roth had hoped to, free literature from moralist bondage. His method and resources, however, were the opposite of Roth's.

Rosset grew up in Chicago with wealth and privilege, which ironically fueled his passion for artistic rebellion. After college at UCLA and a tour in the infantry during World War II, he moved to Manhattan, where he bought Grove Press and planned his first two strikes in the smut wars: publishing two novels that were banned in the United States., D.H. Lawrence's *Lady Chatterley's Lover* and Henry Miller's 1934 masterpiece *Tropic of Cancer*. Rosset knew he was asking for trouble, and he relished the fight.

Postmaster General Allen Summerfield was not amused when Rosset purposefully had a copy of *Lady Chatterley's Lover* mailed to him from

Europe in 1959. The Post Office habitually confiscated banned books and returned them to their senders, which Rosset knew; he literally wanted to make a federal case out of the situation. Rosset's copy was seized as expected, and he eventually sued to prove that the novel had literary value and did not "appeal to prurient interests" as the *Roth* decision claimed it had to for it to be obscene. In July 1959, Manhattan Federal Judge Frederick Van Pelt Bryan ruled that *Lady Chatterley's Lover* was not obscene (and, moreover, that the Postmaster General had no authority to decide whether a work was obscene or not), thereby lifting the ban and handing Rosset—who had funded the whole case—a landmark legal victory.[18]

Next up for Rosset was the legal fight to lift the ban on *Tropic of Cancer*, Henry Miller's lusty rumination of his time as a Parisian vagabond. It was illegal to bring the novel into the U.S., through thousands of vacationers returned from Paris and London with copies smuggled in their suitcases. Rosset saw a golden opportunity to challenge the ban, and announced a fifty-thousand dollar publishing deal with Miller in April 1961. Legal scholars expected *Tropic of Cancer* to receive the same scrutiny as *Lady Chatterley's Lover*, which Rosset banked on. Author Lawrence Durrell said to the *New York Times*, "American literature today begins and ends with the meaning of what he [Miller] has done."[19]

But the book that caused such consternation among moralists would produce an anti-climactic ruling from the U.S. Supreme Court. On June 22, 1964, without hearing arguments or statements from the defense or the prosecution, the Justices ruled, by a 5-4 vote, that *Tropic of Cancer* was not obscene. The Justices based their decision on *Jacobellis v. Ohio*, an obscenity case they ruled on the same day. In that case, Justice William J. Brennan wrote for the majority, saying that, "material dealing with sex in a manner that advocates ideas, or that has literary or scientific or artistic value or any other form of social importance, may not be branded as obscenity and denied the constitutional protection. Nor may the constitutional status of the material be made to turn on a 'weighing' of its social importance against its prurient appeal."[20] The close vote showed that the Justices were still in conflict with their own standard of judging obscenity, which they had decided in the *Roth* case.[21] For the rest of the 1960s, publishers and the courts would continue to test the boundaries and interpretations of what was considered obscene.

"THEY WANTED KICKS!"

After the *Roth* and Rosset verdicts, many critics complained that the Court had primed the market for pornography. In this dire prediction, they were correct. Without the threat of certain prosecution, publishers and filmmakers were now free to test the legal boundaries of erotic entertainment.

Rapidly changing social mores in the late fifties and early sixties, especially the battle between the sexes, provided all the anxiety, fear and sexual angst needed for a pulp novel. "As the Fifties give way to the Sixties, the paperback is 'the latest'—as much a part of the times as hi-fi and stereo records, compact cars and ranch houses, bongo drums and five-children families, two-week jet vacations to Europe and electric can openers," crowed the *Times* in 1960.[22] Pulp novels, a vast subgenre of paperback books, were quickly produced, cheaply printed books with plots full of sexual situations that made hay of gender stereotypes. These sex novels had their literary antecedents in the film-star magazines of the twenties and the popular fiction of the Depression—detective stories, spy tales, western adventures and the emotional confessions of lonely, fictitious housewives. During World War II, over one-thousand titles were printed on cheap paper, bound with soft cardboard covers and shipped to soldiers overseas, all on the Army's and Navy's dimes.[23] After the war, New York publishers continued to print popular fiction and racy non-fiction on inexpensive stock (thus giving them the "pulp" moniker), distributing these books outside the normal channels where respectable literature was sold, including drugstores, bus station kiosks, newsstands, and less-than-aboveboard booksellers in urban areas—in short, anywhere that young working class men (and a few women)—the pulp's main readership—congregated. The price of a pulp—from a quarter to fifty cents—made them accessible to everyone.

The initial attraction of the pulps for many readers were their flamboyant covers: colorful, lusty, and sensational paintings illustrating seductive women in come-hither poses, along with racy taglines promising "the mysteries of triangular love,"[24] or "a report on scandalous women from society dames and suburban sinners to B-girls, he-girls, and call girls."[25] So-called insider secrets, never before revealed, let readers in on the veiled worlds of go-go parties, wife-swapping, homosexual sex triangles, and the hidden shame of lesbians ("a delicate theme, treated honestly and candidly").[26] Despite the invitation to sexual worlds unseen, the stories in pulp novels were usually based on the time-worn battle between personal morality and the temptation of social transgression, within a rigid framework that ensured that decency and the social order would be restored by the end of the book. Pulps were a cathartic outlet for readers facing anxieties about changing social traditions, as evil characters were punished for their wild sexual appetites, penchants for drugs and jazz, or for daring to buck heterosexuality with wanton members of their own sex. In contrast, the protagonists in pulp novels were often innocent men and women lured into webs of seduction and big-city danger, who, after a taste of the dark side, were saved by marriage or accepted back by the husbands and wives from whom they had strayed. In almost every pulp novel, social value lay in antisocial characters meeting a tragic end. Despite the socially-redeeming formula, many pulps were "badly written, joyless, repetitious, and twisted in their emphasis on the sneaky and the abnormal," opined the *New York Times*.[27]

Given the Pill's impact on sexuality and women's increasing role in the workplace, it is not surprising that the most popular pulp plots involved male protagonists dominating women, either morally or physically. An unnamed pulp writer told the *New York Times* that the novels "allow[ed] men to transfer their guilt feelings about their inadequacies from themselves to the women in the book."[28] A plot in which the protagonist convinces a bisexual woman to marry him and leave her butch girlfriend was quite common for that reason. Nymphomaniacs and sadomasochists also proved irredeemably twisted, while lesbian or gay characters usually endured public shame or suicide.

Though many primarily heterosexual pulp novels starred gay characters as villains and sadists, by the late fifties and early sixties, pulp novels were beginning to explore homosexuality as a major theme. "Heterosexual love has become a rare commodity in current pulp novels. Nymphomania was the first aberration to be explored, and even that has given way now in popularity to lesbian and male homosexual themes," the *New York Times Magazine* reported in 1966.[29] There were far more lesbian-themed pulps than gay-themed, presumably because pulps were targeted toward a heterosexual male readership. Lesbians represented the dark and powerful side of sexuality, in which temptation was a weapon. They seduced innocent girls, stole wives from their husbands, and occasionally redeemed a self-loathing gay sister with love and acceptance, to the dismay of the rest of society.

Pulps also exploited society's image of the antisocial Beatniks, the poets and musicians who carved out alternative lifestyles in Greenwich Village. In the late fifties and early sixties, the Village defined free love and unconventional sexuality, just as it had in the years prior to World War I (even if the true Beat writers preferred Times Square). Because of this, New York City became an actual character in many pulps, instead of just a setting. When a small-town girl bought a bus ticket to New York, the reader knew that she was either going to find herself and recognize her deepest desires, or else run away from her past by losing herself in the big-city madness of jazz, dope and sex. Greenwich Village and New York represented the other side of American identity, where pulp readers could escape suburban complacency with "sex weirdos in search of offbeat thrills."[30] For *69 Barrow Street* by Sheldon Lord (a pseudonym for the mystery writer Lawrence Block), an actual address in Greenwich Village was all the title the steamy novel needed. "Their love was right! But their sex was wrong—a startlingly frank novel of love in the shadow world of the third sex," crowed the cover, fulfilling the homo hi-jinks implicit in the title.[31] The same went for another of Lord's novels, *21 Gay Street*, which offered "Greenwich Village, where angels and addicts, lovers and lesbians, bohemians and bawds live and love."[32] For the characters torn between "normal" love and lesbianism, or simply harboring desires beyond the narrow parameters of acceptability, the city was a launch-pad for their dreams.

"RAW, NAKED REALISM"

While the pulps proved that lurid advertising and sensationally sexy plotlines could sell consistently, especially in places where the novels provided the only form of commercial stimulation, the written word could only describe the lustful eyes of the heroines in black and white, not show them glittering with nymphomania in larger-than-life Technicolor. New York-based filmmakers thus saw an opportunity to bring the pulp phenomena to the big screen, which would result in the arrival of "sexploitation" films in the city's sexual epicenter, Times Square.

Exploitation or "sex-problem" films had been popular since the invention of the motion picture. The 1913 films *A Traffic in Souls* and The *Inside of the White Slave Traffic* were just two of the best-known of the silent era, thrilling and frightening audiences with their melodramatic portraits of immorality, without actually showing the evildoers in action. Fifty years later, exploitation movies of the mid-sixties used implicit sexuality and artfully obtuse camera techniques to achieve the same effect. The cinematic precursor to hardcore pornography, "sexploitation" movies combined the sensationalism and social anxieties of the familiar dime-store paperback with low-budget moviemaking. It was like pulp had come gloriously to life on the silver screen.

Audiences went to see the films in small theaters in Times Square that had been converted from gutted bars and other businesses.[33] Seating from one hundred to three hundred people, these theaters came into being expressly to show sexploitation pictures—unlike their antecedents on 42nd Street, which had begun as legitimate live theaters and devolved into grindhouses—and business was apparently booming. Times Square joints like the 50th Street Cinema, the Avon-on-Love, and the New Mini Cinema raked in six to seven thousand dollars daily (with tickets prices ranging from $2.50 to five dollars). "Productions for the mini-theaters, a New York specialty, abound, enabling such theaters as the Capri on Eighth Avenue to book features two or three months in advance," reported the *Times* on this new phenomenon.

Locally, New York fostered a community of commercial filmmakers whose aesthetic was tailored to score a profit. One of the most influential was Doris Wishman, a self-taught filmmaker and the only woman to make heterosexual sexploitation movies. Wishman was born in Forest Hills, Queens, but the actual year of her birth is a mystery, as she was as fond of fabricating the details of her life as she was of creating her films from scratch, usually acting as director, editor, writer and casting agent (she often used pseudonyms in the credits to disguise the fact that she couldn't afford a larger crew).

Wishman's cousin was a film distributor in the city, and she took a job as a secretary with him after studying acting at Hunter College. Initially, Wishman was not looking to create films, but after the death of her first husband, she set about making a movie to assuage her grief. In 1957, a Maryland appeals court had ruled that simply showing a nude human body in a film was not sufficient grounds for banning it.[34] Wishman thus saw an opportunity to flex her creative muscle and set about writing her first script. The result was *Hideout in the Sun* (1960), a no-budget classic set in a South Florida nudist camp. Wishman quickly fell in love with the filmmaking process, and the modest success of *Hideout in the Sun* prompted her to make six more nudist flicks between 1960 and 1965, all filmed on location in Miami-Dade County, where she lived at the time. Wishman eventually moved back to New York, where she joined a community of filmmakers and distributors with offices on Ninth Avenue, west of Times Square. The New York scene was very different from the idyllic nudist colonies of sunny Florida: it was gritty and existential, and the films' nudity was hypersexualized. Wishman's style was transformed by the city's mien as well as the market, in which darker and violent films were prized. While her first films, including *Hideout in the Sun*, *Diary of a Nudist* (1961) and *Nude on the Moon* (1962) exemplified the comparatively innocent "nudie" genre, influenced by the increasing tendency of the pulp novels and magazines to tackle taboo social subjects, Wishman and other directors (such as Russ Meyer in Hollywood) turned to more complex storytelling, developing characters by translating cultural anxieties into film.

The intellectual process behind Wishman's best films was counterintuitive, relying only peripherally on the narrative formula that ensured an audience's erotic stimulation. She began with a title—her most memorable included *Bad Girls Go to Hell* (1965), *Indecent Desires* (1967) and *Too Much Too Often!* (1968)—then created a tagline and a basic plot. Certain scenes, dictated by the pulp formula, were mandatory. Remembered Chuck Smith, the cameraman on fifteen of Wishman's movies, as well as the director of his own sexploitation flicks: "you had this piece of paper in front of you, and you thought, 'okay, these are the obligatory scenes.' You got a rough sex scene, a masturbation scene, a lesbian scene. Now you invent a script that illustrates those to the point where you don't offend the censor. I used to write on file cards."[35]

Wishman's films were characterized by idiosyncrasies that eventually became emblems of her singularity as a director: recycled actors, post-synched dialogue, and demure cut-away shots to inanimate objects when characters had sex. "There was a small group of actors in New York doing that kind of work, the exploitation work, at the time. Almost everybody that used the talent used the same people because they were not averse to disrobing and simulating sex," recalled Smith.[36] Soundtrack music often replaced complicated dialogue (another Wishman trademark), and the audience was always informed of plot developments by changes in music: bebop bongos anticipating a sex scene, or clarinets signaling the heroine's crisis of conscience.

While few sexploitation directors managed to elevate their storytelling above the limitations of their financing, Wishman, on the other hand, was a resourceful, creative director who utilized New York City as both a setting and a character in many of her films, just as many authors had in the pulp novels. On a typical investment of ten thousand dollars, she created claustrophobic scenarios of sexual subjugation, feminine vulnerability, and masculine violence, perfectly (and perhaps unconsciously) illustrating the shifting sexual values of New Yorkers in the mid-sixties.

The advertising for Wishman's films were often as important as the actual content: the trailer for *Bad Girls Go to Hell* exploited the story's "raw, naked realism." As the black-and-white scenes flickered in theaters, a man's voice warned, "See the boldest and most intimate scenes ever shown on screen in *Bad Girls to go Hell!* See sex without shame…see violence in a story that is brutally honest! These are the men, possessed with sex, corrupt, immoral! Who prey upon women—they are the thrill-seekers!"[37]

As "shocking" as sexploitation was to mid-sixties tastes, the films shared a format with mainstream Hollywood movies. Audience members paid a few dollars at the box office, sat down in a multi-seat theater, and watched a standard two-hour screening of a movie with a beginning, middle, and end. Because of this similarity, sexploitation could still be seen as an extension—albeit lowbrow—of typical movie-making, with productions that were far more acceptable than what was about to invade Times Square.

FOR YOUR EYES ONLY

The popularity of the sexploitation genre was waning by the mid-sixties, as audiences were looking for the next, more graphic trend in visual eroticism. Fulfilling this desire would be a thirty-three-year-old Brooklyn business-man named Martin Hodas. Hodas wanted a piece of the now saturated sexploitation market, but he needed to reinvent the product if it was going to succeed. Eventually, he would develop a scaled-down version of a sexploitation movie theater, but with none of the overhead or film distribution costs. Thus, the sexual "peepshow" was born.

Hodas began life as a scrappy Brooklyn kid with a knack for answering the door when opportunity knocked. He learned salesmanship from his father, who supported the family by selling eggs door-to-door, and by age eight Hodas was shining shoes for spending money. He eventually graduated to selling newspapers outside subway stations and, after a stint in the army and at community college, to servicing a gumball machine route in Brooklyn, until he had an epiphany one day that would change his life and alter the landscape of Times Square. It happened at a roadside arcade in New Jersey farming country. As Hodas walked into the room, he came upon the most impressive peep-machines he'd ever seen. They were as tall as a man and, when a quarter was dropped in the slot, played sixteen-millimeter loops (which could play continuously without being rewound) of women go-go dancing, belly-dancing, doing a striptease, or posing suggestively.

The earliest peepshow machines had been invented by Thomas Edison in 1891, and by the nineteen sixties, eight-millimeter peeps were common in arcades in Coney Island and Times Square. Until Hodas came along, however, people thought of peepshows as innocent children's entertain-ment, and arcade owners threaded the machines with cartoons or slapstick comedy clips. Attempts to put adult clips into machines in kiddie arcades did not, for obvious reasons, sit well with the public.

Hodas bought all twelve peeps he saw that day in New Jersey, with the hope that these sixteen-millimeter machines could play actual films of nude women and thus might be placed in adult bookstores. He approached adult bookstores in Times Square with a profit-sharing deal, but the owners refused to install the peep machines when Hodas admitted he didn't have a license. While his own lawyer thought it would be next to impossible to get one, he did come up with an equivalent, a letter from the City Department of Licenses stating that, in fact, no license was needed to "install in the New York City area a coin-operated machine that shows movies."[38]

However, most of the storeowners still weren't buying. Only Hyman Cohen, the owner of Carpel Books at 259 West 42nd Street, took the chance. For him, however, there was little or no actual risk: Hodas covered all of the leasing, maintenance and repairs and would split the proceeds fifty-fifty. Less than a week after four of Hodas' twelve 16mm peepshows were installed in mid-1967, Hodas was called in to fix two that had broken down. He discovered that so many quarters had been jammed in the slot that the collection box had overflowed and gummed up the machinery. While he fixed the problem, the line of men with quarters in hand stretched around the block. Soon after, Hodas installed the rest of his peep machines in stores at 113 West 42nd Street, 210 West 42nd Street and 1498 Broadway.[39]

In order to meet what was now becoming a great demand, Hodas bought more 16mm machines from a Kentucky manufacturer. By 1968, Hodas had incorporated into East Coast Cinerama Theater, with an office above the street-level fracas at 233 West 42nd Street. The money was rolling in, literally, in quarters. On an average day, his associates dragged trunks through Times Square, collecting Hodas' half of the profits from each machine. In one afternoon, Hodas deposited fifteen thousand dollars *in quarters* into one of his four bank accounts.[40]

That same year, Hodas diversified his business by launching 42nd Street Photo Studio, where, at ten dollars for a thirty-minute session, Hodas supplied a Polaroid camera, a girl, and privacy for enterprising photographers. The model received a cut of the fee plus tips. But Hodas knew what happened when a man and a naked girl were in a private room together for half an hour. Naturally, he wanted a piece of that pie as well, so he set up a studio, Dynamite Films, in a 14th Street basement and set about making his own peep loops. He found willing girls through advertisements offering seventy-five dollars for a fifteen-minute loop. With titles like *Flesh Party* or *Elevator Orgy*, the loops would be cut into two-minute segments to thread into the peep machines. With bare-bones production values, Hodas could churn out three films a week. Ingeniously, he then had the store where the two-minute peeps played also sell the original, uncut reels for eighteen to twenty dollars a pop; one storeowner reportedly moved twenty-five hundred reels in a week.

The two-minute duration of the loop meant there wasn't much room for storyline, so Hodas had to keep them relatively clean. Most had a single woman posing or dancing topless, while others showed two women, or a man and woman, with only the upper portion of their torsos visible.[41] Novel scenarios were introduced—sex in an elevator, sex in a car, sex at the office. Hodas knew his place in the industry. "My short films are the finest in the business. The average persons viewing these machines are normal American men who admire nude beautiful women," he claimed. "Show me a man who doesn't admire a beautiful woman and I'll show you a degenerate."[42]

Up until this point, organized crime had mostly left Hodas alone, but the peeps' phenomenal profit-making ability proved to be irresistible. As a result, the mob openly competed for a stake in the game. While masturbation or actual sex never took place in the mainstream loops, a lively underground racket in hardcore loops developed when the mob began siphoning Hodas' control over the peep industry. These illegal loops were often filmed in cheap Times Square hotels, and introduced bestiality, necrophilia, massive orgies, erotic blood sucking, and coprophagia to the cinematic pantheon. Some of the best-known porn stars of the next decade got their start in this cruel theater, including Linda Lovelace, John Holmes, Annie Sprinkle and Vanessa Del Rio.[43]

By the late sixties, about four hundred peeps littered Manhattan, with the greatest concentration along the nexus of 42nd Street and Eighth Avenue.[44] However, the non-peeping public was getting fed up with the unmitigated degeneration of the city. "Cannot something be done about this rapid proliferation of so-called 'adult peep-show' shops?" a plaintive 1969 letter to the editor at the *New York Times* began. "They peddle out-and-out pornography, display disgusting pictures in windows and attract in the main youths and rather disreputable types as potential customers…Who is for spring cleaning with a vengeance?"[45]

CLOSING THE FLOODGATE

By the early sixties, the forces of decency were already concocting an anti-porn strategy, though it received little notice in the media. Along with perennial organizers Francis Spellman and Joseph McCaffrey, a Jesuit priest named Father Morton A. Hill embarked upon his own morality crusade in 1962, spurred on, as so many of his brethren were, by a dirty magazine.

The Brooklyn-born Hill was affiliated with the St. Ignatius Loyola School on the Upper East Side when he was approached by a young mother who complained of sadomasochistic literature circulating among the sixth-grade boys. Hill dutifully looked into the situation, and though the actual facts of his investigation and identity of the offending literature remain hazy, he was sufficiently moved to create a community opposition force called Operation Yorkville. As its most vocal leader, Hill used his pulpit to sermonize against the alleged accessibility of hardcore pornography to minors, likening it to a violation of "parental civil rights."[46] He told worshipers that pornography led to sexual violence and drug abuse, and it "sews [sic] the idea of perversion that soon leads to experimentation and finally fixation." He warned that young boys, in answering mail-order ads for free stamp collections or x-ray glasses, could wind up on the mailing lists of pornographers. The boy might then be bombarded with flyers for "material that illustrates sadism, masochism, homosexuality, and other perversions."

On October 25, 1963, Hill announced that he was fasting indefinitely, subsisting only on water, to protest Mayor Robert F. Wagner Jr.'s inaction toward curbing porn sales, despite Wagner's promise to Operation Yorkville that such sales would be vigorously prosecuted. However, Hill's noble fast lasted only three days, as on October 29, Wagner vowed that the city would use every available resource to ban sales of porn to children. The *New York Times* noted that, "The Mayor acted in response to the demand of a Jesuit priest…and [arranged] for city officials concerned to meet with the priest."[47] Hill had by then made a second career out of touring tri-state communities with a talk-and-slide show about the dangers of pornography (137 stops in just a year), complete with a thirty-minute educational film called *Perversion for Profit* and displays of dirty books and magazines, no doubt solely for the purpose of disgusting his audiences.

The Wagner administration, for its part, was staunchly behind Hill's crusade. Deputy Mayor Edward F. Cavanaugh Jr., the mayor's liaison to the anti-porn groups, justified the city's position thus: "It's one thing to allow adults to buy smut. The law is clear in its respect of adult rights. [The Mayor's action] is confined to minors."[48] Nearly a year later, in August 1964, Mayor Wagner called a press conference to announce the formation of the Citizen's Antipornography Commission, a task force which was charged with determining legal ways to enforce the moral standards of the city. "A veritable floodgate of obscenity [has been] opened in the last twelve months in the form of obscene pocket books, magazines, and greeting cards, to such an extent that it is unbelievable," Wagner declared.[49] He was extending the anti-smut drive instigated by Father Hill, which had been recently seconded by the omnipotent potentate Cardinal Francis Spellman. The day after Wagner's announcement, Spellman congratulated the mayor in a speech for "acceding to our request."[50] The proliferation of pornography "represent[s] an acceptance of degeneracy and the Beatnik mentality as the standard way of American life. Let us have a crusade that will deal a mortal blow to the powerhouse of pornography, reaffirm the ideals of the family, and preserve the traditions of a free America," Spellman wrote.[51]

The 1964 drive was the latest incidence of the New York City government capitulating to the wishes of self-appointed moral guardians like Hill and Spellman, and it gained steam quickly. At a closed-door meeting in December, the twenty-one members of the commission (mostly Wagner administration officials and businesspeople) decided upon its strategy: rather that pursue the small storekeepers and retailers that disseminated the allegedly obscene material to the public, they would go after the publishers of such material themselves—mirroring Comstock's M.O. of nearly one hundred years before. However, unlike Comstock, the commission was afraid that the obscenity drive might backfire in a city with such a live-

and-let-live attitude. Either the commission could please the religious leaders, like Spellman, who constantly called for moral improvement and held
enormous influence over politics; or it could err on the side of the First
Amendment and public opinion. A compromise of sorts was determined,
in which "persuasion" would be the primary weapon in the fight for decency.
No massive book raids, no new legislation passed; instead, the commission
would try to change the hearts and minds of the people. It would not be
easy, conceded deputy commission chairman Cavanaugh; "while we try to
influence judicial determination, we cannot pressure the court. We hope
that by making public the commission's opinion on specific public actions,
we may be able to sway public opinion." Besides, "newspapers can't print the
language that's in these magazines," he remarked, thumbing through some
evidence, "golly, these things are just unbelievable."[52]

Meanwhile, the city Transit Authority was busy mounting its own
cleanup campaign in the subways' underground newsstands. At least 225 of
the stands were owned by the American News Company, a major publisher
of pulp novels and magazines. A TA worker, John Gilhooley, wrote an official letter of protest to American News Company vice president W.A. Mc-
Cullogh, declaring the TA's intent to confiscate materials sold in the transit
system that appeal "to the prurient interest" and contain "photographs of
semi-nude women [and] articles devoted to illicit love, sex, nudism and
violence." Echoing the Comstockian imperative of protecting children
from moral degradation at the expense of adult pleasure, Gilhooley added
that, "Thousands of impressionable schoolchildren are in the subways daily.
While they are on our property we consider ourselves custodians of these
children. We do not intend to permit them to see the filth of the type
above mentioned." Gilhooley went on to justify his intended crackdown
with a desire to halt the rising crime rate within the transit system, another
common reasoning for censorship. It was noted that the TA had in its possession several "lurid" magazines, including *"Mister, Dude, Police Detectives,
Secret Confessions, Male, Personal Romances, Intimate, Real Confessions, and
Real Stories."*[53]

City License Commissioner Joseph C. Di Carlo took up Gilhooley's
cause, also in the form of a protest letter to the publishing industry, de-

manding that its news-sellers forbid the sale of erotic material to anyone under sixteen. But instead of ordering compliance, Di Carlo asked each of the one thousand city newsstands to monitor itself, without clarifying the consequences for noncompliance. "It is not the intent or desire of this department to act in any case as a censor, but I sincerely believe we owe an obligation to the citizenry of this city to protect the young without interfering with the freedom of the press," Di Carlo wrote. Specifically, he added, he was "disturbed" by the homoerotic magazines on display. At the press conference announcing the protest, "he showed newsmen an expensively printed magazine containing color photographs of teen-age boys posing in the nude, bought by one of his inspectors from a sidewalk newsstand where it had been prominently displayed."[54]

"A REALLY GOOD MAGAZINE ABOUT LOVE AND SEX"

While the dual anti-obscenity campaigns were heating up, a thirty-two-year-old magazine publisher and author named Ralph Ginzburg was living a quiet life in Jackson Heights, Queens, with his wife, children and a "large collection of Bach and Jazz."[55] Ginzburg was a slight man, with rounded glasses, a weak chin and a receding hairline—to some, the very picture of a pornographer, which is exactly the opposite of how he saw himself. Rather, he viewed his publishing efforts as an exercise in the free exchange of ideas, specifically, ideas about sex, love, and desire, as well as ideas that could be cheaply printed and sold for fifty cents each. Ginzburg was not as flagrant a copyright infringer as Samuel Roth, but his goal was the same: let the people read, and decide for themselves what was obscene.

Ginzburg had first been inspired by an article in the *New York Daily Compass*, where he was a freelance reporter, noting the retirement of John Sumner, Anthony Comstock's handpicked successor at the New York Society for the Suppression of Vice. It was 1950, and Ginzburg was on his way up the New York publishing ladder, freelancing and managing the advertising budget at *Look* magazine. From there he jumped to *Esquire*, where he became the articles editor ("the pillars of communications industry respectability," he noted dryly many years later).[56] As the story goes, in lieu of a pay raise, *Esquire's* publisher gave Ginzburg back the rights to one of his

articles for the magazine. Titled *An Unhurried View of Erotica*, the piece
was a rather scholarly examination of British erotic works. But with an
already developing knack for sensation, Ginzburg published it in pulp form
by himself in 1958. It became a bestseller at fifty cents a pop.[57]

Ginzburg's appetite for exposing sexual hypocrisy was permanently
whetted. In 1962, flush with royalties from his book, he decided that a "really good magazine about love and sex" was needed in America. Though his
Chicago-based rival *Playboy* had begun publishing almost a decade before,
Ginzburg felt only the "grimiest of publications" were devoted to the glori-
ous miracle of sex.[58] He envisioned *Eros*, a hardcover journal of sexuality
meant to be savored by intellectuals, not a cheap newsstand magazine; he
hired Herb Lubalin, the industry's best typographer and art director, and
collected articles from the renegade writers of the day. Despite his disdain
for the "pillars of respectability" in the publishing world, he desperately
wanted *Eros* to be among them.

The first issue of *Eros* was published on Valentine's Day 1962, containing eighty pages between an elegant ochre cover featuring a naughty
playing card on the front.[59] Among the contributions were a short story
by science-fiction writer Ray Bradbury and a new translation of a Guy de
Maupassant bodice-ripper with drawings by Edgar Degas, which filled sixteen pages. A dirty dictionary and a selection of poems from the Earl of
Rochester, rumored to have been the lover of England's King Charles II in
the seventeenth century, was also included. The Summer 1962 issue opened
with a meditation of women's adoration of the youthful president John F.
Kennedy. If Ginzburg was at all concerned that *Eros* might be singled out
for obscenity violations, this was perhaps unwise: the president's brother
Robert was the Attorney General. The issue's other distractions were photo
essays on Parisian prostitutes and Indian phallic statuary, and reprints of the
thousands of mostly supportive letters Ginzburg had received upon publication of the first issue.

By the third issue in Autumn 1962, *Eros* actually contributed something to the cultural zeitgeist: an eighteen-page spread of Marilyn Monroe,
photographed six weeks before her death. With his previous focus on President Kennedy and the rumors of his affair with Monroe, Ginzburg was

directly or indirectly tempting the Attorney General to take action against him, which would finally occur with the next issue, when *Eros* was cited for obscenity. The material deemed illegal was an eight-page "photographic tone poem" by the critic Ralph Hattersley Jr., in which a black man and a white woman cavorted unclothed yet chastely in a photo essay.[60]

Like Samuel Roth before him, Ginzburg was charged with mailing obscene material. However, Ginzburg's cheeky ploy shot him in the foot: it looked like he was advertising explicit sexuality, which he wasn't, as even he wanted the public to believe that *Eros* was not obscene and therefore respectable. He was also indicted for sending salacious advertising through the mail (though the magazine so advertised, *The Housewife's Handbook on Selective Promiscuity,* was not itself obscene). Ironically, Ginzburg was writing a biography of Anthony Comstock at exactly the same time he was charged with breaking his law.

Ginzburg was aware that the "blue-noses" in New York City had him in their sights. "The New York smut-hunting Catholic priest Morton Hill persuaded U.S. Attorney General Robert Kennedy to have me in indicted, as Father Hill later boasted, for distributing 'obscene' literature," Ginzburg remembered. Hill and Ginzburg were familiar enemies by this time. When Operation Yorkville succeeded in getting the Wagner administration to crackdown on smut in 1964, *Eros* had already been forced to suspend publication; neverthess, Ginzburg answered Hill's sanctimonious hunger strike with one of his own to protest "the obscenity panic that is plaguing our city and the country."[61]

A lower court in New York City convicted Ginzburg in 1963, and sentenced him to the unusually punishing term of five years in federal prison with a fine of $28,000, significantly more than Roth had to pay for his similar offense,[62] but much less than Attorney General Kennedy's request of a $280,000 fine and 280 years in prison.[63] After a series of appeals, the Supreme Court agreed to hear the case in early 1966. At issue: was it a violation of the *Roth* rule to advertise something as obscene, even if it was not? It would be the first Supreme Court case to put the *Roth* standard to the test, and even obscenity foes thought Ginzburg would walk on the case's arbitrary evidence. But both prosecution and defense were stunned when the

Justices ruled, five to four, to uphold Ginzburg's conviction. Justice William Brennan, writing for the majority opinion as he had for *Roth*, seemed to add another dimension to the obscenity standard when the Court "decided that 'titillating' advertising could be proof that the advertised material was obscene."[64] For the first time, a publisher's intentions and motives could be the deciding factor between obscenity and protected speech—even if the material itself wasn't explicit. Brennan chastised publishers that "would make a business of pandering to the widespread weakness for titillation by pornography."[65] Dissenting Justice William O. Douglas fired back that "the advertisements of our best magazines are chock-full of thighs, ankles, calves, bosoms, eyes, and hair, to draw the potential buyers' attention to lotions, tires, food, liquor, clothing, autos, and even insurance policies."[66] The only clear thing decided in *Ginzburg* was that advertising sexuality could be just as obscene as writing about it.

The ruling had an immediate and chilling effect on adult bookstores in Times Square, whose salacious advertising were their stock-in-trade: the sensual harlots and giddy college girls on book jackets, the suggestive blurbs promising literary thrills, the allure of "sex hungry men and women."[67] Storeowners quickly removed from view "sadomasochistic and homosexual publications that the Court appeared to deem offensive," noted the *Times*. Respectable novels took the place of obscure publications like *The Spanker's Monthly* and *Simulated Spanish Inquisition Tortures*.[68] Police arrested six men in a raid at a peepshow reel distribution center in Brooklyn, netting a payload worth millions.[69] A few months later, one hundred thousand dollars' worth of hardcore porn was seized and two men were arrested at a 42nd Street bookstore.[70] But even Father Morton Hill was circumspect. "People have been calling to congratulate me all day,' he said. "But I'm not sure we're to be congratulated."[71]

Ginzburg and the literary community in New York were outraged. After a lengthy appeals process, during which time he was free on bail, Ginzburg's conviction was finally upheld. He began serving his sentence (now reduced to three years) at Allenwood minimum-security federal prison camp in Pennsylvania on February 17, 1972, almost ten years to the day after publishing the first issue of *Eros*. A sensitive soul, Ginzburg wrote about the stripping away of humanity from he and his fellow prisoners. "He is allowed no sexual outlet—I, like the other men, became a robotlike eunuch, and it was painfully clear to me that deprivation of manhood is really what prison is all about."[72]

On the outside, his wife and comrades fought for his parole, which was finally granted after eight months of imprisonment. Upon his release, Ginzburg was defiant. As he walked from the prison gate to the crush of reporters and photographers, he read a prepared statement. "I, Ralph Ginzburg, paroled prisoner, U.S. Bureau of Prisons convict number 38124-134, do hereby accuse the United States Supreme Court…of mocking the Constitution, trammeling Freedom of the Press and playing fast and loose with one man's liberty—mine," he declared. "My work has been defiled. My publications have been suppressed. My family has been tormented…for what? What is the hideous crime for which I have been so mercilessly flogged and declared an enemy of the people?" His voice rose. "In this supposedly civilized, professedly free society, [I] was manacled and muzzled for trying to tell the truth about sex."[73]

6.

YOUR MOST FANTASTIC FANTASIES

1969-1979

By the end of the nineteen sixties, New York City was well into the throes of sexual revolution. However, while manifestations of heterosexual lust and torment were highly visible in subway newsstands, movie theaters and chic cafes, realistic portrayals of homosexual life were still mostly hidden from view, available only to those who searched beyond the muscle magazines and pulp novels. Even as radical youth culture shunned sexual tradition and family obligation, homosexuals were still seen by moral arbiters as a separate species, banished to the fringes for their unorthodox behavior and ideas. Discretion, if not secrecy, was still expected from gay men, and the consequences of living an honest life could be harsh.

"Homophile" organizations, first convened in the early fifties, sought recognition of gays as a legitimate minority group, as well as legalization of consensual gay relationships. Composed of nascent gay rights collectives (such as the Mattachine Society and Daughters of Bilitis) the homophile movement had gained enough political ground by the mid-sixties to warrant a front-page article in the *New York Times*. The paper of record analyzed the peculiarities of so-called "sexual inverts," interviewed eminent psychiatrists, and observed police action against the homosexual community in order to examine "the city's most sensitive open secret."[1] In providing a snapshot of heterosexual attitudes towards homosexuality in the early years of the sexual revolution, the investigation revealed homosexuals' modes of dress, favorite publications, and preferred leisure activities and behaviors, all of which had evolved despite (or because of) an avowedly intolerant heterosexual society. Gay men could easily spot each other on the street because "they have their favored clothing suppliers who specialize in the tight slacks, short-cut coats and fastidious furnishings favored by many...male homosexuals."[2] For an evening on the town, "homosexuals are traditionally willing to spend all they have on a gay night. They will pay admission fees and outrageous prices for drinks in order to be left alone with their own kind to chatter and dance together without pretense or constraint." The article attributed these signifiers to the "basic emotional instability," frivolity and sexual licentiousness particular to the homosexual.[3]

Contrary to Alfred Kinsey's research published in *Sexual Behavior in the Human Male* in 1948, the American Psychiatric Association classified same-sex desire as a mental illness in the early fifties, officially removing it from the arena of religious sin and placing into the realm of pathology. Socially accepted views of homosexuality in the sixties continued to stem from the medical establishment. A majority of physicians and psychologists, the *Times* found, believed homosexuality was not biological, but the result of poor parenting. Therefore, "[psychiatrists] assert that homosexuality can be cured by sophisticated analytical and therapeutic techniques."[4] Such psychiatrists may have assumed gay men would seize the opportunity to be "cured"—though few men investigated this possibility. One member of the Mattachine Society's New York chapter asked three hundred gay men if they would take a cure, even if it were easy and quick; 97 percent would have refused.[5]

Except in the sensational pulp novels of the previous decade, lesbianism too remained under society's radar. Many Americans doubted the existence of female libido or sexual autonomy; even fewer believed a woman could truly desire other women over men. The prevailing wisdom was that women were sexually impressionable, and that lesbians were simply confused by sex; thus, they could be easily flipped back to heterosexuality. New York medical psychoanalyst Dr. Charles Socarides, the go-to guy for opinions on homosexuality well into the seventies, stated the condescending view of the medical profession: "with many women, a homosexual relationship evolves or devolves into a kind of compassionate pair...they protect each other and depend on each other; there is often very little actual sexual contact."[6] One report, however, recognized the growing presence of "the woman homosexual" as a threat to social order. At the time, being a lesbian was not a crime in the state of New York, though it was illegal to "perform a Lesbian act." In 1969, the *New York Times* uncovered "a marked increase in the number of women picked up by New York City police for 'loitering,' a charge applied 'for soliciting another for the purpose of engaging in deviate sexual intercourse.'" In 1968, ten women were so arrested, while forty-nine were picked up in the first nine months of 1969—suggesting that the police were becoming more adept at arresting women.[7]

THE STONEWALL REBELLION

The first taste of freedom for gays and lesbians depended on the decriminalization of private consensual sex acts among same-sex partners. Legalization of gay and lesbian intimacy would eliminate the need for constant police scrutiny of the places where gays and lesbians congregated. And the police excelled in entrapment, the easiest method to maintain control by fear. "Cruising gay bars, effecting mannerisms of homosexuals, members of police vice squads try to ensnare individuals in the act of solicitation," a 1967 *New York Times Magazine* piece disclosed. "Depending on police vigor, imagination and zeal, the homosexual flirts with arrest, fines and a criminal record every time he tries to make a new homosexual contact." About 120 men were arrested under the New York sodomy statute in the sixties, and not a few were tricked into it.[8]

Gay bars acted as the battlefields on which gay men fought their war with the police, and the organized crime syndicates that owned the establishments. Mafia investment in gay bars was a natural extension of its longtime interest in shaking down businesses that catered to easily controlled clientele, dating back to the gambling machine rackets of previous eras. By 1967, ten years after first investing in the bars, organized crime families owned most of the gay establishments in Greenwich Village. Ruthless owners easily exploited customers with exorbitantly-priced drinks, sub-par facilities, and abusive bouncers, knowing that gay men wouldn't want to attract police suspicion for any reason.[9]

The Stonewall Inn at 53 Christopher Street, just off Seventh Avenue South, was one of the most popular Village bars because it allowed dancing as well as drinking. In an unpretentious, working-class atmosphere, Stonewall offered a bar in the front room and a dance floor in the back, where young and flamboyant queens sipped fizzy cocktails and posed. Teenage hustlers who worked the Times Square beat often wound up at the Stonewall at the end of a hard night. Women were scarce, though a few brave butches occasionally blended in.[10] Like all gay bars, the windows were blacked out and covered in plywood to protect the patrons' identities. Bartenders watered down the overpriced drinks as per Mafia policy, since the Genovese crime family was Stonewall's proud owner. Sanitation was an afterthought: an hepatitis outbreak among gay men in the Village was rumored to have been caused by the Stonewall's unwashed glasses.[11]

Stonewall had a system in place devised to deal with police, typical of gay bars of the era; a system of warning lights strung through the bar alerted patrons when the cops were coming. Usually, officers would charge in, check out the patrons, and then leave without too much disruption. The *Village Voice* reported that "generally men dressed as men, even if wearing extensive makeup, were always released; men dressed as women are sometimes arrested; and 'men' fully dressed as women, but upon inspection by a policewoman prove to have undergone the sex-change operation, are always let go."[12] As a additional line of protection, the bar's owners brazenly paid off corrupt officers at the nearby Sixth Precinct (at a rate of about two thousand dollars a week), who would let them know when a raid was planned.[13]

The trinity of mafia, law enforcement, and gay men maintained an uncomfortable détente until early on the morning of Saturday, June 28, 1969. After mourning the death of Judy Garland, who had died June 22, groups of gay men gathered at Stonewall to dance and drown their sorrows in watery gin-and-tonics. It was like any other night at the bar, except that the police raid came as a total shock. There was no tip-off because the officers weren't from the Sixth Precinct, or even the State Liquor Authority, but from the federal Bureau of Alcohol, Tobacco and Firearms (ATF), investigating a mob-connected bootlegging scam run out of Stonewall's basement. ATF agents had just discovered the cozy financial relationship between Stone-wall's owners and the Sixth Precinct, and therefore notified cops of the raid at the last possible moment, offering them no opportunity to alert the bar.

ATF agents and police rushed in at 1:20 A.M., at the height of the night's merriment, taking patrons and staff by surprise. The officers asked everyone for identification, and then rounded patrons up for handcuffing and arrest. The procedure was so unlike the usual catch-and-release that most men immediately realized that this "was no ordinary raid."[14] Sensing they could be in real danger of arrest or exposure, the patrons resisted. A paddy wagon pulled up to the door to take the detainees away; at the same, a growing crowd of onlookers outside the bar began to boo and taunt the cops. When those not under arrest emerged from inside the bar, they did not disperse, but instead stood around, talking with a group of men gathered in the small park across the street. Eventually, the crowd increased in size and anger.

Suddenly, a lesbian in drag started fighting with the officers as she was led to the paddy wagon. Catcalls rose from the onlookers, and "it was at that moment that the scene became explosive. Limp wrists were forgotten," reported the *Voice*.[15] Some in the crowd tried to push over the paddy wagon, while others began hurling bottles, coins, beer cans and bricks at the police.[16] Drag queens being led from the bar tried to wriggle out of their handcuffs as officers wrestled them to the ground. (A few cops got platform heels to their kneecaps.) At one point, someone found the key to the driver's side door of the paddy wagon and freed the arrested queens.

Realizing they were outnumbered, and completely taken aback by the gay patron's unprecedented resistance, the officers blockaded themselves inside the Stonewall. A group of men tried to ram the reinforced door with an uprooted parking meter as shouts of "I'm a faggot and I'm proud of it!" rose from the crowd.[17] *Village Voice* reporter Howard Smith, barricaded inside the ransacked bar with the officers, watched as a stream of lighter fluid trickled in from a broken window, followed by a lit match.[18] Fortunately, the fire caused only minor damage, though the inside of the bar was already a mess; bar stools broken and overturned, broken glass everywhere, the cash register drawer empty, the contents of the cigarette machine gone.

Outside, stunned officers belatedly called for backup. Eventually, scores of cops in riot gear formed lines to sweep the street clear of people; instead of dispersing, the crowd taunted them. The melee continued until 3:30 A.M. The next day, the *New York Times* reported "Four Policemen Hurt in 'Village' Raid."[19] One cop, with delicious irony, had suffered a broken wrist. The story didn't comment on the injustice of the raid itself, saying only that "hundreds of young men went on a rampage in Greenwich Village" when plainclothes cops entered a bar that was "wellknown [sic] for its homosexual clientele."

On the evening of June 28, crowds of protestors gathered in Sheridan Square, the small park across Christopher Street from the Stonewall. The group grew to four hundred tense people, who threw cans and bottles at the police guarding the area. The feared Tactical Patrol Force, a police unit skilled in riot control, was ultimately called in. With their arms linked, the squad formed a line spanning Christopher Street and repeatedly tried to clear the block between Sixth Avenue and Seventh Avenue South. The protesters eventually dispersed, but the violence wasn't over. On Sunday, Sheridan Square and Christopher Street teemed with gay men and lesbians who had heard about the riot and wanted to be a part of the historic struggle. "Allen Ginsberg and Taylor Mead walked by and wanted to see what was happening," wrote the *Voice* reporter on the scene.[20] "[They] were filled in on the previous evening's activities by some of the gay activists. 'Gay Power! Isn't that great!' Allen said. 'We're one of the largest minorities in the country—10 percent, you know. It's about time we did something to assert ourselves'."[21]

Stonewall proved to be the turning point of the sexual revolution in New York City, for gays as well as straights. It culminated the first wave of the sexual transformation of the city—from a culture controlled by sycophantic bureaucrats and moralists to a renaissance of hedonism, experimentation, sensation and sex. It also began a secondary wave of liberation, freeing men and women imprisoned by society's homophobia, as well as opening a vast palette of possibility for heterosexuals that went beyond marriage and the missionary position. The public saw the power of a few sexually disenfranchised people to bring historic social change on that late

June weekend. Stonewall promised that much more could be accomplished if everyone joined in the fight for sexual equality. The next phase of the revolution—political power, social acceptance and radical expressions of sexual desire-- was just over the horizon.

THE STRIKE IS HOT

At the same that the gay rights movement was breaking new ground in New York City, the analogous push for women's liberation was already riveting the nation's attention. Betty Friedan, author of *The Feminine Mystique*, had founded the National Organization for Women (NOW) in 1966 at a conference in Washington, D.C. with like-minded members of the Equal Employment Opportunity Commission and other feminists. "We organize to initiate or support action, nationally, or in any part of this nation, by individuals or organizations, to break through the silken curtain of prejudice and discrimination against women in government, industry, the professions, the churches, the political parties, the judiciary, the labor unions, in education, science, medicine, law, religion and every other field of importance in American society," boldly stated NOW's mission statement. Friedan, the author of the declaration, strongly believed that women must seek "truly equal partnership with men" to reach these goals, and argued that men, too, suffered from the "half-equity" of the sexes. "We believe that a true partnership between the sexes demands a different concept of marriage, an equitable sharing of the responsibilities of home and children and of the economic burdens of their support," she wrote. When such goals were met, "women will develop confidence in their own ability to determine actively, in partnership with men, the conditions of their life, their choices, their future and their society."[22]

NOW's early platform demanded federal legislation mandating equal pay for equal work and non-discrimination in the labor market—an achievement that would allow women to gain financial independence, the first step in their liberation. To boost support, Friedan and NOW organized the Women's Strike for Equality on August 26, 1970, to commemorate the fiftieth anniversary of women winning suffrage, with the main demonstration held in New York City in solidarity with spontaneous, grassroots actions all over the country. The message: despite making up 51 percent of the U.S. population, women were underrepresented, even absent, from positions of power in government, law, industry, education, and the arts, and they weren't going to take it anymore.

Friedan led the march down Fifth Avenue from 59th Street to Bryant Park flanked by her sisters in the movement, including New York Congresswoman Bella Abzug and Amy Swerdlow, an activist who had organized a Women's Strike for Peace a few months earlier against the Vietnam War. Followers carried signs and shouted, "Don't Iron While the Strike is Hot," "For This I Went to College?" and "Don't Cook Dinner: Starve a Rat Tonight!" The media reported that there were thirty-thousand marchers, though organizers estimated a much higher number. Independent of NOW, simultaneous demonstrations occurred in ninety other cities in forty-two states.[23] Friedan was thrilled at the turnout and support from ordinary women, if not from the news media, which treated the feminists' message with pronounced skepticism. Nevertheless, the Women's Strike for Equality incited the feminist movement on a national scale.

Even at that crucial moment of unity, however, philosophical cracks had already started to appear in the movement. In particular, the views of the old guard women who came of age during World War II, like Friedan and Abzug, seemed too conservative to the younger, more radical members. The founders of NOW and their allies preferred to play by the rules set by those in power in order to win equal rights. In contrast, younger feminists were personally radical in their dress and lifestyle, and demanded the same level of radicalism from the movement. This group included Gloria Steinem, whose heterodoxy would become more pronounced as the seventies wore on; Kate Millett, author of *Sexual Politics*, virtually a handbook for the feminist movement; and Germaine Greer, whose book *The Female Eunuch* argued that women's disassociation from their libidos contributed to their own subjugation. The new feminist polemic of 1970 considered the U.S. government inherently sexist and patriarchal, and radical feminists believed that no gains could be made by working within a corrupt system. They would not wait for token handouts; they would take their anger and demands to the streets, where no politician could afford to ignore them.

Nothing less than total revolution would suffice.

Nowhere was the schism between old and new attitudes greater than when it came to the lesbian question. While lesbians made up a large part of the movement, the old guard questioned the wisdom of their visibility in the struggle. The mainstream media already portrayed feminists as man-hating, braless lesbians, and feminist leaders did not want to give credence to their insults. Betty Friedan emerged as the most forceful opponent of lesbian presence within the movement (in 1969 she dubbed it "the lavender menace"). In her opinion, sexual nonconformity was anathema to the acceptance of women as equals in society; and worse, it was a distraction from the real goal of gender equality.[24]

That view went out of style very quickly when Kate Millett revealed, in a 1970 *Time* article, that she was bisexual, thereby exposing the danger and hypocrisy of excluding gay women from the struggle. "[Feminists] bravely talk about liberating themselves from dehumanizing sexual-role definitions, but then employ the same odious treatment in dealing with women who have found a sexual, emotional and spiritual companion in another woman," wrote Lois Hart, a member of the radical organization Gay Liberation Front, to the *New York Times*.[25] *Time* mused that homosexuality was still a scarlet letter, even among feminists: "[Millett's] disclosure is bound to discredit her as a spokeswoman for her cause, cast further doubt on her theories, and reinforce the views of those skeptics who routinely dismiss all liberationists as lesbians," it predicted.[26]

The opposite happened. Millett, along with Steinem, writers Susan Brownmiller and Sally Kempton and NOW's Ti-Grace Atkinson, called a press conference in New York to announce their support of Millett in particular, and gay women in general. "Lesbian is a label used as a psychic weapon to keep women locked into their male-defined 'feminine role.' The essence of that role is that a woman is defined in terms of her relationship to men," they asserted in a prepared statement. "A woman is called a lesbian when she functions autonomously. Woman's autonomy is what Women's Liberation is all about."[27] The press conference also signaled a permanent break from the more conservative origins of the women's movement, and announced feminists' intention to foment revolution until equality became reality. Because radical feminists rallied to Millett's defense rather than ostracize her, lesbians gained more leadership power within the movement.

"THE CONSUMER REPORTS OF SEX"

The gay and women's liberation movements depended on making the personal political—and vice versa—which often required utter seriousness and emotional concentration on the goal at hand, leaving little room for humor, an underappreciated but essential part of the sex business since the days of vaudeville and burlesque. Perhaps it was therefore inevitable that an irreverent, gleefully filthy foil to the essentialist brow-beating would emerge and provide a dose of self-deprecating amusement to the seventies' sex wars.

That counterweight was the sex newspaper *Screw*, founded in 1968 and thus coinciding with the countercultural demands for sexual and gender equality. While Stonewall and the women's movement were expressly for gaining political power, *Screw* provided the ballast of absurdity, standing at the journalistic crossroads between honest commentary on sexuality and politically-incorrect skewering of traditional mores. The paper published the first gay-interest column of any newsstand paper, "Homosexual Citizen" by Lige Clarke and Jack Nichols, two prominent activists in the gay liberation movement (as well as lovers). Many scholars of gay history credit Clarke and Nichols' *Screw* column as the first to use the term "homophobia" in print. At the same time, *Screw* also reviewed porn movies on the "Peter Meter" (a scale based on the number of erections the reviewer experienced while watching), made fun of staid elected officials, printed off-color cartoons and became the platform for the unorthodox views of its founder, Al Goldstein.

Goldstein was a mordant, thirty-two-year-old Brooklynite who followed his Pace University education with a stint in the U.S. Army Signal Corps, then eked out a living as a freelance news photographer. To pay the bills, he drove a cab, sold life insurance, and worked as an industrial spy for a subsidiary of the Bendix Corporation in Queens. Goldstein was not very good at earning regular pay, but he was obsessed with getting laid—two conditions that did not naturally facilitate each other. Perhaps, he thought, publishing a sex tabloid might help in the latter department. He also had a lot of opinions on things besides sex, from mail-order catalogs to the First Amendment.

When he tried to sell an exposé of his Bendix experience to a start-up radical paper, Goldstein met editor Jim Buckley, with whom he shared a loathing of the mainstream media's derision of sex. "We talked about how the sexual act was warped and sick in these puritanical papers. Why weren't skin flicks and fuckbooks reviewed? Why were pussy pictures reserved only for the rich who could afford them? Where was the equality and democracy of smut?" Goldstein remembered.[28]

Goldstein and Buckley each invested 175 dollars in the first issue of *Screw*, a twenty-five-cent, twelve-page newsprint tabloid. The first issue came out the day Richard Nixon was elected president—November 4, 1968.[29] "The sexual revolution was exploding. We embraced a huge market no one knew existed. What was missing from *Playboy* centerfolds, sexploitation films, automobile and cigarette ads with sex—was simple honesty," Goldstein recalled. "We were now the sword of the sexual revolution, the *Consumer Reports* of sex."[30]

The cover of the inaugural issue featured a girl in a bikini suggestively holding a torpedo, over which the issue's contents had been pasted: "How to Buy Sex Books," "Exposing a Fake Vagina," "*Screw* Reviews a Beaver Film," et cetera. Aside from glorifying sex in all its forms, *Screw* editors provided an "exclusive testing service for consumers in the sexual market:" critiques of skin flicks, "fuck books" and sex products to inform readers whether they were getting their money's worth—a service never before offered by any other publication. Goldstein's first review was the "Premier Vaginal Prosthesis, or artificial vagina," and he was not impressed. "Depersonalization reached its zenith when Premier Products in California introduced its artificial vagina for the approval of the American buying public," he began. "Ingenious in theory, it is a failure in practicality." After describing the product in detail, Goldstein lamented, "we are saddened to report that we were unable to give a realistic test of the fake vagina under laboratory conditions. We found the whole concept of trying to fuck a burlap-type bag with breathing gill-like apertures much too ludicrous to get aroused over."[31]

By the eleventh issue, circulation exceeded 50,000, though the magazine was sold only in Manhattan. By the fifteenth issue, the NYPD had Goldstein and Buckley arrested on obscenity charges; the pair retained First Amendment lawyer Herald Price Fahringer to fight the charges, as well as the fifteen similar arrests that would follow, all in 1969. Father Morton Hill, the Morality in Media honcho who had persecuted Ralph Ginzburg, also preached against Goldstein as his profile rose in the daily papers.

Screw signaled the maturation of the sex market from a clandestine, euphemism-laced trade to a consumer-reviewed industry by elevating products to the standard of mainstream consumer items. As a result, it emerged as the authority on the New York sex trade by virtue of its dedication to the market's changes and innovations. The legitimacy *Screw* bestowed on the sex industry would set the tone for the rest of the seventies.

"PORNO CHIC"

With *Screw* now dispensing its expert opinion on porn movies, the time had come for hardcore filmmaking to rise to the expected standards of production. Stag reels of implied sexual intercourse and the sexploitation films of the previous decade lacked the erotic substance and degree of fantasy that seventies audiences wanted; they needed the full experience, from seduction to money shot.

In 1972, Gerard Damiano, a former hairdresser from Queens turned pornographer, was thinking about making a hardcore flick about fellatio, inspired by the singular talent of a stag star he had met through some friends a few days earlier. No filmmaker had ever done a movie just about oral sex. Among heterosexual couples, giving head wasn't on the level of actual intercourse; it was considered a lesser act, base and dirty, something only whores did. Damiano proposed a film that would promote fellatio from the gutter to the boudoir and redefine it as an activity that enhanced a couple's sexual experience.

Much like Doris Wishman, Damiano first came up with the title—*Deep Throat*—before writing the script. He hired Harry Reems, a well-known performer on the stag circuit (Reems would go on to co-star with Chesty Morgan's seventy-three-inch bust in Wishman's *Deadly Weapons* later that year) as a production assistant before casting him as the male lead. But Damiano's real score was signing up twenty-one-year-old New Yorker Linda Boreman as the main character, and changing her last name to Lovelace.

Boreman's life up to that point had been a series of ironic contradictions. She had been raised in Yonkers, New York, a colorless, working-class city just north of the Bronx, and attended Catholic school. Her first ambition was to be a nun, and she kept herself chaste even during the hormonal high school years, though she eventually abandoned the idea in favor of trying to open a clothing boutique. However, a devastating car accident at age twenty again reoriented Boreman's priorities. In the summer of 1971, she was recovering from serious injuries at her family's new home outside Fort Lauderdale, Florida. Under her strict mother's thumb, lazily chain-smoking two packs a day and reading romance novels, Boreman was in the front yard, laying on a chaise lounge in a bikini despite her scarred body, when Chuck Traynor sidled up and introduced himself.

By most people's standards, Traynor was not a catch. He was frequently broke, and when he did have money, its source was murky, as he dabbled in drug pushing, collecting guns and pimping girls. He was a master manipulator, though, and the naïve, sheltered Boreman quickly fell under his spell. To her, he was strong and decisive, and she needed a caretaker; her battered body mirroring her fragile mental state. "I curse the day she ever met Chuck Traynor," recounted Barbara Boreman, Linda's sister, in the 2005 documentary *Inside Deep Throat*. "Unfortunately he died before I could kill him."[32]

The couple moved to New York City, where Traynor found jobs for Boreman as a topless dancer in 42nd Street dives. Perhaps it was her natural shyness, or her imperfect beauty, but she was ultimately offered roles in stag films, and Traynor was more than happy to steer her in the direction of the burgeoning porn market. "Those first eight-millimeter movies were shot in a loft near 48th Street and Broadway by a man named Tom…the first film was a relatively straight one, if you can believe that," Boreman, now Lovelace, wrote in her memoir, *Ordeal*, referring to her first loop in which she had sex with a man and a woman.[33] With another director, she was forced into her most infamous loop. "They had the dog lick me. All this time they were telling me to smile and to laugh. I was supposed to look very excited," Lovelace recalled. "[They said] 'Okay, Linda, get down on your hands and knees. No, down on all fours. That's right...' When they pulled the dog away from me, I was in the deepest valley I'd ever been in, devastated."[34]

Rumor had it that Damiano hired Lovelace based on one particular talent she had displayed in the loops. *Deep Throat* is the story of Linda Lovelace ("as herself"), a young woman who is tormented by her dissatisfaction with sex—"I don't enjoy it," she tells her pal Helen (Dolly Sharp). Helen arranges an orgy to see what will float Linda's boat. Even after panting and sweating up a storm with a succession of mustachioed hunks, Linda still isn't satisfied. At the end of her rope, she visits Dr. Young (Harry Reems), who gives her a physical examination, where he discovers that Linda doesn't have a clitoris. Or does she? Peering inside her mouth, Dr. Young is tickled to discover it lodged deep in her throat!

The good doctor then recommends a strict regimen of fellatio for Linda. She is put to work as a "physiotherapist," helping members of the community suffering from impotence. She meets her match in patient Wilber Wang (William Love), who falls for her. Linda initially rejects his advances ("The man I marry has to have a nine-inch cock!") but she's happily surprised when Wilber whips out his manhood. Naturally, they live happily ever after.[35]

Deep Throat had its world premiere at the New Mature World Theater on West 49th Street on June 12, 1972. It was an immediate smash. Each week, five thousand New Yorkers went to see Linda Lovelace take it all the way down. The film's appeal went far beyond the trenchcoat set, luring celebrities, politicians, artists, and many women. Public figures such as Jack Nicholson, Johnny Carson, film director Mike Nichols, and actress Sandy Dennis went to see the film and, most remarkably, told everyone they did. Truman Capote, always the gadabout, "thought the girl was charming."[36] Vice President Spiro Agnew, perhaps in the interest of getting to know the enemy, took in *Deep Throat* during its first run.[37] Tourists, kids playing hooky, and businesspeople on their lunch breaks also filled the New World's seats. Famously, *Washington Post* reporter Bob Woodward, who broke the Watergate scandal, named his White House source after the movie.

Unlike standard porn movies, *Deep Throat* gave audiences a story line with a clever gimmick, prompting laughter among ordinarily silent

porn audiences. The soundtrack was filled with catchy melodies, campy lyrics and bizarre marching rhythms. The popular Coca-Cola ad jingle *I'd Like
to Teach the World to Sing* received a makeover with the new lyrics, "I'd like
to teach the world to screw/in perfect harmony/I'd like to see you all get
laid," and so on.[38] Al Goldstein, reviewing *Deep Throat* in *Screw*, remarked
that it was "the best X-rated film ever made" and gave it a perfect score of
one hundred on the "Peter Meter." "Suddenly, I see a movie that knocks my
socks off. And here's the wonderful thing: this film, *Deep Throat*, is funny.
And Linda's a wonderful, wonderful cocksucker. God, I wish my wives could
suck dick like that," Goldstein remembered wistfully. Even cops sent in to
monitor the audience sensed that the film "was something different."[39]

Most viewers credited Lovelace as the strength of the movie. Her
fresh-faced smile, slight snaggletooth, and girlish innocence was light-years
from the bored harlots and faked orgasms of average porno. She seemed to
truly enjoy herself during the coital scenes, and fellated with genuine gusto.
While *Deep Throat* was not a feminist film, it was considered a step in the
right direction for female viewers. In a little more than six months, the film
grossed roughly seven hundred thousand dollars in New York City alone,
and $3.2 million nationwide.

Deep Throat also hit theaters at the precise moment when porn actors
looked like counter-cultural heroes, artists who bravely challenged society's
traditions of sexuality by baring it all. "The American public was tired of
words like 'coitus.' They wanted words like 'fuck,' and 'suck,' and 'eat my
cunt,'" said Goldstein. A *New York Times* reporter, Ralph Blumenthal,
penned an article in January 1973 that encouraged even more publicity and
summed up *Deep Throat's* impressive cultural impact: "Porno Chic."

CUT THROAT

As *Deep Throat's* profits (and Al Goldstein's seal of approval) seemingly legitimized hardcore porn, the forces of public morality launched a counter-
attack. This led to a police raid of the New Mature World Theater in April
1972, with *Deep Throat* seized on obscenity charges. The non-jury trial began
in Manhattan Criminal Court on December 18, 1972, and proved nearly as
entertaining as the film. Almost immediately, journalists referred to the trial

as a landmark case because the owner of the theater, Mature Enterprises, Inc., was charged with promoting obscenity, rather than an assortment of building code violations as was typical in city efforts to close down porn theaters. If *Deep Throat* was found to have any redeeming social value, it would be protected from the obscenity death-sentence.

Expert witnesses distilled the movie's fifteen sex acts into crisp, factual testimony. Five witnesses testified for the defense, including prominent film critic Arthur Knight, who argued that it was "the first film of this genre to acknowledge the importance of female sexual gratification."[40] Two academics asserted that the film was merely a spoof of contemporary sexual mores, and therefore had social value. The final witness was the controversial medical psychologist Dr. John Money, a flamboyant presence at Johns Hopkins University who delighted in flaunting sexual conventional wisdom. A brilliant researcher in the field of psychological endocrinology and transsexualism, an advocate of open marriage and recreational sex, and the originator of the term "gender identity," Money had no particular expertise in film criticism but nonetheless praised *Deep Throat* for offering viewers an opportunity to adopt less shameful attitudes about sex.[41]

The witnesses for the prosecution proved to be less than convincing. Seventy-one-year-old retired psychiatrist Dr. Max Levin, who had "frequently testified for the prosecution in obscenity cases," took the moral high road. "My objection is both to the message, which I found outrageously misleading, and to the presentation, which I found obnoxious," he stated. Viewers, he said, were in danger of being "blinded" to the facts of female sexuality, which could cause them to believe that women could only reach orgasm by clitoral stimulation. "I think that vaginal orgasm is superior to the clitoral," he declared, despite his obvious lack of firsthand knowledge. His credibility suffered when it was discovered Levin had confused the subject matter of *Deep Throat* with another hardcore film showing in the same theater.[42]

In the end, Judge Joel J. Tyler, who had been the City License Commissioner prior to being appointed to the bench, remained unmoved by the defense's plea for sexual freedom. In a particularly caustic guilty ruling in March 1973, Tyler referred to the low-budget flick as a "feast of carrion and squalor," "the nadir of decadence," and most picturesquely, "a Sodom and Gomorrah gone wild before the fire." In addition, the filmmaking techniques "were directed toward a maximum exposure in detail of the genitalia during the gymnastics, grations [sic], bobbing, trundling, surging, ebb and flowing, eddying, moaning, groaning and sighing, all with ebullience and gusto."[43] After the ruling against the New World Theater, Bob Sumner, the theater's twenty-six-year-old manager, replaced the advertisement on the marquee with a clever headline: "Judge Cuts Throat, World Mourns."[44]

Mature Enterprises appealed Tyler's ruling, but the police immediately confiscated the theater's print of *Deep Throat* and prevented its further screening in the city. Just a few months later, in June 1973, the U.S. Supreme Court decided an unrelated obscenity case, *Miller v. California*, which would have ramifications for *Deep Throat*, and other sexually explicit material. The Court ruled that such material would be tried against local community—rather than national—standards, and would be judged obscene if it, "taken as a whole, lacks serious literary, artistic, political, or scientific value."[45] Any community where *Deep Throat* was being shown could thus bring charges based on the community's particular sense of decency. Such ambiguity promised to keep the film entangled in the courts for the near future.

PUBLIC DESIRES

Because of its celebrity endorsements and legal notoriety, *Deep Throat* greatly increased porn's profile among the mainstream, resulting in it gaining popularity and a degree of acceptance, if not actual respectability, in the early 1970s. As explicit sexuality became entrenched in the consciousness of New Yorkers, many sought additional, more tactile experiences. Passive viewing in a movie theater just did not rate as high on the thrill scale as actually taking part in scenes like those on the big screen. As a result, a culture of active sexual participation—in public, and in group settings— grew to include commercial spaces dedicated to sexual exploration and sensual horizon-broadening. The market evolved in turn to meet the needs of a sexually sophisticated public, with club owners tailoring their services to distinct segments of the population based on sexual preferences. No matter the scene, however, clients sought to express sexual desire, explore boundaries, and be included in the trend toward greater sexual freedom.

In the gay male community, the baths regained their notoriety as hot pick-up joints after two decades out of the spotlight, in the process evolving from unofficial, semi-covert meeting places for gay men to elaborate sexual entertainment complexes that doubled as gay community centers. While owners retrofitted basic shower facilities into saunas, pools, private cabins, porn-viewing lounges, cabaret stages, and discotheques to attract self-aware and sophisticated hedonists, guests could also find political information from the gay liberation movement on bulletin boards, or get tested for sexually-transmitted diseases on the premises. For the first time, many baths were owned, operated, and patronized by gay men (rather than owned and operated by straights with a gay clientele), a sign of the gay community's growing sense of identity and social responsibility.

Bathgoers now had an astounding variety of settings and services in which to engage their whims. After nearly eighty years as a mixed club, the Everard Baths in Chelsea, the most popular of the wartime bathhouses, re-opened as an exclusively gay paradise. (Though the Everard was "*the* bath," according to activist Larry Kramer, "it was hideous, like Kafka. There were wire-mesh walls, and the floors were filthy and stank.")[46] The new gay owners of the St. Marks Baths, originally a turn-of-the-century Russian spa, refurbished and reopened as a gay establishment for the leather and S/M scene. Men also roamed the steam room and showers for willing partners in almost total darkness at Man's Country, the Barracks, Beacon Baths and the Wall Street Sauna.[47] A national chain of gay bathhouses, the Club Baths, opened in 1970 and featured the latest in hippie-style décor.[48]

The Continental Baths, though, were a class apart. "I think the Continental Baths changed things more than Stonewall did...the Continental Baths were like ancient Greece. They were clean, and you could talk to people...[they] were like a candy store," remembered Kramer. Billed as "a unique, total gay environment," the Continental Baths occupied the basement of the Ansonia Hotel at 230 West 74th Street and offered live entertainment, a pool with a waterfall, sex rooms, juice bars, and theme parties.[49]

A 1975 indie film, *Saturday Night at the Baths*, memorialized the Con-
tentintal Baths' heyday. Filmed on location and directed by David Buckley,
brother of *Screw* co-founder Jim Buckley,[50] the film employed a basic plot
in which Michael (Robert Aberdeen), a pianist from Montana, moves to
SoHo with his girlfriend Tracy (Ellen Sheppard) and is hired to play at
the Baths by the cute, voluminously Afro'd manager, Scotti (Don Scotti)—
the real-life entertainment director of the establishment—and Steve (Steve
Ostrow, the Baths' owner, in a cameo appearance). Scotti develops a crush
on Michael, who initially rebuffs him. When Tracy encourages their friend-
ship, however, Michael is forced to re-evaluate both his prejudices and his
sexual orientation.

Though the characters act out the story, the setting is the real star of the
film. During a daytime rehearsal, the baths are mostly empty, with only a few
hirsute men in white towels mingling about. But when Michael returns for
the evening's performance, the Baths have come to life: half-naked men (and
a few hip women) boogie to disco music on the dance floor, people frolic
under the swimming pool's waterfall, and two young hunks soap each other
down in a steamy shower scene. As the emcee of the show, Scotti announces
the night's line-up of drag performers in a Cabaret-esque costume. Real
drag stars of the time perform as Judy Garland, Diana Ross, Shirley Bassey,
et al., followed by a modern-dance vignette by men in tighty-whiteys.

Saturday Night at the Baths opened at the RKO 59th Street Twin I Theater in Manhattan on June 11, 1975. Though clearly a low-budget movie,
it rated a brief review in the *New York Times*, which noted it was filmed on
location and "is, like the baths, slightly steamy and enervating." After a brief
mention of the raunchy sex scenes, the reviewer sniffed, "this gay life in the
'Baths' is somewhat sad and pointless."[51]

The Continental Baths' popularity proved, unfortunately, to be its down-
fall. After attracting struggling artists such as Bette Midler (with Barry Ma-
nilow on piano), Cab Calloway, and Tiny Tim to its poolside stage, slumming straight couples began to outnumber the sexually adventurous queers.
When the higher-profile cabaret acts started to overshadow the cruising—
the original reason for the Baths' popularity—the gay clientele moved on to
greener pastures. The straight crowds then noticed that the Bath was losing

its erotic edge (Ostrow seemed determined to appeal to the widest possible customer base with grandiose live entertainment, diluting the focus on sex) and stopped coming. The last straw came when Bloomingdale's began selling reproductions of the Continental Baths' monogrammed towels. With the Baths' sell-out complete, business fell off, and Steve Ostrow was forced to close shortly thereafter.

However, the storied space would come back to life in 1977 under new ownership as Plato's Retreat, (allegedly) the world's most famous sex club. As the Continental Baths, the Ansonia basement had drawn gay men like a beacon, providing identity and easy sex; as Plato's, the twenty-three thousand square foot oasis would become the shrine of swinging, "America's fastest-growing leisure-time activity."[52]

THE CULTURE OF SWINGING

Swinging, "Westport roulette," key parties, wife-swapping—whatever the terminology, it meant strictly heterosexual sex between two or more couples.[53] The trend originated in the suburbs of California, but quickly swept eastward throughout the late sixties. "Carol" and "Tim," the pseudonymous authors of *The Swinger's Handbook* (1974), recounted an anecdotal story from the early days of swinging in New York. "Not long ago, two couples met at one of the few, but well-populated, Manhattan bars open only to swinging couples. After a few drinks, they decided to go to one of the couples' apartment to get better acquainted," they wrote. "During the cab ride from the bar to the apartment, one of the two men looked quizzically at the other couple and said, 'you know, I have the strangest feeling that we've met somewhere before.' The foursome started comparing notes on who-was-where-when and who-knew-who. It wasn't long before they all realized they had swung together some fifteen years earlier, as one of them told a mutual acquaintance, when 'there were only seven swinging couples in the entire city of New York.'"

In the beginning, swinging provided an outlet for sexual experimentation within the staid confines of middle-and upper-middle class suburban life. Most swingers were husband and wife; singles were gently discouraged, and it was exceedingly rare for one partner in a marriage to swing without the other, even if he or she (usually she) had to be coaxed into the scene. Swingers threw meet-and-greet cocktail parties in their private homes, perhaps smoked a little grass, and rarely, if ever, went out to a public bar or nightclub to meet other swinging couples.

As the fad gained popularity through word of mouth, swingers placed personal ads in dedicated magazines to connect the scene across the United States, using deliciously-coded language to indicate personal tastes. "Husband and wife seeking playmates into French culture" indicated a fondness for fellatio, "Greek culture" meant anal sex, "Roman culture" meant orgies, and "English culture" intimated whipping and flagellation.[54] According to "Carol" and "Tim," most swingers were white (as were most suburbanites), and unfailingly heterosexual—though, of course, many husbands encouraged their wives to explore bisexuality, as they watched. "Carol" mentioned that 80 percent of swinging women had bisexual experiences.[55] But the husband never engaged in homosexuality, a social line even the sexually-enlightened wouldn't cross. Women often sought sexual validation from swinging, to be reminded that they were attractive to the opposite sex even after marriage. Husbands encouraged wives to follow the orgasmic urges, and through orgasm find a new sense of self-esteem. Men, by and large, enjoyed having their egos (and other things) stroked.

In cities like New York, urbanites viewed swinging as a suburban phenomenon for bored housewives and sexually-frustrated husbands, since people in the scene were mainly conservative and conventional in every way but their marital boundaries.[56] Group sex, on the other hand, was a different animal—a urban recreational fad based on hedonism, rule-breaking, and thrill-seeking. Places like Plato's Retreat were purpose-built for orgies. Every modern convenience had been provided, from a full buffet dinner service to small trysting rooms overstuffed with Oriental pillows to locker rooms dispensing tiny white terrycloth towels. The Olympic-size swimming pool, giant dance floor and whirlpool of the Continental Bath days still remained, but the patrons were now straight couples from Connecticut rather than hedonist homosexuals. Public group sex had arrived as a mass-marketed fad; it was therefore not surprising that the owner of Plato's, Larry Levenson, was a former manager of a McDonald's franchise in Brooklyn.

In many ways, Levenson personified the typical early-middle-age, completely heterosexual customer at Plato's. At forty-one, he was divorced, and after being drawn into swinging by a date, had become the scene's biggest booster, creating Plato's with an investment of $250,000 and the zeal of an infomercial huckster. "This is a mellow atmosphere; a nice place to be. You come here for complete freedom to do anything: nude bathing, dancing, meeting dynamite people," he told a reporter for the *Washington Post* in 1978. "Now if people go in for [making love], that's something else. If a boy meets a girl here—that's beautiful. Dynamite."[57]

Sexual spontaneity came at a price, though. Couples paid twenty-five bucks for admission, plus a five-dollar temporary membership fee (as a sex club, the law required that Plato's only admit private members). Strict rules at the entrance read: "couples and single women only;" "when the female leaves, the male must leave also;" "no one admitted fully dressed."[58] No food was allowed in the mattress room or pool areas, there was no smoking permitted, and by law, no alcohol was served.

Despite the stringent behavioral guidelines, Levenson implored audiences, via late-night cable television ads, to "come down and fulfill your most fantastic fantasies and stimulate your wildest dreams."[59] It was not difficult, at the height of the sexual seventies in New York City, to convince the public to try out the club. Levenson admitted as much. "This club runs itself…anyone with half a brain can run a club. I wish they had said I was a genius for thinking up Plato's Retreat, but it just happened," he shrugged to a *Screw* reporter. "No great idea, nothing brilliant. I just happened to be the first one to go public with swinging. Swinging shot through the roof. Now I'm riding the crest."[60]

SEX CAPITALISTS

As the sexual milieu of the city became more mainstream and flamboyant during the seventies, the old-time X-rated bookstores, where mostly male customers browsed plastic-wrapped magazines in furtive privacy, now seemed like the sad relic of a bygone era. "Lighting is fluorescent and harsh, the décor nonexistent, the silence oppressive…about a dozen men, mostly middle-aged and dressed in business suits, stand alone at the racks in the approved porn-shop posture: book or magazine held tight against the chest, head bent, eyes never straying to another customer," sniffed *Newsweek* in 1976.[61]

In contrast, the new breed of sex capitalists invested in slick new porn emporiums, exploiting pornography's low overhead and high profit margins. Of these so-called "sex supermarkets," Show World Center, which opened a few steps from the Port Authority Bus Terminal at 8th Avenue and 42nd Street in 1975, was the first and most notorious by virtue of its comprehensive displays and spaciousness, array of products, and different sections for magazines, video, and live entertainment. As *Deep Throat* had legitmized hardcore films, Show World owner Richard Basciano wanted to liberate porn retail from its usual place in shifty storefronts and give it the makeover it deserved as one of the most profitable business segments in the city. He envisioned selling porn and pleasure as one would display fresh vegetables at a grocery store, not unlike Larry Levenson's fast-food marketing approach at Plato's Retreat. Basciano started small, with two dozen peep booths equipped with video and twelve private booths featuring live girls, and met with immediate success.

Basciano also owned the building which housed Show World (as well as many other properties in Times Square), which freed him from the snags of renting from easily offended landlords. But one major obstacle Basciano did encounter was organized crime. According to an investigation by the *New York Times*, by 1971, organized crime dominated sex retail as well as a significant percentage of the prostitution market.[62] A reason for this may have been the Supreme Court rulings in the sixties that broadened the interpretation of pornography, which resulted in a greater volume of sexually explicit goods on the market and increased scrutiny on the goods' producers and distributors. This scenario offered opportunities for mob agents to extort "protection" money from porn manufacturers, who were not likely to go to police, especially if their merchandise rode the line between legal and illegal.

Mob control was accomplished in several ways: through directing payment to writers and actors, intimidation of store owners and distributors, and extortionate merchandise price markups. For example, porn books and magazines, bought wholesale for less than fifty cents each, were sold to the public for five dollars apiece; erotic photo collections that wholesaled for a quarter were eight dollars at retail, and three-dollar stag films were sold for thirty five dollars. One member of the Lucchese crime family reportedly scored a million dollars in one year this way, tax-free and in cash. Peepshow king Martin Hodas himself was involved in an apparent mob turf war, as he was indicted in 1973 for fire-bombing two massage parlors on 42nd Street, allegedly in connection with the Colombo crime family.[63]

Mob extortion and the increasing violence associated with pornography prompted city leaders to issue calls to action. While the religious community prodded Mayor Abraham Beame and city officials to do something about the increasingly immoral and shameless industry, civic leaders declared it humiliating to have Times Square, Manhattan's most famous neighborhood, overrun with pornography. Additionally, legitimate business owners in the area blamed the sex shops for ruining property values and attracting shady male customers instead of middle-class tourists. Regular New Yorkers' outrage at the municipal inability to contain the porn explosion reached a boiling point in the mid-seventies, when, after twenty years of relying on "moral suasion" to fix the problem, the city finally got serious about restoring Times Square to its former glory.

THE CLEANUP (REPRISE)

In 1970, the President's Commission on Obscenity and Pornography, a group of clergymen, lawyers, journalists and sociologists (only two of the eighteen members were women) released the results of a two-year study on the effects of pornography on popular culture.[64] While few expected the report to exonerate the Hugh Hefners of the world, not only did the commission find sexually explicit material harmless to adults, it surmised that it was probably *helpful* to sexual communication between couples. Morton A. Hill, the reverend who had pursued Ralph Ginzburg all the way to the federal penitentiary, was a member of the commission, and wrote a scathing, contemptuous dissent. Calling the majority's conclusions fraudulent, he declared, "The Commission's majority report is a Magna Charta for the pornographer."[65]

Anyone walking through Times Square would have agreed with Hill.

On the five blocks of Eighth Avenue between 42ⁿᵈ and 47ᵗʰ Streets, at least fourteen massage parlors were running full tilt. "The Show World Center advertised 'Hottest Live Acts in U.S.'... at the Cameo theater on the next block, 'Bordello Girls' and 'House of Kinky Pleasures' were said to be 'Two of the Hottest Porn Flicks of the Year'...a block uptown, a few doors from the Pleasure Palace, the pink entryway to Hungry Hilda's bore a sign saying simply, 'topless...' ...the Eros I offered the 'Finest All-Male Films in NY' and a 'Live Male Show'. For anyone still unsatisfied, the House of Happiness, on the corner of 46ᵗʰ Street, had a sign that said, 'Come In and Be Satisfied...Girls*Girls*Girls," wrote the *New York Times.*[66]

For the most part, the city had little idea how to combat the porn problem in Times Square through legal means, and often resorted to below-the-board tactics. For example, a landlord whose building's ground floor was occupied by the Hidden Desires massage parlor hired three detectives from a private security agency to bust the shop. After the agents, disguised as customers, asked for and received happy endings, police rushed in.[67] When the landlord was asked why he had hired the detectives to entrap the women, he said that Sidney Baumgarten, the Mayor's assistant in midtown matters, had recommended the plan.[68]

It was now time to get tough. On November 11, 1976, Mayor Beame introduced zoning legislation to ban sex shops from within five hundred feet of a residential area, and to allow no more than three shops within a one-thousand-foot radius of a commercial area.[69] The terms were based on a similar bill enacted in Detroit and approved by the U.S. Supreme Court in 1975, which ruled that these types of zoning laws did not violate the First Amendment. However, Beame's bill went further in restricting the places where sex shops could legally operate. The bill needed approval from the City Planning Commission and the Board of Estimate (a body that included the Mayor, the City Comptroller, the City Council President, and the five Borough Presidents). If both groups passed the bill, all sex shops on 8ᵗʰ Avenue would be banned, while on 42ⁿᵈ Street, only three would be allowed to remain open. This marked the first time that large-scale rezoning had been used specifically to try and eliminate sex shops in New York City.

Though faced with possible eviction, sex shop owners were unfazed.

Previous efforts to close massage parlors and sex clubs on building code violations and other technicalities had only resulted in New York City having
"the cleanest, safest, and most well-lighted brothels in the country," according to one cop.[70] Owners knew that any political campaign to rid the city
of porn would have to consider the enormous profits—and tax revenue—of
the sex industry. "[Richard Basciano's] got over half a million invested in
Show World," said its manager, "if it wasn't lucrative, he wouldn't be in the
business."[71]

In debating Beame's proposed zoning bill, officials discovered that it
would inadvertently ban sex shops in the entire borough of Brooklyn, as
every "adult-use" zone in that borough happened to overlap a residential
or commercial area. This small oversight sounded great, however, to the
Brooklyn borough president, and to the Queens and Bronx borough presidents as well, all of whom wanted to eliminate sex shops in their boroughs.
With a little tweaking of the legislative language, the bill was amended to
ban porn shops in Brooklyn, Queens, the Bronx, Staten Island, and almost
all of Manhattan.

The City Planning Commission approved the plan in January 1977.
However, soon after insisting on the amendment, members of the Board
of Estimate started having second thoughts about the bill's ability to with-
stand legal scrutiny. While consumers still had the constitutional right to
buy whatever legal products they wanted without restriction, Beame's bill
would seem to put undue hardship on residents of the outer boroughs, who
would have to travel all the way to Manhattan for a stag reel. When the
Board of Estimate finally did vote on the proposal, it became clear after
only six votes that the auspicious bill to rid New York City of sex shops
would fail, waylaid by the Borough Presidents' fears that the bill was too
restrictive to pass legal muster, even though they *wanted* the restrictions for
the betterment of their boroughs.

After a disorganized meeting at which the members blamed each oth-
er for the spectacular demise of what should have been a political victory,
Beame attempted to get the original, non-restrictive bill passed by the city.
That too failed. To save face, the Mayor personally led a police raid at Show

World and at Jax Three-Ring Circus the following day (though both businesses reopened a few hours after the raid.) A crowd gathered on the street
to watch Beame's entourage of police officers, press people and fellow po-
liticos traipse through smut alley. "Almost everyone was angry at the mayor.
'Fascist!' yelled one man from the crowd, who identified himself as 'Joe
Citizen.' Another man climbed a pole to shout down at the crowd, 'Forget
porno. We need jobs!'"[72]

After four months of bureaucratic wrangling and grandstanding, the
entire saga ended in disaster for the city. The political melodrama had dis-
tracted the Beame administration from more pressing municipal problems,
and New Yorkers had lost confidence in elected officials' ability to handle
the porn issue. Sex entrepreneurs emerged unscathed, and Abe Beame ultimately lost his job as Mayor to Edward I. Koch in November 1977. But if
the defeat taught city officials anything, it was that zoning was the way to
curb pornography in the city—the challenge was figuring out how to make
it stand up in court.

While the lawyers toiled, a powerful group of conservative feminists,
headquartered in the heart of Times Square, would pick up the street fight
where the Beame administration had left off.

"WE SAY NO!"

As the mixed crowds that had lined up to see *Deep Throat* showed, women
were enjoying the fruits of the seventies sexual revolution, having more access to commercial pleasures than at any time since World War II. Clubs
like Plato's Retreat argued that women deserved sexual freedom as much
as men; the belittling term "wife-swapping" was deemed passé and replaced
by the more egalitarian phrase "swinging." While *Playboy* and *Hustler* were
familiar fixtures on city newsstands, new soft-core magazines for women
like *Playgirl*, *Viva*, and *Foxy Lady* were launched in the mid-seventies to
capitalize on the desire for more romantic, less graphic porn.

Some feminist leaders, however, claimed that this new freedom was
emblematic of the pornography problem, as there could be no such thing
as "women's porn," because all pornography was, by definition, violent and

abusive toward women. Though feminists had united to legalize abortion and to try and ratify the Equal Rights Amendement in the early seventies, thereby expanding women's political and sexual power, those efforts had had, to some, an unpleasant side effect: a "climate of acceptability" regarding sex that posed a threat to women's continued liberation. The ideological schism that had split the movement along conservative and radical lines in the mid-sixties and (as seen in Betty Friedan's dislike of lesbians in the movement) appeared to resurrect itself over the issue of porn.

This time, however, many women who had fought on the liberal side in the early seventies, such as Gloria Steinem, took the conservative, anti-porn position, claiming that women who professed to enjoy pornography were too brainwashed by popular images of sexuality to realize their role in their own subjugation. Andrea Dworkin, the hardcore anti-pornography feminist, articulated the central belief that pornography was the manifestation of the inherent masochistic submissiveness of all women in a male-dominated society. "Heterosexuality...can be defined as the sexual dominance of men over women," she said in a typical speech at the Massachusetts Institute of Technology in 1975. [73] "It is necessary to understand that pornography is a kind of propaganda designed to convince the man that he need not be afraid; that he is not afraid, to shore him up so that he can fuck...[to] provid[e] a pornographic fantasy of pleasure from which he can learn as a creed and from which he can act to dominate women as a real man must."[74]

In her 1979 essay "Let's Put Pornography Back in the Closet," fellow writer and activist Susan Brownmiller quoted Chief Justice Warren Burger's majority opinion from the 1973 case *Miller v. California*: "To equate the free and robust exchange of ideas and political debate with commercial exploitation of obscene material demeans the grand conception of the First Amendment and its high purposes in the historic struggle for freedom."[75] Brownmiller insisted that the feminist position on porn did not stem from a desire for censorship; rather, "the feminist objection to pornography is based on our belief that pornography represents hatred of women; that pornography's intent is to humiliate, degrade, and dehumanize the female body for the purpose of erotic stimulation and pleasure."[76] She also took issue with those who insisted that no one was compelled to look at porn if they don't want to, saying that any person buying a newspaper at a newsstand was exposed to the covers of *Penthouse*, *Hustler*, et al. Pornography was obscene, Brownmiller argued, and belonged in the category of speech restricted by the First Amendment because it posed a clear and present danger to the well-being of women.

Dworkin and Brownmiller were two founding members of a New York-based feminist anti-pornography organization that eventually became Women Against Pornography (WAP). Dworkin drifted from the group in its early days, but former *Newsday* reporter Dolores Alexander and activist Dorchen Leidholdt completed the core leadership of WAP with Brownmiller by 1978. The group's purpose was to blast porn off newsstands and out of theaters, removing it from the public consciousness. Brownmiller was convinced that "New York, the home of Times Square and the national media, was the only place to launch a national feminist anti-pornography campaign."[77]

From the beginning, their tactics were purposefully confrontational. WAP asked the city for space for its headquarters at 579 9th Avenue, in the center of Times Squares' porn industry.[78] To show municipal support, especially after Abe Beame's embarrassing zoning failure, the city leased the space to WAP far below market value. "Pornography is a matter of concern to both the city and the feminists," said Carl Weisbrod, head of the Mayor's Midtown Enforcement Project, and "the city needed all the help it could get on that score."[79]

WAP surmised that people who did not frequently buy or watch pornography were dangerously unaware of the scope and menace of the porn industry. The group took its message to the streets—42nd Street in particular—by leading walking tours of Times Square's sordid spectacles, much in the spirit of Reverend Charles Parkhurst's forays into the Tenderloin, with the hope of turning public opinion against porn through exposure and education. Led by the group's members, each two-hour tour began at WAP headquarters with a slide show designed to highlight the most egregious violent sexual images in the media. Examples were culled not from just men's magazines and books, but from record albums, mainstream advertisements, and movie posters. Among the images was the infamous 1975 *Hustler* magazine cover of a woman being fed into a meat grinder and coming out as hamburger. Perfume ads from *Vogue* showed female models being dragged across the floor or slapped by male counterparts, and enjoying it. Women in the audience unsurprisingly expressed disgust at the show.

Next, attendees paid a donation of five dollars and received maps of Times Square and the day's itinerary, which included visits to Show World Center and the Roxy Burlesque on 42nd Street, a glimpse inside a shop specializing in racist porn, and a grand tour of a classic dirty bookstore (a quaint and disappearing fixture in Times Square). The tour would end at a typical topless bar, the Melody Burlesk at Broadway and 49th Street.[80]

The tours proved so popular that WAP organized a two-day consciousness-raising conference in September 1979. In one speech, Dolores Alexander claimed that "pornography is antiwoman propaganda" and was just one of the many manifestations of male hatred of women in society, which had to do with violence, not sex. "We've eroticized being submissive," said writer Robin Morgan, rationalizing the seeming contradiction of women who were erotically attracted to sadomasochism. *Ms. Magazine* founder Gloria Steinem explained why porn had become such an explosive and topical issue for feminists: "Pornography is the instruction, rape is the practice."[81]

Following the conference, WAP's efforts culminated in a massive march against pornography on October 20, 1979. Gathering at Columbus Circle, five thousand to seven thousand mostly female marchers held signs with anti-porn slogans. In the late fall sunshine, the crowd aligned itself behind the women carrying the Women Against Pornography banner, including Steinem, Bella Abzug (a recent losing candidate for mayor), and Brownmiller. Marching down Broadway, the crowd chanted "Two, four, six, eight! Pornography is woman-hate!"[82] The sea of women eventually reached 42nd Street, where they slapped fluorescent stickers on the windows of massage parlors and peepshows to mark them as complicit in the war against women. The march snaked on to a rally site in Bryant Park, the square of green behind the New York Public Library, a favorite hangout of drug dealers and vagrants. On stage, Steinem and other luminaries gave speeches, castigating

porn profiteers and vowing revolution. Andrea Dworkin spoke out in typically stark terms. "There is one message basic to all kinds of pornography
from the sludge that we see all around us, to the artsy-fartsy pornography
that the intellectuals call erotica, to the under-the-counter kiddie porn, to
the slick, glossy men's 'entertainment' magazines," she began. "The one message that is carried in all pornography all the time is this: she wants it; she
wants to be beaten; she wants to be forced; she wants to be raped; she wants
to be brutalized; she wants to be hurt. This is the premise, the first principle,
of all pornography."[83] The crowd cheered.

When comparing the 1970 Women's Strike for Equality and the 1979
WAP March, significant differences in ideology and method emerge. First,
the Strike was a loosely-coordinated effort of thirty thousand New York
women and women's groups across the country, spontaneously joining in
the spirit of liberation in creative and often humorous ways. The WAP
marchers, in contrast, focused purely on the menace of pornography and
employed very little humor or creativity, or indeed individuality, in getting
their message across. Secondly, the Strike pulled together many different
demographics of women—rural and urban, working- and middle-class, old
and young, racially heterogeneous—with the goal of creating a unified front
against women's inequality in all forms. WAP's march was a women's offensive against men, painting men as the problem instead of inequality itself.
Finally, the Strikers in 1970 realized that the reform of sex laws—regarding
access to contraception, abortion rights, divorce, and marital equity—were
the linchpins in assuming parity with men. In 1979, having achieved the
goals of lawful abortion and non-discrimination legislation, the WAPers
turned against sex as a positive vehicle for change, and instead demonized
it as a weapon against women, as if women had no right to sex at all.

Though covered extensively on the nightly news and in magazines,
WAP's actions did less to affect change in Times Square than to officially
form a coalition against pornography, comprised of conservative feminists,
city agencies, real estate developers and, most ironically, the fledgling New
Right movement of fundamentalist Christians. All had the same goal in
mind: erase sexual expression, no matter how violent or harmless, from
the landscape. Brownmiller, as she recalled in her memoir *In Our Time*,

personally conferred with the enemy in an attempt to build the unholy coalition when she and other WAP members met with Morton A. Hill, by now an ageing but still formidable opponent of sexual expression. "We honestly believed that radical feminists, with our deeper understanding of porn and our sophisticated knowledge of sexuality, would succeed in turning around public opinion where the old-fashioned moralists had not," she wrote. Brownmiller confessed "terror at being lumped with religious conservatives," but that is exactly what happened.[84] WAP's actions ultimately backfired, causing a rift in the leadership of the group and in the feminist movement in general, just as pro-sex feminists, especially pro-porn lesbians, began to form an opposition movement against the perceived conservatism of mainstream feminism.

One unlikely supporter of WAP was Linda Marchiano, née Boreman, formerly known as Lovelace. In the years since *Deep Throat* had hurled her into notoriety, Marchiano had distanced herself from her pornographic persona. In 1980, she held a press conference to announce the publication of *Ordeal*, her tell-all memoir of how Chuck Traynor had forced her into the peep loops and prostitution, rendering her helpless and often suicidal from the hellish cycle of spousal abuse and degradation at the hands of the pornography industry. At the photo op she was flanked by feminist anti-porn lawyer Catharine MacKinnon, several WAP members, and Andrea Dworkin, who presence undoubtedly legitimized Marchiano's story. It was exactly the kind of testimonial the anti-porn movement wanted to hear.

However, the pages of *Ordeal* contradicted Marchiano's claims of victimization, particulatly during the filming of *Deep Throat*. On the set, Traynor was so annoying that director Gerard Damiano frequently sent him out on errands, offering Linda regular reprieves from his presence. Furthermore, as the star of the movie, Linda was treated like a celebrity by Damiano and co-star Harry Reems, with whom she got with along especially well. "*I was laughing along with the rest of them*...I hadn't laughed, really laughed, in so long that my face had to carve new smile lines [emphasis hers]," Lovelace wrote. "For the first time in many months, I was thrown in with other people, other people who weren't perverted and threatening. I became part of a group." Instead of constant torment and physical abuse, "we laughed a lot on the first day of shooting while we were doing the poolside shots, the walking-down-the-street shots and the knocking-on-the-door shots. And no one was asking me to do anything I didn't want to do."[85]

DON'T VISIT HOUSES OF ILL-FAME

If in doubt call at the nearest Hospital
for free and confidential advice

SAVE YOURSELF & YOUR FAMILY FROM V.D.

Used in a 1940s health campaign, this poster, directed at soldiers during World War II, urged servicemen to avoid visiting "Houses of Ill-Fame", so as to not contract sexually transmitted diseases. (*Centers for Disease Control*)

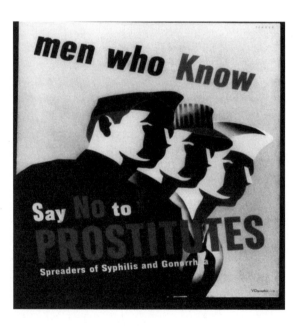

This 1940 wartime poster urged servicemen to "say No" to prostitution to reduce venereal disease cases among soldiers during World War II. (*Centers for Disease Control*)

A sailor sits on a barstool with his arms around a girl on Navy Day, October 27, 1945. (*Getty Images*)

Hubert's Flea Circus in New York City, in 1954, another mainstay of 42nd Street's honky-tonk. (*Daily News*)

The Stonewall Inn in the late 1960s, site of the riot that ignited the gay rights movement. *(Diana Davies/New York Public Library)*

Gay Liberation Front Supporters march through Times Square in 1969. *(Diana Davies/New York Public Library)*

Protestors object to a New York theater showing *Deep Throat* in 1980, a typical occurrence in the feminist-led anti-porn movement that began in the late seventies. *(AP)*

ACT UP Poster featuring Ed Koch. *(New York Public Library)*

7.

RISE AND FALL
1980-1993

To many heterosexual New Yorkers, fads like swinging or going to a porn theater had grown passé by the early eighties. At the same time, the burgeoning home video market allowed couples to stay home to satisfy their sexual desires, eliminating the need for them to venture out to places like Plato's Retreat. However, as the taste for hedonism began to wane, the physical repercussions of the seventies culture of swinging and anonymous casual sex began to emerge with a vengeance, as incidences of sexually transmitted diseases increased among both gays and straights.

Of the seven thousand new cases of syphilis in New York each year, half were now in gay men. Contributing factors included their reluctance to go to straight doctors, their unwillingness to disclose the gender and number of their sexual partners, and the fact that "the homosexual man's lifestyle often provides for easy access to anonymous sex in bathhouses."[1] To educate gay men about syphilis and its prevention, the city began offering free treatment and counseling at the baths. Patrons of the Club Baths, the Everard Baths and the Continental Baths were thus able to consult with doctors in an environment where they felt comfortable, inevitably increasing the number of men who had access to treatment, and hopefully decreasing the number of infections. "If we are going to encourage gay men to be examined and treated, we must attempt to make our clinics as hospitable and responsive to their needs as possible," said Dr. Yehudi Felman of the Bureau of Venereal Disease Control.

Among the heterosexual population, there was a national outbreak of genital herpes in 1980. A virus that had only come to be properly understood in the mid-seventies, herpes "may be a prime mover in helping to bring to a close an era of mindless promiscuity. The monogamous now have all the more reason to remain so…[herpes] may inadvertently be ushering in a period in which sex is linked more firmly to commitment and trust," opined *Time*. [2] Herpes would become so indicative of sexual promiscuity over the course of the eighties that it would eventually be coined "Jerry Falwell's revenge," illustrating an intensified relationship between venereal disease and personal morals at a level not seen since the early twentieth century. [3] In the case of incurable herpes, one man lamented to *Time*, "I have a guilt trip that won't quit."[4] The American Social Health Association, formerly the American Social Hygiene Association (the name had changed in 1959), launched a national VD hotline in 1979, and reported that 40 percent of the calls it received concerned herpes. [5] *Screw* publisher Al Goldstein, in a moment of uncharacteristic regret, told *Time*, "it may be there is a god in heaven carving out his pound of flesh for all our joys."[6]

Concurrent with the herpes epidemic, there was an unexpected rise in a strain of penicillin-resistant gonorrhea among heterosexuals in New York. Seventeen cases of the resistant strain were discovered during a period when 3,300 cases of normal gonorrhea were reported to the Health Department. Dr. Felman feared that many more cases of the resistant strain were out there, and that aggressive, if legally controversial, action was needed.

As it was believed that prostitutes and other sex workers were the main sources of the strain, health inspectors from the Bureau of Venereal Disease Control personally began visiting brothels and sex clubs to test workers on the spot. "We've had excellent cooperation from madams, prostitutes and pimps," announced the city's Health Commissioner, David Sencer. In less than three months, inspectors visited forty brothels and tested three hundred prostitutes, 40 percent of whom carried the strain. The police, for their part, turned the other cheek, in this case ignoring the legal issues in favor of curbing a public health risk. [7]

For once, city health officials and the sex industry were able to work out a solution that made both sides happy: the city was able to prevent a public health crisis, and sex workers and their clients avoided police action for taking part in the program. In both of these cases— offering treatment in gay bathhouses and testing for infections in brothels—city officials realized that health problems could be solved more efficiently by meeting with patients on their own terms. Unfortunately, this did not become standard operating procedure for the Health Department, with disastrous consequences.

"RATHER DEVASTATING"

Despite the poential risk of catching an STD, gay men continued to pursue sex as if though they were in Never-Never-Land. Since the late sixties, the market for gay sexual experience had continued to expand until it seemed that there was barely any place in Manhattan not appropriated by men for sex *al fresco* or *sub rosa*. Few penalties existed for following one's bliss, especially if it led to Central Park or the West Side piers. In 1978, *New York* writer Doug Ireland confirmed the longevity of the Park's Ramble as "the city's best-known outdoor gathering place for gays."[8] Accompanying a few regulars there one evening, Ireland discovered casual sex among gay men, hidden from censure by the cover of foliage and darkness. At the West 81st Street gate to the park, "the iron bars have been bent back to allow easy access to a well-worn, narrow dirt path among the bushes. Paul follows that path until he comes to a series of turnings. Choosing one, he enters a grotto within a grotto. There, around a large, gnarled old tree—the 'orgy tree'— there are little confessional-like spaces created by the untrimmed flora." In this idyllic setting, where the sounds of traffic are muffled and few streetlamps cast a glow, "the nighttime sex scene…is conducted in silence, lest the voice dissipate the mutual fantasy evoked by the look, the pose, the costume, the attitude. Body language is the only language needed for success here." Even as the number of gay social outlets had exploded after Stonewall, drawing middle-class men away from public spaces, working-class young men continued to utilize the Ramble as a refuge from cramped homes and disapproving families. "I can't bring my boyfriends home—it would kill my ma," said one nineteen-year-old. "So we have sex in the park. It's beautiful smelling the grass and not even feeling like you're in the city."

Gay clubs in Manhattan's meatpacking district cultivated a less bucolic environment, characterized by rougher, masculine sexuality, sadomasoch-ism and public eroticism. At the Anvil, a bi-level club on the corner of 14th Street and Eleventh Avenue, hundreds of men surrounded a bar on the upper level where go-go boys shimmied under strings of red lights and deafening music. Drag shows transpired on a corner stage, which most men were too busy cruising to notice. The real action, though, took place in the dimly-lit basement. Patrons checked their shirts and entered a subterranean cavern, where black and white porn movies flickered on TV sets, barely il-luminating the couples or groups of men having sex. Each sense heightened in the dark near-silence, gay men found the Anvil experience seedy, dank, and liberating.

Nearby, the Mine Shaft felt more jagged around the edges. The club's strict dress code demanded Levi's and leather boots; once inside, one meshed into a crowd of similarly-attired men, bringing to mind the dungarees-and-studded-belt uniform of the fifties-era hoodlum. The murky atmosphere smacked of danger, of boundaries pushed, of fantasies of dominance or submission made real. There was little prelude to sex scenes. "It was really wanton, wild sex. It was really, really free. A lot of fist-fucking. And a lot of S&M," one regular told historian Charles Kaiser.[9] The Mine Shaft even provided the setting for William Friedkin's 1980 film *Cruising*, in which a police officer (Al Pacino) goes undercover in the gay leather scene to find a serial killer.

In the words of the screenwriter and soon-to-be activist, Larry Kramer, "We didn't have a political movement back then. Sex wasn't a political act. It was just pure and simple exuberant hedonism."[10] That changed on July 3, 1981. A short article appeared in the *New York Times* that day, a sliver of text along the left-hand margin, buried in the middle of the paper. Lawrence K. Altman's now-famous report, "Rare Cancer Seen in 41 Homosexuals," would be the first mention in a major newspaper of a puzzling new medical mystery. Altman reported that doctors in New York City and San Francisco had, over a recent five-week period, assessed forty-one cases of Kaposi's Sarcoma (KS), an extremely rare form of skin cancer, in young homosexual men. The collected cases had been diagnosed up to thirty months previously, indicating that some of the patients had come down with KS symptoms as early as 1979.[11] While KS was not usually fatal, the data showed that eight of the forty-one men had died less than two years after being diagnosed.

Dr. Alvin Friedman-Kien, a microbiologist at New York University Medical Center, called the KS outbreak and its high mortality rate "rather devastating." He reported that most of the cases involved gay men who had had up to ten sexual encounters a night, four times per week—an easy feat at the baths and leather clubs. Most of the patients had also used poppers (amyl nitrite) for heightened pleasure, which had shown the ability, though uncommon, to cause cancer in lab animals.[12] Significantly, Friedman-Kien also noted abnormalities in the patients' immune systems that left them susceptible to several relatively rare but fatal opportunistic infections: pneumocystis pneumonia, a virulent lung infection; herpes simplex; Hepatitis B; and cytomegalovirus (CMV), a virus that caused swollen lymph glands, fever and weight loss. He suggested that the gay patients' promiscuous sexual behavior had repeatedly exposed them to more common diseases like gonorrhea and syphilis, which could account for their overtaxed immune systems, opening the door to additional infections. Ultimately, there were many questions and few certain answers. "It could be the bugs out of the pipes in the bathhouses," sighed Dr. Felman of the Bureau of Venereal Disease Control, whose work never seemed to end.[13]

The new syndrome was initially named Gay-Related Immune Deficiency (GRID), but at the request of gay activists, was changed to the less-stigmatizing Acquired Immune Deficiency Syndrome (AIDS) in 1982. By then, New York City had the nation's largest concentration of cases (259) and gay men were beginning to panic: health clinics were overwhelmed with calls from men terrified that their sore throats, bruises, insect bites or common colds were signs of the deadly illness.[14] Medical professionals were generally at a loss. Said one social worker, "What's unique is that, in the presence of such sophisticated medical technology, we seem to be so powerless. AIDS reminds people of cancer, yet it has the sense of contagion about it."[15]

In the absence of facts, gay men were encouraged to curtail their sexual activity, have fewer partners on fewer occasions, and if they did have sex in the baths, get their partners' names. Such careful planning, however, was completely antithetical to the seventies' style of gay sexuality. Fourteen years after the Stonewall rebellion, "AIDS is torturing not only its victims but also the whole ethic of the 'gay life style,' which, roughly translated, has meant the freedom to live as one felt, openly, and to seek sex as one wished," reported the *New York Times* in 1983. Breaking the "bathhouse habit" meant changing the definition of one's own sexuality. While some sufferers felt guilt about being gay, and assumed AIDS was somehow a punishment for transgressive sexuality, many were reluctant to radically change their behavior. "The problem is that safe sex is boring sex," complained a thirty-two-year-old art director in New York.[16] A forty-two-year-old man added that it was harder to be openly gay: "these days you're not just coming out of the closet...you're dragging a skeleton out of the closet with you."[17]

"THIS COUNTRY WOULD NOT KNOW WHAT HAD HIT THEM"

Even before the days of his AIDS activism, Larry Kramer stood as the sometimes unwelcome conscience of the gay male world in late-seventies New York City. Though a respected writer with Hollywood cred—Kramer wrote and produced the subtly homoerotic film adaptation of D.H. Lawrence's *Women in Love* in 1969, for which he received an Academy Award nomination—gay Manhattan provided his artistic inspiration and fueled his flair for controversy.

Kramer deplored the "gay lifestyle" centered on anonymous promiscuity, scoffing at the idea that sexual liberty meant that gay men had achieved political power and identity. He expressed this view in his unambiguously-titled 1978 novel *Faggots*, in which the gay men of Manhattan and Fire Island revel in orgies worthy of Caligula and prize fleeting sexual passion over real love. *Faggots* polarized gay readers and painted Kramer, in the context of the hedonistic seventies, as a prude.

However, in the early eighties, when AIDS started picking off the very men on whom Kramer had based his *Faggots* characters, his detractors realized he had been more prescient than they dared to realize. Perhaps there were unknown consequences of sexual freedom. People began to listen, and Kramer found a vehicle for his abrasive, take-no-prisoners style of direct activism at the *New York Native*, a gay newspaper.

Kramer felt that the mainstream press either sensationalized or purposefully ignored AIDS at the expense of its gay sufferers, and that it was gay men's responsibility to fight for their own lives. "The men who have been stricken don't appear to have done anything that many New York gay men haven't done at one time or another," he wrote.[18] "Money is desperately needed…this is our disease and we must take care of each other and ourselves. In the past we have often been a divided community; I hope we can all get together on this emergency, undivided, cohesively, and with all the numbers we in so many ways possess."[19]

Soon after the appearance of the *Times* article in July 1981, Kramer invited Dr. Friedman-Kien to his Greenwich Village apartment to speak to a group of concerned gay men about the few known facts about AIDS. Doctors had only just surmised the way the disease attacked the body: the Human Immunodeficiency Virus (HIV) was transmitted via sexual contact or infected needles, breaking down the body's immune system and leaving the infected person vulnerable to opportunistic diseases that a healthy person could easily fight off. There was no test to determine whether a person was infected until the opportunistic symptoms appeared.

Eighty men listened as Dr. Friedman-Kien explained the need to limit sexual partners and anonymous encounters. At the end of the evening, a hat was passed around for donations. In all, $6,635 was raised. The meeting gave Kramer and five other attendees, including the writer Edmund White, the impetus to organize the Gay Men's Health Crisis (GMHC) in January 1982. The group set up an information hotline, which received one hundred calls on its first night of operation. It was remarkable that the all-volunteer staff at GMHC even had information to give out, such was the lack of interest in AIDS at the time outside the most at-risk groups.

Eventually, GMHC printed brochures and flyers explaining what the newly-coined concept of "safe sex" meant. In a controversial departure from what most physicians advised at the time, GMHC did not recommend that gay men simply give up all sexual activity, which they knew was an impossible and inhumane request; they also believed that bathhouse culture was an important and viable part of gay life. Rather, GMHC's strategy accepted that gay men would continue having sex with multiple partners, and worked around the fact by posting safe-sex information in baths and bars, along with free condoms and the GMHC hotline number.

Within its first year of existence, GMHC had recruited three hundred volunteers, raised more than one hundred-fifty thousand dollars for research, distributed thousands of copies of the GMHC Newsletter, printed three hundred thousand safe sex brochures in four languages and answered five thousand calls on the hotline, offered legal advice and implored elected officials to take action. In essence, GMHC was providing services for the needs of people with AIDS that the city of New York should have already been supplying.

As the leader of GMHC and a natural rabble-rouser, Larry Kramer quickly grew into his role as the AIDS-affected community's mouthpiece in the press. "For two years now we've…grasped at straws of possible causes [of AIDS]: promiscuity, poppers, backrooms, the baths," he wrote in a landmark 1983 essay "1,112 and Counting," which appeared in the *New York Native*. "If all of this had been happening to any other community for two long years, there would have been, long ago, such an outcry from the community and all its members that the government of this city and this country would not know what had hit them."[21]

Kramer and others in New York's AIDS community put the blame for the city's apathy squarely on Edward I. Koch. "Our mayor, Ed Koch, appears to have chosen, for whatever reason, not to allow himself to be perceived by the non-gay world as visibly helping us in this emergency," Kramer wrote. "The Mayor of New York has an enormous amount of power—when he wants to use it…with his silence on AIDS, the Mayor of New York is helping to kill us."[22] Former Times Square hustler-turned-artist and essayist David Wojnarowicz, eloquent in describing his rage at the apathy, homophobia and stupidity of elected officials in the face of the crisis, agreed with Kramer. "Koch has stalled, ranted and raved, and in general done everything he could to avoid dealing with the AIDS crisis," he wrote.[23]

For its part, the Koch administration insisted it would not be bullied into negotiations or discussions with anyone from the AIDS-affected community. Aside from creating the Office of Gay and Lesbian Health Concerns under the auspices of the city's Health Department in 1983, the Koch administration had few suggestions for AIDS prevention. The Office's director, Dr. Roger Enlow, asserted at a 1984 health conference that the city "really has no business trying to regulate individual behavior—these things are totally unpoliceable."[24] For a mayor who proudly dispensed opinions on any topic that came to mind and was as garrulous as they come, Koch's reticence in answering his critics was highly unusual.

Despite the mayor's seeming indifference to the AIDS epidemic, the city, as well as New York State Governor Mario Cuomo, supported the baths' function as community centers where AIDS information could be effectively distributed, and thus were in favor of keeping them open. The city's passive allowance of the baths' continued existence, however, was not enough to placate activists' calls for more public services and money for AIDS patients.

While Kramer and Koch bickered, the number of AIDS cases in America doubled from March to September 1983, to 2,339. Nine-hundred-seventy-five of those were in New York City. In his follow-up essay, "2,339 and Counting," Kramer let the ugly facts speak for themselves. "The sum total of this city's contributions to the AIDS epidemic to date [September 1983] is $24,500" for its nearly one thousand AIDS patients. In comparison, San Francisco had spent more than $4 million on its 284 cases.[25]

"IT IS OUR DUTY TO PROTECT THESE PEOPLE FROM THEMSELVES"

Nineteen-eighty-five would be a politically and emotionally tumultuous year. The New York City mayoral election would take place in November, and the still popular Koch was running against three long-shot opponents: the Liberal Party candidate, City Council President Carol Bellamy; Republican-Conservative Party candidate Diane McGrath; and the Right-to-Life Party nominee, Rabbi Lew Y. Levin. The latter two candidates introduced bathhouse-closure as a major issue in the race, forcing Koch to respond with an AIDS policy that would need to please both noisome AIDS activists and moderate voters.

The political storm erupted on October 3, when McGrath announced a proposal to close "bathhouses, bars, theaters and pornography shops" where gay men congregated in an attempt to curb AIDS. "It is our duty to protect these people from themselves," she declared. "[These establishments] are a clear and evident menace to the health of their patrons."[26] McGrath later reported receiving death threats.[27] For his part, Rabbi Levin picketed "an East Village bathhouse" (probably the St. Marks' Baths, whose owner, Bruce Mailman, was vocally opposed to closure) and promised to go to court if necessary to get the baths closed.[28] Koch shot back that he hoped no one would make "political the calamity of AIDS," but it was clearly too late.[29]

The next day, McGrath's salvo prompted Koch and Governor Cuomo to reevaluate their shared opposition to closing the bathhouses. The assumption that the bathhouses served as places for AIDS education had been formally challenged, and Koch needed a politically acceptable strategy to the AIDS question if he was to win reelection. Cuomo asked State Health Commissioner David Axelrod, and Koch asked City Health Commissioner Dr. David Sencer, to evaluate whether the educational approach was viable, or if more drastic measures were needed.

In the meantime, a *New York Times* editorial questioned how efficient, if the government's true aim was to curb AIDS transmission, bathhouse closure would actually be. The editorial hinted that upholding public morals was the real inspiration behind the fight for closure: "The bathhouses seem to respond to an important need for some homosexuals," it noted carefully. "Though closing them might win some votes, that need will remain, to be satisfied in ways and places that are less safe."[30]

On October 24, Commissioner Axelrod submitted his AIDS policy evaluation to Cuomo, revealing a stunning about-face. Though he'd previously recommended that bathhouses remain open in order to continue dispering AIDS-related information, Axelrod now asked that places allowing or encouraging "dangerous heterosexual or homosexual sex"[31] on the premises be closed. He defined "dangerous" as blood-to-blood or semen-to-blood contact through anal sex or oral sex, and singled out the bathhouses as the primary spots where these acts occurred. Axelrod did not address the issue of safe sex or the condom-distribution efforts in the baths, instead announcing that he would offer an amendment to the State Sanitary Code that would specify the incidence of "dangerous" sex as grounds for closing bathhouses.

In news coverage of the announced amendment the following day, Axelrod did not explain why he had changed his mind about closing the bathhouses. Governor Cuomo, for his part, simply said that he had been dissuaded from the argument that bathhouses should be allowed to remain open to educate the public about the dangers of AIDS. "My perception is that the Governor is caught in a political bind," Michael Callen, a member of Cuomo's AIDS Advisory Council, told the *New York Times*. "He has to be seen doing something...nobody knows quite what to do, so it's all show. If he has presidential ambitions, he doesn't want to be confronted in a debate with the charge: 'You're the one who kept the bathhouses open'."[32]

Cuomo had also announced his change in position and the state's approval of the amendment without first running it by Koch, who was irked at being sidelined on this crucial issue during the heart of the mayoral campaign. And though Koch had admitted prior to Cuomo's announcement that "the governor's position is basically my position," the city's Health Commissioner, David Sencer, in fact came to the opposite conclusion as State Health Commissioner Axelrod on the efficacy of bathhouse closure.[33] Sencer felt the new law would add "little if anything to the control of AIDS." In a letter to Koch, he claimed that bathhouse sex had actually decreased, while sexual activity had increased in "movies, book stores, public restrooms and peepshows." Sencer wrote that "The issue is human behavior, not where the behavior takes place."[34]

AIDS activists were angry, though unsurprised, with the admendment. "1985 was ...the height of the AIDS crisis, and people were dying, and there was no explanation," remembered activisit Lenny Waller. "But none of these clubs or baths [that the city closed] because of a threat to the public health was *forcing* people to do anything."[35] The people who ran the baths scoffed at the government's apparent belief that unsafe sex would cease to occur if the baths were closed. "The Governor's trying to close the bathhouses without actually coming out and saying so," fumed Jack Stoddard, a manager at the St. Mark's Baths.[36] Tim Sweeney, executive director of the

Lambda Legal Defense Fund, asked, "If the authorities drive this underground, and it [reappears] in some district where there is no supervision, what health purpose is being served?"[37]

To many activists, the abrupt reversal reeked of election-year expediency, and played political football with their very lives. After hearing of the amendment, Bruce Mailman pointed out that there would be no reason to close the baths if patrons abided by the sex safe guidelines. However, if the baths were to close, "dangerous" sex would still continue. "Theoretically," he warned, "you could have sex safely with one hundred people or unsafely with one."[38] In an op-ed published in the New York Times, Mailman wrote, "By failing to distinguish between safe and unsafe sex, the amendment takes us a step backward in the highly successful educational effort that we and other responsible establishments have undertaken."[39]

"IT MUST BE HORRIFIC, HORRENDOUS IN ITS ACTUALITY TO WITNESS"

Though the new State Sanitary Code empowered the city to shut down places where high-risk sexual activity supposedly occurred, Koch still needed to determine the best method of enforcement. The Sanitary Code didn't outlaw the baths themselves—each establishment could remain open, *unless* unsafe sex practices occurred on its premises. To determine if this type of activity was going on, Koch decided to employ undercover inspectors in the baths, who would issue summonses if they witnessed forbidden sex acts.

While the city's ten baths were immediately put under surveillance, specific guidelines for witnessing sexual behavior were still hazy. If an inspector saw just one sex act in an establishment packed with hundreds of men, was that enough to warrant closure? Did a pattern of violations need to be established? What if the sex was safe sex? And, to top it all off, how was evidence supposed to be collected? "Do you have somebody peer over the top [of bathroom stalls]? Do you issue an order that states you have to take the doors off?" asked one city lawyer.[40]

On November 7, 1985—two days after he was re-elected for a third term as mayor—Koch put his money where his mouth was, closing the Mine Shaft, the notorious leather bar in the meatpacking district, for violating the health code, operating as a public nuisance and serving liquor without a license. City inspectors, sent in to the bar to enforce the new rules, claimed that they'd seen half-naked men groping each other, and, in the open, engaging in fellatio and anal sex. They also claimed to have observed men having sex with multiple partners over the course of a single night, and that condoms were not being used, though they were offered for free by the club. Koch praised the courage of the inspectors, saying, "It must be horrific, horrendous in its actuality to witness."[41]

Lenny Waller thought the bust was a charade. "The inspectors who originally went in to the Mine Shaft were from the Department of Consumer Affairs. They went in to this notorious gay leather club, and saw these things going on—of course they were shocked and terrorized! [The city didn't send] cops from Public Morals or Anti-Crime who see this every day. They sent the most vanilla person they could find."[42] According to Waller, one inspector said that it was so dark in the bar that he couldn't see his hand in front of his face, yet he testified as to what was happening in the same room fifty feet away. Another inspector said he heard moaning and the sound of whips snaking through the air, but "there were two big black men watching the room, so for his own safety he wouldn't go in."[43]

Ultimately, the city's action had a chilling effect on other longstanding clubs and baths. Some clubs with popular backrooms, like the Anvil on 11th Avenue and West 14th Street, voluntarily shut down "until further notice."[44] The Ramrod, the Badlands, and the Spike closed their backrooms, but kept their bar areas open for the diminishing crowds.[45] AIDS activists were furious that there were no corresponding closures of the heterosexual massage parlors and prostitute-friendly hotels where high-risk sexual activity occurred, which they felt proved the city's homophobia. This view seemed to have a strong basis in fact, as by 1985, New York City health officials had begun to seriously consider the possibility of female prostitutes spreading the disease to their male clients. Officials believed that up to one-third of the city's street prostitutes injected drugs, and that 50 to 60 percent of IV drug users carried the AIDS virus, resulting in a substantial, if unconfirmed, population of HIV-positive prostitutes. "Scores" of unexplained AIDS cases among low-risk groups were thought to have been contracted from prostitutes or their clients. Yet, perhaps due to the health department's over-whelming focus on the gay male population, not one of the city's nearly five thousand AIDS cases had officially been attributed to sex with a female prostitute.[46]

Almost as an afterthought, the city dispatched inspectors to Plato's Retreat in December 1985, still in operation long after its seventies' glow had worn off, at its new location on West 34th Street. In searching for health code violations, an inspector was solicited by a transvestite offering bondage and a blowjob for ten bucks. On that evidence, the city shuttered the club for prostitution, despite having never observed any unsafe-sex practices in violation of the health code. "We will not permit premises to be used for prostitution or high-risk sexual practices, whether they are heterosexual or homosexual," Koch claimed.[47]

While the Mayor's intent was to reassure gay activists, the two offenses he cited—prostitution and high-risk sex—were not equivalent under the law. Allowing heterosexual prostitution on one's property was a crime; allowing gay men to engage in high-risk sexual activity was not. But with their actions, the city and state had enabled the health department to shut down, if it wished, the entire gay club/baths industry, with curbing AIDS as the ostensible justification. At best, this seemed hypocritical and homophoic, as the activists had claimed; at worst, it revealed the erroneous belief that prostitutes and their clients were safe from the disease.

More than a year after the new Sanitary Code had into effect, resulting in closures and drop-offs in patronage of the city's gay establishments, the cumulative number of AIDS deaths in New York City jumped, from 9,822 in 1987 to 14,102 in 1988.[48]

UNITED IN ANGER

By the mid-eighties, AIDS activists' list of enemies was long, in addition to being national in scope. In addition to Koch and city and state health officials, the list now included the pharmaceutical industry, which was responsible for the agonizingly slow and expensive development of AIDS drugs; the Food and Drug Administration, which did not make AIDS treatment approval a priority; President Ronald Reagan, whose administration was totally indifferent to the epidemic; and New York's anti-homosexual, anti-condom Archbishop John Cardinal O'Connor. A backlash was brewing, and Larry Kramer felt that things were ready to boil over. "We can point out until we are blue in the face that we are not the cause of AIDS but its victims," he warned, "but other frightened populations are going to drown out these truths by playing on the worst bigoted fears of the straight world."[49]

Though still indelibly connected to GMHC in the public consciousness, Kramer had in fact quit the organization in 1983 after become painfully disillusioned with the group's mission. Kramer's original vision had been to form an organization for advocacy and action, "primarily to spread information and fight in every way to help the living keep living."[50] Over time, however, he saw the group calcifying into an overworked social services provider, and as a consequence losing what he thought was that necessary spark of anger.

That spark would reignite for Kramer on March 10, 1987, when he was asked to fill in at the last minute after writer Nora Ephron abruptly canceled a speaking engagement at the Lesbian, Gay, Bisexual and Transgender Community Services Center in New York. With no material prepared, Kramer ad-libbed one of the most moving and impassioned speeches of the AIDS era to about 250 attendees. "Sometimes I think we have a death wish. I think we must want to die. I have never been able to understand why for six long years we have sat back and let ourselves literally be knocked off man by man—without fighting back...this is more than denial; it *is* a death wish," Kramer began with typical candor. He then asked two sections of the audience to stand up, and said, "At the rate we are going...two thirds of this room could be dead in less than five years."[51] He went on to tell his listeners that asking for help was no longer working; they needed to *demand* it, and hold those in government and the health department accountable if their demands were not met. He recalled that at a recent meeting of the Centers for Disease Control, a gay activist group called the Lavender Hill Mob had repeatedly disrupted the proceedings by yelling, screaming, and being "blissfully rude to all those arrogant epidemiologists who are ruining our lives." *That* was the way, the only way, Kramer argued, to make the people in City Hall and Washington pay attention. The crowd was galvanized.

Two days later, three hundred people packed into the Center to organize the first meeting of a new group devoted to direct action on behalf of people with AIDS—the AIDS Coalition to Unleash Power (ACT UP). Unlike GMHC, which had been founded by and was run mostly by gay white men, ACT UP was committed to diversity, and thus included in its ranks members of the most at-risk AIDS groups, in addition to gay men: I-V drug users, minorities, and women. Also unlike GMHC, ACT UP had no elected leaders or official spokespeople; shared anger was members' common thread.

Many of the founding volunteers were artists, graphic designers, and advertising executives, lending ACT UP a sense of media-savvy that no other AIDS organization possessed. The group's signs and banners bore simple yet starkly compelling messages (for example, a bulls-eye next to a smirking Reagan with the caption "He Kills Me" or "AIDSgate") with a graphic flair easily readable in newspaper photographs.[52] Many of the posters specifically condemned Ed Koch with slogans like "10,000 AIDS Deaths—How'm I Doin'?," echoing the mayor's signature greeting.[53] Soon after ACT UP's founding, black, white and pink "Silence=Death" stickers peppered bus shelters, phone booths, store windows and park benches in Manhattan.

The group's first major public event occurred on March 24, 1987, only two weeks after Kramer's inaugural speech, at the New York Stock Exchange. With flyers that shouted "no more business as usual!," six hundred protesters demanded that the big pharmaceutical companies release experimental drugs and end ethically questionable drug trials on AIDS patients.[54] They specifically targeted the drug giant Burroughs Wellcome, maker of azidothymidine (AZT), the first AIDS drug. When AZT hit the market in March 1987 (costing $10,000 for a year's supply), patients improved so dramatically that many considered it a virtual cure. However, doctors soon discovered that the virus quickly developed resistance to AZT, rendering the treatment ineffective. What should have been a turning point in AIDS treatment instead became an expensive failure for most patients, and ACT UP wouldn't let Burroughs Wellcome get away with it.[55]

Eventually, some protestors crossed police barricades to lie down in the street, obstructing traffic while passively resisting arrest. Others strung up an effigy of Frank Young, then the head of the Food and Drug Administration. The police wound up arresting nineteen protesters, and the *New York Times* ran a photo of the event with the erroneous caption "Homosexuals Arrested at AIDS Drug Protest."[56]

"STOP THE CHURCH"

Besides fighting for attention on financial and legislative fronts, ACT UP also waged war against religious leaders who demonized homosexuality, forbid condom use, and believed AIDS was unsubtle retribution for sufferers' sins. In New York City, John Cardinal O'Connor—who Gloria Steinem once called the worst thing to happen to the city, along with AIDS—personified this collection of misconceptions.[57]

In 1987, Ronald Reagan had chosen O'Connor to be a member of his Presidential Commission on AIDS, despite the fact that the Cardinal was New York's most outspoken critic of condom distribution, homosexuality, and AIDS education. Like his predecessors Cardinal Hayes' aversion to burlesque and Cardinal Spellman's Communist paranoia, AIDS became O'Connor's *cause célèbre*. He carefully adopted the "love the sinner, hate the sin" ethic and strenuously opposed homosexuality as immoral, saying that "the Church does not reject those persons who engage in such behavior, only the behavior itself."[58] AIDS activists saw his opposition to condoms as unconscionable, but O'Connor countered by opening Catholic hospices for AIDS patients, while at the same time insisting that homosexual sex was the cause of the epidemic. David Wojnarowicz wrote that O'Connor was "the world's most active liar about condoms and safer sex."[59]

O'Connor pugnacious defense of anti-gay attitudes also had an effect on the city's increasing hostile actions against gay establishments. In February 1989, health officials closed two gay movie theaters, the Bijou Cinema and Cinema 14 (neighbors at 100 and 133 Third Avenue respectively) for "essentially operating an AIDS breeding ground with profit being the driving force," in the words of the new Health Commissioner, Dr. Stephen C. Joseph.[60] Similar to the bathhouse inspections four years earlier, the city had sent in inspectors from the City Department of Consumer Affairs—not the Health Department—to observe acts of unsafe sex. The *Times* noted that this was the first closure of a theater for sex acts not involving prostitution, inferring that the theaters were shut down for allowing high-risk sexual activity among men. Said Michelangelo Signorile, a member of ACT UP (and today a well-known journalist and blogger), "if you close down a place like that, [sex] just happens underground"—the same dispute from 1985, now argued with more urgency.

To protest what they saw as the immoral beliefs of the Cardinal, on December 10, 1989, ACT UP staged its biggest and most controversial act yet: a massive "Stop the Church" protest inside St. Patrick's Cathedral, in collaboration with Women's Health Action Mobilization (WHAM!). Five thousand protestors blocked Fifth Avenue with their bodies, carrying signs with condoms attached reading "Take One and Save Your Life." One protestor screamed, "the Church claims to be pro-life and their policies are killing people."[61] Eventually, a few dozen people infiltrated the church and staged a "die-in" by lying motionless in the aisles. Protesters also shouted down Cardinal O'Connor's oration, while others chained themselves to the wooden pews. Television cameras, alerted to the action, swarmed over the bodies, while the rest of the congregation remained trapped in their seats, terrified and aghast.

Vainly trying to keep order, O'Connor continued with giving Communion, until he was challenged by gay parishioner Tom Keane. Instead of accepting the consecrated bread, Keane quietly told O'Connor that opposing safe-sex education was murder. He then let the wafer fall to the stone floor—an act of desecration, as the bread represented the body of Christ to Catholics. "Church ushers grabbed me while priests and altar boys rushed in like ecclesiastic paramedics," Keane remembered.[62]

Eventually, police and EMTs in latex gloves came in to the church, but the activists did not comply with demands to stand up and vacate the premises. "Some of the protesters were taken out on orange stretchers, and they were so frail, I could have picked them up myself," remembered one policewoman. "It was just one of the saddest things I've ever seen."[63]

O'Connor was visibly enraged the following day. "It would have to be over my dead body that the Mass will not go on," he spat. "And no demonstration is going to bring about a change in church teachings and it's certainly not going to bring about any kind of yielding on my part...I'm the Archbishop of New York and I have to preach what the church teaches."[64] Ed Koch, who was present in St. Patrick's during the action, was similarly incensed. "If you don't like the church, go out and find one you like—or start your own,"[65] he said, calling the action an "excrescence."[66] ACT UP member Jay Blotcher retorted, "unfortunately, the dead bodies that the Cardinal is stepping over are the bodies of the people with AIDS who have already passed away. And what he faces are more bodies of people who could potentially contract the disease because the church refuses to give them access to safe-sex education."[67]

Despite the agressive rhetoric, the membership of ACT UP was in fact divided over whether the "Stop the Church" action did more harm than good. A few activists thought that the message was obscured by the notoriety and camp of the protests: one said "the [St. Patrick's] act did provide the mass media with a focal point away from the issues."[68] *Time* magazine reported that the "sacrilegious scene at St. Patrick's was the latest in a series of increasingly militant demonstrations...ACT UP's demonstrations are designed to shock." Jay Blotcher later admitted that the St. Patrick's action "weakened our position somewhat."[69]

After the St. Patrick's action, ACT UP's influence on public policy waned, but not before the group had loudly advocated for the rights of people with AIDS, and had brought media attention to the government's and society's indifference to the disease. However, its main goal, a cure for AIDS, had yet to be reached.

"SOCK IT TO THE PIMPS AND JOHNS"

The decimation of New York's most gregarious and visible sexual subculture in the early nineteen-eighties in many ways mirrored the physical decay of the city itself. In the same way that AIDS let loose its deadly symptoms on a handful of specific risk groups, so too was the city's decomposition confined to a few notorious neighborhoods, with Times Square the primary pocket of putrefaction. The dominant belief was that there could be no civic rebirth in New York City without a physical and moral cleansing of Times

Square, and implicit in the area's future was the destruction of its present—namely the pervasive sex industry and associated businesses that hogged some of the most valuable real estate in Manhattan.

Unlike the wrath of a single virus in the case of AIDS, the catalysts for New York's decay—poverty, crime, inept municipal management—were well-known and decades old by the early eighties, so much a part of the city's character that a succession of mayoral administrations was unable to put a dent in them. Rather, every mayor since La Guardia had tried the same cosmetic approachs: smash the slot machines and burlesque houses, sweep the streets of prostitutes, and get rid of the signs of poverty and crime, without solving the causes of poverty and crime. The question at the dawn of the eighties was: Would the Koch administration and its counterparts at the state level be able to stem the tide of decay, and, by extension, restore Times Square to its former glory?

In 1978, the city and state made two different moves to crack down on the presence of prostitution and massage parlors, the first salvos in the latest attempt to tame Times Square. On July 28, Governor Hugh Carey, Mario Cuomo's predecessor, signed a law that made the penalties for hiring a prostitute the same as those for being a prostitute. Johns would now be charged with a misdemeanor, upgraded from a simple violation. Commenting on the state's action, Ed Koch said it would "sock it to the pimps and johns" and eliminate the sexist double standard that had existed within the law, along with presumably reducing prostitution itself.[70]

On November 18 of the same year, the Board of Estimate unanimously approved an amendment to the city's zoning code that would place a moratorium on new massage parlors and force many existing ones to close. The amendment stipulated that any new "health establishments" must meet carefully defined standards, and required a special permit to operate. If they fell short of these standards, they had to close within a year. Former Mayor Abe Beame must have been irritated, considering that the BOE had doomed his zoning proposal in 1976 while now heartily approving a similar (though less far-reaching) bill under Koch. The director of the Office of Midtown Enforcement (OME), Carl Weisbrod, gloated that the bill was "a terrific preventive device." One might even have said a great prophylactic.

The 1978 amendment built on an existing moratorium from May 1977, which prevented any "adult physical culture establishments" from opening for one year. This broad category included "any establishment, club or business that offers massages, rubs, baths, or similar treatment by members of the opposite sex," but excluded licensed physicians, barbershops, beauty parlors, martial arts studios, and by the nature of its "opposite sex" designation, gay bathhouses. Massage parlors were definitely "adult physical culture establishments," but so were legitimate gyms and spas; the definition was purposefully vague to give police wide range in inspecting and shutting down such establishments for criminal violations or "lack of a proper certificate of occupancy." In the eighteen months between the 1977 and 1978 amendments, the number of massage parlors in midtown Manhattan fell from sixty-four to just twenty.[71] "We are confident that by December 1979 there will be very few, if any, left," Carl Weisbrod stated a bit too confidently, as enforcement of zoning amendments rested on whether a judge found them constitutional. Fortunately for the amendment's proponents, a federal judge upheld the new rules in December 1979, claiming that "Regulations to protect the health, safety, morals or welfare of a community is a constitutionally valid use of a state's police power."[72]

With the new zoning rules in place, city officials felt that they now had a solid foundation for further regulation of the local sex industry. Curbing the sex shops would buttress the argument for Times Square's revitalization and assure potential investors and real estate developers that the city meant business.

Two major construction projects in Times Square were under development by the late seventies, focusing on reclaiming the streets from illegal and sexual activity and making them safe, suburban-style thoroughfares. The Portman Hotel/Broadway Mall project called for a new $261.5 million hotel to be built on the west side of Broadway between 45th and 46th Streets by the Atlanta-based architect John Portman, necessitating the demolition of the Helen Hayes, Morosco, and Bijou Theaters and the Piccadilly Hotel. Though the project had been floated since the Lindsay administration, financing difficulties had prevented it from coming to fruition; in 1978 the Koch administration saw an opportunity to revive the project as the anchor upon which the revitalization of Times Square would be tethered.[73] City planning officials also proposed a pedestrian mall fronting the Portman Hotel, on Broadway between 45th and 47th Streets, which would divert vehicular traffic to adjacent avenues.[74] While the Broadway Mall would feature the TKTS booth for discounted Broadway show tickets, relocated from 47th Street, developers couldn't agree on further amenities. Some argued that providing places to sit, for example, might attract loiterers and vagrants from the non-revitalized parts of Times Square to the south.

The second major revitalization project, called the City at 42nd Street (CA42), was spearheaded by the 42nd Street Development Corporation (42DC), also called the 42nd Street Redevelopment Project. Founded in 1976 by Frederic Papert, a successful Manhattan adman-turned-developer, the 42DC was an entirely private entity created to spur public and private development in West Midtown, financed by the Ford Foundation and Papert himself. A familiar character in the drama of Manhattan real estate, Papert sat on the Board of Directors of the Municipal Art Society, an influential civic group involved in the preservation of historically significant buildings and urban areas. He also boasted of a working relationship with Jacqueline Kennedy Onassis, a champion of the historic preservation movement who had been instrumental in having Grand Central Terminal protected as a landmark in 1967. Papert saw the revitalization of West Midtown as a logical expansion of that effort (Grand Central was on East 42nd Street, Times Square on West 42nd Street); perhaps as an early show of support for the new Times Square, Onassis became a 42DC board member and donated twenty-five thousand dollars to the organization.[75]

Among the 42DC's successful early development efforts were Manhattan Plaza, a 1,700-unit affordable-housing complex for artists between 42nd and 43rd Streets and Ninth and Tenth Avenues in 1977; the "Operation Crossroads" NYPD substation, replacing a notorious porn outlet, in the Times Building in 1978; and Theater Row, a strip of off-off-Broadway theaters and studios, across 42nd Street from Manhattan Plaza, also in 1978.[76] As a local development corporation, the 42DC enjoyed many perks from the city and state, such as the right to buy or lease city-owned properties without having to go through the usual bidding process against other companies.[77] Though the 42DC's mission was to create private real estate development to benefit the public, such incentives blurred the group's status as a private entity.

THE BRIGHT LIGHTS ZONE

As a backer of 42DC, the Ford Foundation saw the benefit of evaluating the socioeconomic factors of the area to be redeveloped. In 1978, the Foundation commissioned sociologists William Kornblum and Terry Williams of the City University of New York Graduate Center to perform a study assessing the conditions of West 42nd Street between Seventh and Eighth Avenues. While not specifically issued in conjunction with the 42DC, the study was meant to "assist governmental leaders and the business community in revitalizing this blighted section of 42nd Street," Kornblum wrote in the introduction.[78]

Eventually published in 1979 as a monograph titled *Times Square: The Bright Lights Zone*, Kornblum and Williams' assessment provided "an understanding of the human ecology of the area and how it had emerged historically, describing the influence of the various moral crusades that swept through central city entertainment zones—starting with Prohibition, the bans on burlesque houses, the drug crusades, and so on."[79] Kornblum noted two assumptions in the undertaking: one, that a "change in the present conditions which plague the street is desirable," and two, that "change will depend on increased public understanding of the present conditions and of their underlying causes."[80] In other words, *Times Square: The Bright Lights Zone* was designed to sway decision-makers toward development initiatives and perhaps influence the public's opinions of the area. Along those lines, Carl Weisbrod contributed "all the help and encouragement" the authors could have asked for, while Fred Papert personally offered suggestions about "how the study could assist them in their efforts to revitalize the district."[81]

A fascinating visual picture of 42nd Street life in the late seventies emerged from the pages of Kornblum and Williams' study. "Friday afternoon, 5:15, April 8, 1978: A tall high yellow harlot strolls down the street streaking with tight-tight pink-pink pants on pink blouse, pink high-heeled shoes, cold black underpanties wrapped around her bottom," Williams wrote. Pimps, or "players" in Times Square argot, were similarly attired in distinctive costumes: "The players are dressed in an assortment of colorful hats and clothing, their hair in a 'superfly conk' style. Their hands held backward, high stacked heeled shoes, wide-brimmed hats, manicured polished fingernails."[82]

Among the prostitute underclass, gay men and "transvestites" (a contemporary term describing gay men in drag, used interchangeably with "queens") were omnipresent. "The gays [in Times Square] are increasingly black former convicts who share little of the middle-class gay culture of the village or the West 70's. Gay men and transvestites cruise 42nd Street regularly. Some are flamboyantly attired in women's apparel and others distinguish themselves with short cut-off pants and white socks and t-shirts. The range of clothing does not lend itself easily to description."[83] It was assumed that most of the queens and young gay men on the street were hustlers or their johns, and the study noted one transvestite's similarities in dress and mannerisms to a female prostitute: "Friday afternoon, 4:00, April 7, 1978: A lone transvestite strolls by wearing heavy rouge, red lipstick, black wig, stacked heels, earrings, red Danskin top, ballooned-bottom pants. Looking, cruising, searching for anyone who will notice."[84]

The *Bright Lights Zone* also revealed that, far from being the domain solely of the poor and derelict, 42nd Street was actually the most racially-integrated street in Manhattan. Most customers of the sex shops and massage parlors were middle-class white males, while young black and Latino males constituted much of the audience for action-adventure movies. In addition, working-class white males patronized the bars and restaurants, while men of all ethnicities patronized the fast food joints, electronics stores, and other shops along 42nd Street. Women in the area, numbering far fewer than men, were similarly ethnically diverse.

Kornblum and Williams also noted the sex industries' adaptability to downturns in the market and to increased police pressure. Like any other business, "the sex entertainment industries would not continue functioning if they were not profitable. They turn profits even though they pay enormous rents, high legal fees, and are subject to various kinds of monitoring."[85] Though loathed by the ruling classes, the sex industry contributed was a major part of New York City's economy. Reverend Bruce Ritter, the media-savvy director of Covenant House, the shelter for teen runaways on Eighth Avenue, estimated that consumers spent more than one billion dollars annually on sex in Times Square.[86] "Sex and entertainment has become legitimized," he said. "We have the sex industry here because we want it."[87]

Ultimately, Kornblum and Williams found an entrenched industry that would not disappear even if the area was redeveloped. "The fact that 20 percent of [survey] respondents report patronage of adult bookstores (most of which now include peep shows as well)…supports our conclusion that economic development of the Bright Light District will not eliminate the commercial sex industry from the Times Square area since that is where it finds its most concentrated market."[88]

Undaunted, the 42DC created a redevelopment scheme that removed the sexual element from Times Square; in the planners' thinking, revitalization equaled elimination of the sex industry from the properties it occupied. Rather than a building-by-building cleanup, as had been the city's pattern before, the 42DC envisioned the wholesale renovation of the blighted area. Fred Papert and a colleague, former City Planning Commission chairman Donald Elliott, initialized an offshoot of the 42DC called the City at 42nd Street Inc. specifically to draw up a blueprint for the new Times Square. Influenced by the findings in the *Bright Lights Zone* and driven to return Times Square to its historic origin as a glamorous entertainment center, Papert and Elliott designed the $600 million CA42 in 1979 (again, with financial backing from the Ford Foundation) as a combination amusement park, cultural destination, and corporate headquarters zone, with an element of historic preservation mixed in.[89]

Encompassing the eight acres between 40th and 43rd Streets and Broadway and Eighth Avenue, the CA42 renewal area included eight Beaux Arts theaters then operating as cheap movie houses. Under the plan, the Victory and the New Amsterdam theaters would be restored for nonprofit use, while the Selwyn, Apollo, and Harris would be given over to commercial companies after renovation. The facades of three other theaters, the Lyric, Times Square, and Empire, would be preserved but the structures themselves gutted to make way for purposes other than live theater.[90]

The CA42 also included millions of square feet of commercial and office space, long considered the bedrock of any economic revitalization plan. A new two-story shopping mall containing four-hundred-thousand square feet of retail space would connect to the Port Authority Bus Terminal via bridges across 42nd Street. Three forty-two-story office towers would add another four million square feet of office space on lots circling the old Times Building at the intersection of 42nd Street, Seventh Avenue and Broadway (the *Times* tower itself would be slated for demolition). In addition, garment manufacturers convinced planners that an enormous Merchandise Mart housing wholesalers and showrooms would bring revenue to the nearby garment industry as well as Times Square; the Mart would anchor the Eighth Avenue corner of 42nd Street with two million square feet of space. The Times Square subway station, housing more than ten transit lines, would also be overhauled and redesigned to facilitate visitors and workers in the new office towers.[91]

The centerpiece of CA42 would be a five-hundred-thousand square foot "cultural, educational and entertainment complex," on Forty-Second Street between Eighth Ave and Broadway. Essentially a New York City-inspired theme park, the complex would house exhibits explaining the city to tourists with dazzling visual technology; a collection of replicated treasures from the city's many museums; an IMAX theater; a "Slice of the Apple" ride simulating a vertical leap from a subway tunnel to the top of a skyscraper; a cone-shaped theater resembling the interior of the Guggenheim Museum; a fifteen-story indoor Ferris wheel; and a skywalk to the *New York Times* headquarters on 43rd Street.[92]

To recoup building costs, it was estimated that admission to the theme park would need to be at least four dollars a head. Papert also planned to sell corporate sponsorships to finance the rides, a model he had observed at Disney World's Epcot Center.[93] In fact, Donald Elliott claimed that CA42 was based, in part, on his observations of how the Disney machine worked. He even approached Disney about taking part in the CA42 project, but was turned down. "Disney didn't want to be involved with any idea that was controversial; they only wanted a visual story, not a talk or text story.

We were told Disney doesn't do these things downtown, in New York City," Elliott recalled.[94]

The CA42 would be financed with $70 million in federal grants, with the rest of money provided by private developers eager to get a piece of Times Square, including Helmsley-Spear and Olympia & Yorke.[95] Papert boosted CA42 relentlessly, and eventually won funding from the city's most formidable corporations and foundations, including IBM, Chase, Exxon, and the Equitable Life Assurance Society.[96] The city's main role beyond contributing municipal money would be condemning property via eminent domain, as the biggest remaining variable to the CA42's success was the constitutionality of kicking out sex businesses that "frighten away out-of-towners and city residents alike."[97]

SELTZER VS. ORANGE JUICE

Mayor Koch and the City Planning Commission, whose support was absolutely crucial for CA42 to move forward, initially championed the CA42. However, by 1980, Koch was having second thoughts. Amidst the gritty glamour of Manhattan, and as a new decade dawned, suburban-style pedestrian malls and theme park attractions suddenly seemed bourgeois, a little cheesy, and very un-New York-like. In June 1980, Koch withdrew any and all city support for the massive project, a shocking reversal that stunned the City at 42nd Street Inc. and its investors. Koch derided the proposal as "Disneyland on 42nd Street" and famously quipped that New Yorkers preferred seltzer instead of Florida orange juice.[98] The Mayor also publicly fumed that the City at 42nd Street Inc. had been designated as the project leader, and the sole contractors were developers like Olympia & Yorke, leaving the city out of the loop. Koch demanded a total re-do, with a formal bidding process independent of Papert's organization. Elliott complained bitterly that killing CA42 was a political maneuver.[99] In withdrawing his support, Koch forced planners back to square one and required them to field bids based on the city's, not the City at 42nd Street Inc.'s, guidelines. Though this new process would supposedly be above-board and transparent, it would also be time-consuming and had the potential to cost the support of the private developers assembled by Papert's group, who would not wait around forever while the city weighed proposals.

In another unexpected move, the city enlisted the state's help in organiz-
ing the municipal plan to save Times Square. In June 1980, the city signed a
Memorandum of Understanding (MOU) with the New York State Urban
Development Corporation (UDC), a state agency with far-reaching power
to enable public/private development. The UDC's authority extended to
negotiating tax incentive packages, enacting eminent domain and overrul-
ing local zoning codes in order to push through real estate deals. The MOU
established a joint city/state partnership known as the 42nd Street Development Project (42DP).[100]

The 42DP's plan was announced on February 11, 1981, and called for
the refurbishment of nine historic theaters between 40th to 43rd Streets, a
new 560-room hotel at 42nd Street and Eighth Avenue, the aforementioned
Merchandise Mart, four new office towers circling the intersection of 42nd
Street and Seventh Avenue, and the Times Square subway station renovation, all conducted by private interests. The plan scrapped the theme park
concept, as Koch had wanted.

Though the 42DP plan and the rejected CA42 were strikingly similar,
there was one notable difference: the UDC would have control over Times
Square's future, not the privately-funded 42DC. Despite this seemingly important distinction, no money for the 42DP's refurbishment plan would
actually come from federal or state sources; rather, private developers would
fund demolition and construction in return for enormous tax breaks. The
UDC would choose the developers, and authorize property condemnation
via eminent domain where needed. While the right of eminent domain had
historically allowed the government to seize private property for public use,
and required that the owners of the seized land be compensated for their
losses, in this case, the UDC would have the power to seize private property
for *private* development—even though the private development was ostensibly for the public good—and in turn the private developers, not the state,
would compensate the property owners.

Not everyone was happy with this cozy city-state-developer relationship or its vision of a squeaky-clean Times Square. Cultural critic Phillip
Lopate lamented the proposed destruction of "that magnetic field of neon"

contributing to "a visual clutter so extreme that it makes the simple traversal of one city block as adventurous as passing through a gantlet."[101] He surmised the city's and state's real motivations behind the revitalization: "What's objected to here are not movie houses and pinball parlors but the people who go into them, who are the wrong class and the wrong color...I wonder if this city knows how lucky it is to have a raunchy street so famous and so densely compacted." Lopate asked if the city understood that "tourists, even the straightest, come to New York City partly because they've heard that we have a real Sodom and Gomorrah?" It seemed that the 42DP orchestrators had never considered the current version of Times Square, organic and disorganized, as a tourist attraction.

Why did the city think that the 42DP project would succeed when so many of its earlier attempts to clean up Times Square had flamed out? Primarily, because the 42DP was unlike any revitiliaztion plan that had come before. First, this was no mere clean-up campaign; it was a ground-up demolition and rebuilding effort. Secondly, the 42DP's motivation was pure capitalism, not moral outrage; the age-old desire to restore a sense of decency to the area had been completely cut from the equation. Third and most significantly, the city embraced the private developers and would allow them virtual free reign over their specific components of the project, once approved by the UDC. Despite these substantial differences in method, there was still no certainty that this latest plan would actually work were so many others had failed before. "No one has ever heard me say it's definitely going to happen," cautioned Richard Kahan, the UDC's president. "All I said is we're going to give it our best shot. It's the right plan at the right time and it's the best shot Times Square is going to have."[102]

BULLDOZERS ON BROADWAY

While all this was going on, the Portman Hotel project on which the city had originally pinned its revivalist hopes was progressing through its bureaucratic paces. In August 1980, the Board of Estimate gave approval to the hotel and, implicitly, to the city's plan for the pedestrian Broadway Mall at the hotel's entrance. However, several controversial aspects of the plan still needed to be worked out. The powerful theater industry vehemently opposed the destruction of the Helen Hayes, Morosco, and Bijou Theaters, and attempted to have the structures hastily declared as landmarks so that they could not be demolished. In addition, automotive groups dreaded the bottlenecks that would result if car traffic was diverted from Broadway. Finally, financing for the multimillion-dollar project was also far from assured; the developer and the city scrambled to find money from state and federal sources. Despite the complications, on March 22, 1982, the hotel cleared its final legal hurdles. Though public support for the mall had evaporated due to concerns over traffic congestion, the three theaters were demolished, and the hotel was built, opening as the Marriott Marquee in 1985, facing southbound traffic on Broadway.

Concurrent with the construction of the hotel, the UDC assembled an 850-page Draft Environmental Impact Statement (DEIS) during 1982 and 1983, assessing possible changes in the immediate vicinity of the 42DP project. On the plus side for the city, the DEIS predicted that the project would generate 23,000 new office jobs, a potential of $860 million in tax revenues over a twenty year period, and improve the transportation infrastructure to ease crowding and traffic. The 42DP would also allow Times Square to reclaim its original character as a grand intersection of entertainment, commerce, and the arts, absent any remnants of the massage parlors and sex shops. In a set of mandatory design requirements, the UDC insisted that new construction harmonize with historic architecture (such as the Beaux Arts theaters) and allow for the expansion of Times Square's signature neon signs and advertisements. The four office towers, which the UDC made possible by overruling zoning restrictions on building height, would have their upper stories set back from the street so that when looking upwards, visiting tourists would see a blaze of LED lights and signage rather than colossal facades.

On the down side, 42DP depended on the UDC invoking eminent domain, a situation that existing property owners vowed to fight. While area sex businesses may have been considered undesirable, they were for the most part legal entities (excluding street prostitution) and composed an economy that brought the city millions of dollars in tax revenues each year. "We're ready to fight the UDC taking away private property for a project that there is no need and no reason for," fumed Leonard Weiss, owner of two huge parking lots slated for condemnation. "Cleaning up Times Square is one thing—this is something else."[103] Herald Price Fahringer, a well-known defense lawyer, was retained by a number of the threatened sex shops to follow the case for possible litigation down the line.

In early October 1984, Mayor Koch, Governor Mario Cuomo, and leaders from the highest levels of New York's political world presented the final 42nd Street Development Project plan to the Board of Estimate.[104] Two weeks later, the BOE approved the plan for four office towers, the merchandise mart, the subway station facelift, the hotel at the corner of 42nd Street and Eighth Avenue, and the renovation of nine historic theaters. The only buildings to be retained under the plan were the Candler Building on 42nd Street and the Hotel Carter on 43rd Street, and possibly the iconic Times Tower at One Times Square; everything else would be demolished or gutted and built anew.

Soon after, four sets of developers signed ninety-nine year leases with the state for parcels of the thirteen-acre area. The UDC chose developer Park Tower Realty for the four office buildings, and its president, George Klein, in turn chose the world-renowned architect Philip Johnson as the master planner.[105] The selection of Klein was a slap in the face to more experienced contenders like Paul Milstein and World Trade Center developer Larry Silverstein; it was quickly revealed that Klein, heir to a candy fortune, had generously supported Ed Koch's reelection campaign in 1981.[106] Further controversy arose when Johnson and his partner, John Burgee, revealed their designs for the four office towers, which were definitely not what the UDC had in mind. The set-back facades and accessibility had been abandoned; instead, the Johnson/Burgee plan called for severe columns of red granite at street level, rising to "virtually identical towers lighted by formal lanterns and floodlights and varying only in their height and girth."[107] Scant space was allowed for the spectacular neon and LED advertisements. The overall effect was more Rockefeller Center sterility than Times Square glamour.

Regardless of design, the 42DP would displace 413 businesses with 3,300 employees, many of them workers in the theater industry; evict twenty-four full-time residents, and erase "42nd Street's role as a movie and entertainment center for many low-income patrons."[108] The proposed office jobs and entertainment offerings—rejuvenated Broadway shows, restaurants, first-run films—were designed to replace working-class customers with educated, cultured, middle-class consumers, in order to increase the city's revenues. The project also promised an end to the sex industry's dominance of Times Square, as 42DP would "reclaim 42nd Street from the pervasive aura of lawlessness and tawdriness that infects it by filling it with thousands of legitimate theater-goers, office workers, tourists and out-of-town buyers."[109] Yet there was one caveat: it was believed that the sex businesses, unlike the second-run cinemas, would most likely relocate to the upper West 40's, Eighth Avenue north of 43rd Street, and to residential side streets in west midtown. Though the UDC did not believe that the shops would be as densely-packed together as they were on 42nd Street, $25 million was included in the 42DP to pacify residents in Clinton, the neighborhood to the west of Times Square, based on the possibility that the displaced sex shops could relocate there.

Despite the added money, civic groups and unions decried the potential damage to the fabric of abutting neighborhoods, the enormous tax breaks to already-rich developers, and the bulldozing of the heart of New York's most famous street. "This plan has so many downsides to it that you're cleaning up Times Square by destroying it," claimed one state senator.[110]

"A PUBLIC PROBLEM"

The implentation of 42DP coincided with a nationwide wave of anti-porn sentiment and a renewed effort by the federal government to combat smut. A decade and a half after the first Pornography Commission in 1970, President Reagan cannily sensed that it was time for another examination of the public-sex problem. "It's time to stop pretending pornography is a victimless crime," he announced. "We consider pornography to be a public problem."[111]

Reagan's statements seemed to indicate that it was already a foregone conclusion that pornography *was* evil and *did* produce victims; nevertheless, Attorney General Edwin Meese III appropriated half a million dollars for a study of this "public problem." Instead of scientific experts, as had been consulted for the 1970 Report, Meese selected several members of the Commission based on their proven anti-pornography, anti-sex stances, including Covenant House founder Father Bruce Ritter (who was later accused of having sex with four male teenagers in his care) and Dr. James Dobson, president of the Christian Right group Focus on the Family.[112]

Rather than conduct empirical, unbiased research, the Commission instead traveled the country, holding public hearings in which self-identified victims testified about being personally harmed by pornography. Not surprisingly, much of the "evidence" the Commission gathered was purely anecdotal, such as this anonymous letter that had been sent to Women Against Pornography: "When I first met my husband, it was in early 1975, and he was all the time talking about *Deep Throat*. After we were married, he on several occasions referred to her performances and suggested I try to imitate her actions... my husband raped me...While he held a butcher knife on me threatening to kill me he fed me three strong tranquilizers...he beat my face and my body. I later had welts and bruises. He attempted to smother me with a pillow."[113] Inexplicably, none of the violence the writer described actually occurred in *Deep Throat*.

Linda Lovelace herself, who had dropped her *nom de porn* and now went by her married name of Marchiano, also testified before the Commission, recounting nastiest vignettes from her memoir *Ordeal*. Al Goldstein, playing the part of comic relief and muckraker, "showed up waving copies of *Dog Fucker*," Marchiano's long-lost, pre-*Deep Throat* stag loop.[114] Conservative feminist Andrea Dworkin, though estranged from Women Against Pornography, opened the second session of the Commission's hearings in New York City on January 26, 1986. "Every year millions of pictures are being made of women with our legs spread. We are called beaver, we are called pussy, our genitals are tied up, they are pasted, makeup is put on them to make them pop out of a page...so that our vaginas are exposed for penetration, our anuses are exposed for penetration, our throats are used as if they are genitals for penetration," she testified. "The major motif of pornography as a form of entertainment is that women are raped and violated and humiliated until we discover that we like it and at that point we ask for more."[115]

Like Parkhurst and Comstock, the committee members educated themselves about their subject matter by visiting peep shows, adult cinemas, and sex retailers. But unlike Parkhurst and Comstock, who had gone in undercover, the identity of the Meese Commission members was obvious. On one visit, the Commission and a squad of cops burst into a peep booth. "As everyone watched, a bullet-headed vice cop yanked open the door and announced in a loud voice, 'and here we have two men engaged in an act of oral copulation!'" recounted a *Playboy* reporter on the scene. "The two men looked up in astonishment at the eleven commissioners."[116]

The highly anticipated final report of the Attorney General's Commission on Pornography was released in July 1986. At nearly two thousand pages, it was an absolutely exhaustive survey of a totally imaginary problem. Among its recommendations for community action against local sources of pornography, the Report included a comprehensive list of 2,325 adult magazine titles, the intricate plot summaries of 725 books, and incriminating dialogue lifted from more than 2,300 X-rated movies.[117] Al Goldstein opined in the *New York Times* that pornographers themselves should foot the bill for such handy reports, instead of the taxpayers. After all, he wrote, "Puritan proscriptions and the cult of taboo is the *raison d'etre* of the whole adult entertainment industry."[118]

THE BEGINNING OF THE END

From the moment the 42nd Street Development Project was approved, lawsuits by passed-over developers and community groups started to fly. Everyone wanted a say in the revitalization of Times Square, as well as a cut of the profits when it was all completed. While the cases played out in court, virtually no demolition or building took place for the rest of the eighties.

Curiously, many of the sex businesses threatened by the 42DP were initially slow to respond to the proposed redevelopment of Times Square. Perhaps, due to its survival in the face of every cleanup campaign of the past fifty years, the sex industry did not take the plan seriously (few people beyond the inner circle of planners were initially aware of the details of 42DP). Years of municipal threats may have also had made the owners of sex-related businesses reluctant to speak up and thus draw unwanted attention to themselves.

On the other hand, maybe the industry felt a greater threat to its survival from more immediate forces. In the wake of the Meese Commission report, eight thousand convenience stores across the country stopped carrying magazines like *Playboy*, *Hustler* and *Penthouse* for fear that store owners would be indicted for the sale or distribution of obscene material. The National Federation for Decency, a Christian anti-porn group based in Mississippi, called for consumer boycotts and picketing of stores that continued to sell such material. "There's a strong moralistic trend in the country today," claimed an expert at the Gannett Center for Media Studies at Columbia University. "I think there's a tremendous reaction in the country generally to what was the sexual revolution."[119]

Just the threat of controversy in such a sensitive retail climate encouraged many establishments to drop publications with even a hint of skin, which of course adversely affected many stores in Times Sqaure and vicinity. In addition, stores that continued to sell a wide range of smut also suffered diminished sales as a result of customers' fear of sexually-transmitted diseases, like AIDS. The most damaging blow, however, were the changes that the porn market was undergoing during the eighties, as videocassettes augmented or replaced magazines and books in adult stores and cable television provided home-based adult content for consumers who found visiting sex shops distasteful.

Pornography producers had initially spearheaded the home-theater revolution, and most of the early videos for sale or rent in the United States were X-rated, such as *Deep Throat* and *Behind the Green Door*. Since a VCR cost several hundred dollars in the early eighties, and cassette rentals ranged from four to ten dollars per tape, the key consumers of these early porn videos were middle-and upper-middle-class white men who could afford the luxury. Even as videos started to flood the market, younger male and working class viewers continued to go to the cinema to see porn movies. It was not until the cost of VCRs and tapes dropped in the mid-eighties that less-affluent consumers had access to them.

By eliminating the middlemen—the sex shops themselves—from the consumer-porn relationship, cable TV presented a second threat to New York's sex industry. After establishing *Screw's* profile in the newsstands and daily tabloids, Al Goldstein had branched out to the nascent public-access cable television market in Manhattan. Launching his show *Midnight Blue* in 1975, Goldstein brought the *Screw* brand to late-night TV. A typical episode of *Midnight Blue* might contain an interview with a porn starlet, an intellectual chat with an actor like Jack Nicholson, and a long segment of Goldstein ranting about his defective Mercedes-Benz and shouting "fuck you!" to the company's CEO. Goldstein and his two long-suffering cameramen also made vignettes satirizing current events and exposing the hypocrisy of sanctimonious politicians and Bible-thumpers. Yet Goldstein always reserved the harshest invective for himself, constantly complaining about his difficulty in getting laid. He also delighted in skewering feminists' anti-pornography rhetoric, as in this exchange with the porn actress Seka: "What about Women Against Porn, who would say that you are being used and abused? Are you being forced to do what you're doing? Are their guns to your head? Do you enjoy what you're doing or do you feel you're being exploited?" Goldstein asked. Seka replied drily, "You can be exploited in any field you're in; it does not matter what you do...I feel that members of Women Against Pornography probably never had orgasms in their lives and probably never will."[120]

Despite (or because of) its haphazard structure built upon the whims of Al Goldstein, *Midnight Blue* became the most popular program on Manhattan cable in the late seventies and early eighties.[121] It also spawned a spin-off cable-access program in 1977, *The Robin Byrd Show*, starring the former stripper and actress. Byrd's format was a bit more low key than Goldstein's—various female and male strippers would dance at the beginning of the show, then Byrd (in her customary black crocheted bikini and white nail polish) would gather her guests for a chat about their scheduled appearances at New York clubs. Viewers could call in and ask questions, and Byrd's enthusiasm for serving her public never flagged. Though the program only aired in Manhattan, Byrd was soon instantly recognizable on the street by her mane of flowing blond hair, frosty pink lip gloss and husky voice. Unlike *Midnight Blue*, *The Robin Byrd Show* advocated AIDS prevention and safe sex.

The growth of the video and cable industries had a chilling effect on the urban infrastructure of the porn industry. In 1980, there were approximately one thousand adult movie theaters scattered across the country; that number had shrunk to less than four hundred by 1986.[122]

"A 42ND STREET ANYWHERE IN THE WORLD"

The courts wrapped up the last of the numerous lawsuits against 42DP in April 1990, giving the UDC permission to warm up the wrecking ball. State officials were also granted the exclusive right to condemn properties within the 42DP zone. Evictions soon followed—240 commercial tenants from thirty-four separate buildings within three years, including many of the despised porn businesses (mission accomplished for the moralists) as well as action-adventure cinemas, offices, delis, and discount retail stores.[123] By 1992 the majority of the 42nd Street strip was blocked off and boarded up, waiting for the second act.

Despite the ongoing pace of demolition, the actual plans for rebuilding had not yet been finalized. George Klein's Park Tower Realty and his investor, Prudential Insurance Company, had formed a joint partnership (Times Square Center Associates, or TSCA) and were itching to start building the first of the proposed four office towers at 42nd Street and Seventh Avenue. Unfortunately, the market for commercial office space had plummeted while the 42DP had been tangled up in the courts, a result of the local and national recession of the late eighties and early nineties. This presented a serious problem for TSCA. They could start building, but tenants might never materialize. Prudential had already sunk more than $240 million into the four towers and couldn't afford to lose its investment.

Meanwhile, at the Eighth Avenue end of the strip, the developers that had been slated to build the merchandise mart and the proposed hotel reneged when the economy bottomed out. A rule in the 42DP stated that construction must begin on any condemned property within one year of demolition—but without anyone contracted to build, the existing structures could not be condemned, thus leaving the sex shops and clubs circling the Port Authority Bus Terminal intact, their neon signs glowing defiantly.

Weakened by this legal catch-22, 42DP was now vulnerable to attack from cultural critics who voiced their dismay at the generic office-park aesthetic of the planned buildings, especially the red granite monoliths designed by Philip Johnson and John Burgee for Park Tower Realty. They feared the rich, nearly century-long history of Times Square as the city's entertainment epicenter would be lost amid the wind canyons and faceless architecture. As their protests grew louder, planners began to reevaluate their strategy: with little demand for office space, commercial real estate did not seem like the financial savior of 42nd Street that it had in the eighties.

The Municipal Arts Society stepped into the void to offer new uses for the area that built upon Times Square's original, historic character. This was a step in the right direction; instead of destroying the culture of the street, perhaps it could be preserved, albeit in a highly sanitized form. In 1992, the office tower construction was put on indefinite hold and Rebecca Robertson, president of the 42DP since 1987, announced a stopgap plan for the already-condemned parcels on 42nd Street, in conjunction with Robert A. M. Stern Architects. Titled 42nd Street Now! (42N!), the plan was based on six principles: "layering, unplanning, contradiction and surprise, pedestrian experience, visual anchors, and aesthetics as attractions."[124] 42N! called for the condemned buildings, including the historic theaters scheduled for renovation, to be quickly and temporarily retrofitted for a variety of entertainment uses: clubs, theaters and live stages. Above the second story of the renovated buildings, blinding walls of lighted billboards, LED advertisements and signage would evoke the razzle-dazzle of Times Square gone by. The overall plan was hailed as a synergy of popular entertainment, modern energy and historical conservation.

A distinguished urban planner, the suave, silver-haired Stern was known for his style of retaining traditional character while modernizing key aspects of public spaces and buildings. That would seem to dovetail with the 42DP's shift from corporate use to tourism and entertainment. It also didn't hurt that Stern's firm had already designed two major projects for the Walt Disney Company—the Beach Club Resort and Yacht Club Resort in Lake Buena Vista, Florida—and that Stern maintained a friendly relationship with Disney's then-chairman, Michael Eisner, and sat on Disney's Board of

Directors. "Disney has taught Americans a lot about what they're missing in the urban life," Stern told *Newsweek*.[125] One could see from 42nd Street Now! that New Yorkers were going to finally get their orange juice.

With the UDC's choice of Stern's firm to lead 42N!, the state was carving a direct line of negotiation to Disney. For all of the planning, bargaining, demolishing and retrofitting, the UDC still did not have the one flagship tenant on the new 42nd Street that would, by example, convince other megacorporations of the financial promise and cultural excitement (not to mention the sweetheart tax incentives) of the new Times Square. With Stern on board, the UDC hedged their bets on Disney.

To support Stern, the city spun off yet another nonprofit corporation, the New 42nd Street Inc. (New42) in 1992 with Cora Cahan, a former dancer, as president, responsible for the restoration of 42nd Street's historic theaters. New42 held ninety-nine year leases for seven of the nine historic theaters and adjacent buildings on 42nd Street (annual rent on each property: ten dollars).[126] The group would be the main lobbyist for the city and state in convincing Disney to come to 42nd Street. *New York Times* publisher Arthur Sulzberger Jr., who had a very personal stake in the future of 42nd Street, convinced his aunt, influential civic booster Marian Heiskell, to chair the New42. Not at all coincidentally, Heiskell was also a very close friend of Michael Eisner. Sulzberger and Heiskell made repeated overtures to Eisner, even going so far as to ambush him with a pitch and a map of 42nd Street at a society dinner.[127]

Eisner, however, was far from certain that the most notorious block in the most infamous city in America was the ideal spot for children's entertainment. Disney's most important requirement for the project was a theater in which to launch its live theatricals. Architect Stern led Eisner on a tour of the New Amsterdam Theater, once the largest and finest Beaux Arts house on the strip and the former home of Ziegfeld's *Follies,* but now abandoned and boarded up. When they stepped through the doors, in hardhats, pigeons were nesting in the intricately carved rafters and mushrooms sprouted through the rotten wooden floors. Beyond the decay, however, Stern and Eisner saw a legendary space that with the right ratio of grandiose history and Disney-style whimsy, could be the ideal setting for the company's first planned show, *The Lion King*. Eisner phoned Heiskell and hinted that he was interested in the New Amsterdam. Other Disney executives were hesitant, however: "To me, it didn't make a hell of a lot of sense to spend thirty or forty million dollars to restore a place that was going to sit nestled between a couple dozen pornographic shitholes," remarked a member of Eisner's staff.[128]

Since the New Amsterdam's potential alone would not be enough to convince Eisner, the New42 drew up an attractive package of financial incentives, generous tax breaks and other perks. Here the city seemed to relinquish its control over the project in favor of Disney's suggestions (unlike the CA42 fiasco in 1980, in which the city and state had elbowed the City at 42nd Street Inc. out of the picture). The estimated cost of renovating the New Amsterdam was thirty-two million dollars, twenty-four million of which would come from New 42nd Street, Inc. as a loan, with 3 percent interest. Disney also demanded that two additional major entertainment companies set up shop on 42nd Street as co-anchors of the strip. It wanted Tishman Construction (which, like Stern, had also built Disney theme properties) to handle the New Amsterdam renovation, which the New42 duly hired. And one other demand: the city had to get rid of every single porn shop on the strip, within one year.[129] "No way around it," said Rebecca Robertson, the 42DP president, "we are going to have glitz on 42nd Street."[130]

The deal between the city, state, and Disney was signed on the last day of the David Dinkins administration, December 31, 1993. The next day, mayor-elect Rudolph W. Giuliani would be sworn in to bask in the success of this unprecedented *coup d'etat*. "It was about as attractive a deal as anyone could ever imagine, especially for a multibillion-dollar corporation that really didn't need the financial assistance," a Disney executive gloated.[131] "We are creating a series of products that are Disney-branded—smaller-than-a-[theme] park products you can put on a 42nd Street anywhere in the world."[132]

8.

DISNEY VS. THE DIRTY DEBUTANTES
1994-2000

B y the mid 1990s, the erotic landscape of New York City was but a pale
shadow of the rollicking, omnipresent flow of sexual commerce it had
been the previous two decades. The era of *Deep Throat*, swinging and Plato's
Retreat was long over, and the city was now paralleling a nationwide wane
of freely expressed sexuality, with sexual eroticism replaced in part by the
battles over sexual politics. Reflecting the well-publicized spectacles of the
late eighties and early nineties—including future Supreme Court Justice
Clarence Thomas being accused of sexual harassment by Anita Hill on live
television, and a *60 Minutes* interview in 1992 that revealed Democratic
presidential nominee Bill Clinton's alleged extramarital activities—the sexual discourse was redirected from eighties-era "pornography victims" and
Christian boycotts of 7-Eleven to official regulation of sexual behavior on a
national scale, in which, for example, corporations adopted zero-tolerance
policies against sexual harassment.

In New York, for many, the sex had been taken out of sexy. No one
seriously advocated a return to the cruising culture or casual intercourse
of the seventies—to do so would negate the reality that AIDS was continuing to rampage through the city's gay, African-American and Latino
communities. By the early nineties, the disease had become the city's worst
public health crisis ever. During the Dinkins administration, from 1989 to
1993, twenty-five-thousand cases were diagnosed, and AIDS had become
the leading cause of death of men aged thirty to forty-nine, and of women

aged twenty to thirty-nine, in the city.[1]

As the 1993 mayoral election approached, many voters and activists began to scrutinize the AIDS policies of Dinkins' rival in the race, Republican upstart Rudolph W. Giuliani. Giuliani's camp, however, offered little in the way of concrete plans for continuing the fight against the disease. In an analysis of both Dinkins' and Giuliani's policies, the *Village Voice* suggested "[using] Giuliani's positions on other issues—crime, homelessness, schools, squeegee men—to gauge what his approach to the epidemic might be." The outlook did not bode well, as his proposals for battling New York's intractable social problems (such as poverty, expanding welfare rolls, drug abuse and violence) included a welfare-to-work program that required welfare recipients to immediately go to work or suffer cuts in their benefits, as well as arguing against the "right" to shelter for the homeless and for limiting shelter stays to ninety days.[2] And as for the candidate's views on gay equality, Giuliani was against a public school curriculum that taught respect for gays, and regularly marched in the notoriously anti-gay St. Patrick's Day Parade.[3] Regardless of these views, Giuliani was elected mayor in 1993. To many, a moderate Republican mayor in Gracie Mansion seemed on the surface as anachronistic as New Yorkers preferring orange juice to seltzer; however, enough voters evidently felt that the city's problems required a new, radical direction in leadership.

THE MAN, THE MYTH

On February 2, 1994, the new mayor announced Disney's lease on the New Amsterdam Theater to the press, flanked by Michael Eisner and the newly elected Governor of New York, George Pataki. As the cameras flashed, Giuliani, who apparently had no qualms taking credit for a deal that the Koch and Dinkins administrations had exhaustively negotiated with the help of the state, gloated, "If a match were made in heaven, this is it."

The first Republican to be elected mayor of America's most Democratic city since the Lindsay administration, Rudy Giuliani was an anomaly in city politics: a fiscally conservative, socially moderate politician who was also a pugnacious, abrasive, condescending opera buff. Like his hero Fiorello La Guardia, Giuliani was also a courageous and shrewd crime-fighter, determined to honor his Italian heritage by smashing the mob. As Associate Attorney General in the Reagan Justice Department from 1981 to 1983, and then as U.S. Attorney for the Southern District of New York, Giuliani had made quite a splash prosecuting white-collar crime and narcotics. However, it was his sustained attacks on organized crime that really earned him a gold star.

For more than twenty years, the federal government had been carefully constructing a case against the major players in New York's Mafia, focusing on individuals in each of the five families. By 1985, Giuliani, as the federal prosecutor for New York City, had expanded the "La Cosa Nostra" case to include the "board of directors" of the Genovese, Gambino, Lucchese, Colombo and Bonanno families on charges of "loan sharking, drug trafficking, labor racketeering and contract murder," a massive prosecutorial effort that had never before been attempted in a single organized crime case.[4] If his efforts resulted in convictions for the leaders of the five families, Giuliani told the *New York Times Magazine* in 1985 that "We can end this debate about whether the Mafia exists. We can prove that the Mafia is as touchable and convictable as anyone. And without their mystery, they will lose their power."[5] On November 19, 1986, all eight indicted "directors" were convicted of racketeering for leading the "largest and most vicious criminal business in the history of the United States" in the words of Giuliani's chief trial prosecutor Michael Chertoff (who was later appointed by President George W. Bush as Secretary of the Department of Homeland Security in 2005).[6]

Giuliani's successful prosecution of the mob leadership had come on the backs on two decades worth of legal work conducted by other attorneys, reflecting what would become one of his signature idiosyncratic talents—namely, being in the right place at the right time to claim glory for other people's labors. "It's like stuffing a pipe," commented G. Robert Blakey, a judicial consultant who had drawn up the anti-racketeering laws Giuliani had used to indict and convict the mob bosses. "You put it in at one end, and for a long time you don't see anything. And finally it shows. Rudolph Giuliani is the guy lucky enough to be standing at the end of the pipe."[7]

In addition to his behind the scenes legal maneuvering, there were also plenty of triumphant moments in front of the cameras for Giuliani. His colleagues in the Justice Department often complained about his flair for publicity, whether he sought it or it found him; after the La Cosa Nostra case hit the headlines, Giuliani defiantly (and with no small degree of glee) told the press of receiving death threats. He also used news stories to launch salvos against his enemies. "He must be running for something," said Dick Brennan, then a WMCA radio producer. "He goes for every lick of publicity."[8]

It turned out that Giuliani would be running for Mayor of the City of New York in 1989, narrowly losing the race to the gentlemanly David Dinkins. Never one to forget a slight, real or imagined, the Doberman-like Giuliani ran for mayor again four years later and won, bolstered by Dinkins' failure to overcome the crime rate, exploding racial tensions, and deteriorating neighborhoods. Candidate Giuliani championed self-reliance for the city, free of federal handouts, and vowed to improve the city's dismal public school system, alleviate poverty, deflate bureaucratic bloat in City Hall, and most importantly, increase public safety by giving police carte-blanche to fight crime. "Today, when we hear those words, 'only in New York,' we don't think of great voices and great occasions," he said in his inauguration speech in 1994. "'Only in New York' has too often become shorthand for the despair of a whole generation of Americans."[9]

QUALITY OF LIFE

Soon after moving into Gracie Mansion, Giuliani introduced a string of plans for the city based on the conservative principles he had picked up while serving in the Reagan administration. His quality of life campaign, an initiative to foster civility in the city, was based on the "broken windows" theory developed by the sociologists James Q. Wilson and George L. Kelling. "Social psychologists and police officers tend to agree that if a window in a building is broken *and is left unrepaired*, all the rest of the windows will soon be broken [their emphasis]," wrote Wilson and Kelling in a 1982 *Atlantic Monthly* article. "One unrepaired broken window is a signal that no one cares, and so breaking more windows costs nothing."[10]

The two men also argued that the presence of "undesirable" people, if tolerated, created a perception of lawlessness that in turn facilitated crime. "We tend to overlook or forget another source of fear—the fear of being bothered by disorderly people. Not violent people, nor, necessarily, criminals, but disreputable or obstreperous or unpredictable people: panhandlers, drunks, addicts, rowdy teenagers, prostitutes, loiterers, the mentally disturbed." (Their argument was redolent of the 1950s, when groups of teenagers were assumed to be "up to no good," even if none had criminal records). For this reason, Wilson and Kelling suggested that municipal officials pay closer attention to so-called "victimless" crimes: "public drunkenness, street prostitution, and pornographic displays can destroy a community more quickly than any team of professional burglars."

To counter these kinds of threats in New York, the NYPD under Giuliani renewed its focus on so-called minor offenses, such as littering, spraying graffiti, jay-walking, panhandling and prostitution. "A civilized society can't let people go around the streets and intimidate other people," the mayor argued. "If somebody was urinating on the street, the reaction [used to] be, oh, we can't do anything about that. Then the idea would start to develop that there must be some inherent human right to urinate in the street."[11] The quality of life campaign would, according to Giuliani and his supporters, turn ideas like that around.

Giuliani's first target was squeegee men, whose M.O. was to stand at an intersection, douse a motorist's windshield with filthy water, then extort money to squeegee it off. During the election, Giuliani and Dinkins had made squeegee men the symbolic broken window that led to social chaos; as mayor, Giuliani vowed to put an end to the practice as a matter of common decency. "Some travelers argued that New York wasn't as bad as Kinshasa, Zaire, where soldiers routinely pulled over tourists' cars and extracted money at rifle point. But at least the soldiers weren't smoking crack," observed a writer for the New York Times Magazine.[12] "The reality for the most part is that the squeegee people are an annoyance and not a crime problem," said a police spokesman in 1994. "But when people see a strange, disheveled person, they immediately perceive that something bad is going to happen to them."[13]

Giuliani and Police Commissioner William Bratton engaged George

Kelling himself to study the problem, with a twenty-thousand-dollar grant from the Police Foundation. Released in February 1994, Kelling's study suggested it would be easy for police to get squeegee men off the streets with aggressive patrolling and arrests for disorderly conduct. It was noted that most of the forty-one squeegee men that were included in the study had prior police convictions for drugs, theft or possessing weapons. Skeptics wondered whether police sweeps and arrests would encourage the squeegee men to seek out more violent means of making a living, since most already showed a propensity for serious crime. Homeless advocates also pointed out that arresting squeegee men did nothing to alleviate the poverty, homelessness and drug addiction that often led them to squeegee in the first place.

These kinds of arguments were easily ignored, however, after police sweeps conducted in October and November of 1993—ironically, under the Dinkins' administration—had resulted in two-thirds of squeegee men being taken in for disorderly conduct and other outstanding warrants.[14] Based on the quick and easy success of the anti-squeegee campaign, in March 1994, Giuliani and Bratton announced a formal crackdown on so-called quality of life crimes. Police brass instructed officers to apply the same tactics they had used to corral squeegee men to perpetrators of a variety of civil irritations, such as public drunkenness, public urination, aggressive begging, or solicitation, as well as issuing summonses to suspects, and, if that suspect had a prior summons, to haul him or her off to Riker's Island on the spot.

As a result of the crackdown, between January 1 and September 21, 1994, arrests in the city jumped sixteen percent compared to the previous year, with the largest increase in "low-level criminal activity," or so-called quality of life crimes. That September, Giuliani ordered the violence-plagued Brooklyn Correctional Facility, which had closed earlier that year to save money, reopened to hold the influx of offenders. Soon after, corrections officers started complaining of overcrowding in the city's detention centers from repeat offenders with records that included nothing more serious than jumping a subway turnstile or street peddling without a license. These complaints, though, were proof to the mayor that his plan for tackling city crime was working.[15]

While the quality of life campaign quickly and admirably achieved its short-term goal—getting petty offenders off the streets, thereby improving citizens' perception of their safety—it ignored any long-term questions or resulting problems. Residents would see this pattern happen again and again with Giuliani: shoot first and ask questions later, or never.

A LOSING PROPOSITION

Bratton's skillful reorganization of the police department included implementing two new programs to tackle crime: saturation patrolling and community policing. In the former, areas with the greatest amount of criminal activity were flooded with with police officers, rather than the usual procedure, which was to have a set number of officers assigned to a geographic area, regardless of the crime rate. Community policing was an approach where officers familiarized themselves with the neighborhoods they patrolled, and solicited residents' help in keeping crime to a minimum. These dual approaches were initially focused on high-crime neighborhoods; as a result, the seven "major" offenses—homicide, robbery, rape, aggravated assault, burglary, grand larceny, and auto theft—dropped 11 percent in the first five months of 1994.[16] While many gave credit to the Dinkins administration, which had hired additional cops and initiated community policing, Mayor Giuliani, as was his wont, was more than happy to take credit.

The mayor's next target in his quality-of-life crusade was prostitution. Operation Losing Proposition, an ongoing prostitution investigation, had been in place since January 1991. Under this initiative, female officers dressed up as hookers in "tight mini-skirt[s], fish-net stockings and high heels" and trawled for customers in neighborhoods with established prostitution activity.[17] If the female officer was solicited, waiting cops would swoop in, arrest the man, and seize his car as an accessory to committing a crime. The hope was that this would deter johns from future solicitation, and force prostitutes to look elsewhere for their business.

By 1993, two years after Operation Losing Proposition had been implemented, officers had made sweeps in more than twenty precincts but had arrested only two hundred johns and seized only ninety cars, anemic numbers considering the prevalence of the problem.[18] The emphasis on arresting johns also meant that prostitutes themselves were often back on the same streets within a few hours. While Operation Losing Proposition may have evened out the sexual bias in anti-prostitution law enforcement (an effort spearheaded by Governor Carey's 1978 bill that made soliciting a prostitute and being one equal offenses), it seemed to do little to curb prostitution itself.

To add some teeth to the program, in October 1994, Police Commissioner William Bratton ordered each precinct in the city to conduct its own Operation Losing Proposition sweep, without waiting for the central command to issue a directive. One sweep in upscale Murray Hill in November bagged twenty men in five hours. "It's like you put a piece of cheese out and the rodents come out," snorted one officer. The NYPD was confident that the extra show of force—dozens of officers, multiple police cars with sirens wailing and paddy wagons at the ready—would convince johns not to repeat their behavior. "The shame factor is a huge deterrent," insisted a police spokesman.[19] Beyond the humiliation of arrest, however, there were not many legal consequences for soliciting prostitutes: if convicted, a john faced a forty-five dollar fine, a day of community service, and a three-hour class that taught men the risks of solicitation.

In the end, some civil liberties advocates objected to Operation Losing Proposition because it smacked of entrapment and meted out punishment (in the form of having one's car impounded) before the person had actually been convicted of a crime. But the quality-of-life argument won out: an expert at John Jay College of Criminal Justice told the *New York Times* that "prostitution usually fosters other crimes, like robbery and drug trafficking, and the presence of prostitutes on the street creates a sense of disorder and vulnerability in the community."[20]

ONE GIGANTIC BROKEN WINDOW

To many New Yorkers, Giuliani's quality of life campaign created a sense of safety and accountability that hadn't been felt in a generation; the across-the-board drop in crime was proof that the mayor's fight against the city's "broken windows" had been a success. From that point, it was not difficult to expand the definition of "broken windows" from prostitutes and panhandlers to include adult businesses.

While Wilson and Kelling had stated that individuals could act as broken windows, Giuliani now refitted the term to include *places* that directly or indirectly caused the same negative, crime-attracting effects. Wherever adult businesses clustered, they supposedly became *one gigantic broken window* that spread harmful "secondary effects" like vandalism, public drunkenness and indecency to the surrounding neighborhood. Under this rubric, a place like Times Square hurt the whole city—informing the entire world that no one in New York cared.

In turning his attention to Times Square, Giuliani was merely continuing the work that Dinkins and Koch had started. In fact, Giuliani had an easier battle to fight than his predecessors: the economic boom of the mid-nineties, fueled by internet-based commerce and investment, had poured money into the city's coffers. Additional funds meant more influence and ability to reorganize and reclaim the city from the sex industry. Here was an ironic twist: Pornography had in part fueled the development of the e-commerce technology that was making New York richer, and the city would now use that wealth to try and destroy pornography.

As soon as the internet had been opened to commercial interests by an act of Congress in 1992, a rudimentary network of sex-themed bulletin boards, chat rooms and websites was up and running. "It comes in all forms: hot chat, erotic stories, explicit pictures, even XXX-rated film clips... The newsgroups that carry it (alt.sex, alt.binaries.pictures.erotica, etc.) are among the top four or five most popular," reported *Time* in 1994.[21] Though lucrative for its purveyors, online porn chipped away at the market share that had been held for decades by brick-and-mortar sex shops and movie theaters—establishments that had been losing customers since the mid-seventies introduction of home video. The adult businesses in Times Square that had escaped condemnation in the late eighties as part of 42DP, then, continued to suffer from declining revenues. To the casual observer in the mid-nineties, adult stores must have looked like low-tech remnants on the shoulder of the sexual information superhighway; Giuliani saw them as pernicious reminders of the bad old days, neat symbols of municipal and moral collapse primed for the landfill of history.

Conditions, therefore, seemed favorable for the success of the city's revitalization plan. Two studies, one by the merchant-friendly Times Square Business Improvement District (TSBID) and a second from the Department of City Planning, were issued to provide statistical support for Times Square's overhaul. The TSBID, a nonprofit organization founded in 1992 and composed of area business and civic leaders in order to create a clean, business- and tourist-friendly Times Square, released its report in April 1994. [22] With an annual budget of $4.6 million, the TSBID represented the interests of four hundred property owners (some of whom, no doubt, leased space to sex shops) and five thousand businesses, and as such, naturally hoped to provide the evidence needed to rid the district of adult businesses.

One major argument against "adult use establishments" (the legal term for sex shops) was that their presence in a neighborhood lowered surrounding property values. The TSBID report analyzed real estate data and concluded that "rates of increases in assessed value for properties with adult establishments is greater than the increase for properties on the same blockfront without adult establishments," immediately dispelling the notion that sex shops harmed surrounding property values. "While it may well be that the concentration of adult establishments has a generally depressive effect on the adjoining properties, as a statistical matter we do not have sufficient data to prove or disprove this thesis," the study concluded. Despite this seemingly clear rebuttal of their position, Times Square business owners continued to cling to the notion that "adult establishments hurt businesses and property values."[23]

The TSBID also failed to positively link adult use establishments with increased rates of crime, seemingly due to a lack of information supplied by the NYPD. To compare the criminal activity on streets with and without adult establishments, assessors chose representative Study Blocks to compare with Control Blocks. The four Study Blocks included the notorious stretch of 42nd Street between Seventh and Eighth Avenues, and the three blocks on Eighth Avenue from 45th to 48th Streets—areas that teemed with adult businesses. The Control Blocks—those with no adult businesses— were 42nd Street between Ninth and Tenth Avenue, and three blocks on Ninth between 45th and 48th Streets.[24] The TSBID discovered eighty-eight complaints for the Study Block on 42nd Street between Seventh and Eighth Avenues compared to forty-five on the Control Block between Ninth and Tenth. Correspondingly, assessors found 118 complaints for the Study Blocks on Eighth Avenue compared to fifty for the Control Blocks on Ninth Avenue. While the figures showed greater criminal activity on blocks with adult establishments, the analysts could not "assert a direct correlation" to them. In addition, the greater pedestrian traffic on the Study Blocks may have contributed to the increased crime stats.[25]

To make their comparisons, assessors had requested statistics based on citizen complaints (not arrests) collected by the NYPD for the period of one year for both Study and Control Blocks. However, "this amount of data appeared too difficult for the Crime Analysis Division to obtain." Instead, the police supplied statistics for only a three-month period, from June through August 1993, for all blocks in the area. While police had received complaints for larceny, auto theft, drug possession, harassment, assault, and robbery, prostitution and drug trafficking complaints were "collected in an incompatible format" and thus not included in the TSBID's assessment, throwing the accuracy of the TSBID's evaluation into question.[26]

Overall, the study's results were ambivalent at best, neither proving nor disproving the crucial secondary-effects link. What the study lacked in empirical evidence (which was significant), it made up in anecdotes from area business owners, community groups and residents, much like the Meese Commission's reliance of pornography "victim" testimonies. And much of that testimony did not support the secondary links argument. For example, two retailers saw "no particular effects of the presence of adult establishments on their own specific business. Both of these condemned the presence of drug and crack dealers in the vicinity. One of these two said that he knew the manager of a gay movie theatre across the Avenue, and considered him a "neighbor trying to do business." An AIDS counselor opposed adult businesses in the area because unsafe sex could occur on their premises, not as a moral menace; he claimed that there was a "double standard" in which much energy was spent on getting rid of such businesses and not enough on preventing AIDS and prostitution. Even block associations representing businesses and residents west of Eighth Avenue, which one would presume to be most concerned about the moral character of the neighborhood, rated drugs and drug-related crimes their number-one concern, followed by prostitution, with "pornography establishments" a distant third. Finally, in a glaring omission, not one adult business owner or worker was interviewed for the study.

Despite the seeming lack of conclusiveness of the study, many property owners and corporate leaders insisted that while the presence of porn shops attracted consumers and their money to surrounding businesses in the short run, "there is no way to encourage increased value of commercial properties in the long run" if they're adjacent to such stores. TSBID president Gretchen Dykstra concluded that, "if you let the market rule on this issue, you'll see that the pornographers move into areas with depressed property values near transportation hubs...you then [see them] destroy the neighborhood."[27]

The Department of City Planning study was commissioned by the mayor to examine legal adult businesses in six city neighborhoods in order to prove that they contributed to negative secondary impacts. Released in September 1994, the study surveyed the upwardly mobile enclaves of Chelsea and the Upper West Side in Manhattan, Fordham in the Bronx, rapidly gentrifying Sunnyside in Queens, semi-industrial Sunset Park in Brooklyn, and South Beach on Staten Island. (Times Square was notably absent from the list.) Giuliani fully expected police records and other data to prove his case against the adult use establishments, but, as in the TSBID report, the Department of City Planning study relied chiefly on anecdotal evidence from merchants, residents, and workers in each neighborhood. And while some blocks with sex shops reported a slight increase in crime compared to surrounding blocks, it could have had as much to do with the proximity of a soup kitchen or bus station as an adult use establishment. Ultimately, it wasn't possible to definitively link the sex shops' presence to any crimes.[28]

THE 60-40 LAW

This lack of hard evidence didn't stop Mayor Giuliani, a seasoned moral opportunist, from introducing a sweeping new zoning amendment designed to eliminate the majority of sex shops from Times Square, as well as the rest of the city. Barely nine months into his first term, at a press conference in front of an adult video store on Queens Boulevard, Giuliani told a welcoming crowd that sex shops "hurt the economy of this city. They cost us jobs. They cost us money."[29] City Councilman Walter L. McCaffrey, representing portions of Queens, concurred that sex shops were "opening up in my district faster than McDonald's and Burger King."[30]

Giuliani's proposal (which lacked a proper title) differed from the failed Beame amendment of the late seventies and other previous zoning rules in that it changed the existing ordinance that allowed adult stores to operate in commercial and industrial zones as if they were a regular business. The mayor now wanted adult businesses to be considered a separate entity, and thus restricted from operating in most of the commercial and industrial zones in the city. If passed by the City Council (the legislative entity that replaced the Board of Estimate in 1989), the amendment would greatly reduce the number of sex shops in Manhattan and banish the rest to the fringes of the outer boroughs.

The amendment defined an "adult establishment" as a business selling "actual or simulated acts of human masturbation, sexual intercourse or sodomy;" "fondling or other erotic touching of human genitals, pubic region, buttock, anus or female breast;" "human male genitals in a discernibly turgid state, even if completely and opaquely concealed'" and many other equally minute differentiations.[31] The amendment would affect establishments selling a minimum of 40 percent adult merchandise; businesses with less than 40 percent adult material (like a corner video store or magazine stand) were exempt. To avoid being caught on the wrong side of the numbers, many shops scrambled to stock at least 60 percent general merchandise—anything from massage oils to kid's video games to, ironically, Disney videos—hence the amendment's nickname, the 60-40 law.

The amendment would also prevent adult businesses from operating within five hundred feet of a school, a house of worship, a residential area, or each other, a move that would finally end their clustering in Times Square.[32] An immediate year-long moratorium on new businesses would also be levied. If caught in violation of the 60-40 law, a sex shop had two choices, neither of which was favorable to the business owner or his consumers: it could close, or it could move to an acceptable (remote) location elsewhere in the city.

The amendment would radically alter the sexual landscape of New York. In Manhattan, sex shops would be banned everywhere except along the West Side Highway and in Washington Heights; Times Square's red light district would be effectively wiped from the map. In Queens, only the industrial sections of Long Island City, Newtown Creek and College Point—home to auto-body shops, warehouses and desolate streets—would be zoned for adult stores. Brooklyn's remote and underdeveloped waterfront, Hunts Point in the Bronx, and isolated pockets of Staten Island would make up the balance of adult zones in the boroughs.

In an unprecedented move, the amendment would also set a cap on the number of sex businesses per borough. (Not even Beame's proposal set such limits.) Though it was highly unlikely that each borough would even reach the cap, Manhattan would be allowed seventy-eight adult use establisments, Queens 124, Brooklyn 165, the Bronx seventy-nine, and Staten Island (which had only three when the law passed) could legally have sixty-eight. "The goal is not to keep pornography out of the city," said Councilman Charles Millard of Manhattan, the chief sponsor of Giuliani's bill. "The goal is to keep the negative effects out of our neighborhoods."[33]

OPPOSITION MOUNTS

Not surprisingly, the adult establishment owners who stood to lose their livelihoods, or at the very least, be forced to move to a location further away from the city's commerical centers, were adamently opposed to the bill, protesting that their rights as businesspeople in a free market economy were being infringed. "We believe in free enterprise, we're Constitutionalists," said a manager at Scores, one of New York's biggest and flashiest topless clubs.[34] Alan Rieff, the owner of Queens Village's EcsXXXtasy video store, complained that his store was unfairly targeted despite his meticulous upkeep of the property.[35] Randy Travers, a former sex store owner, explained that most businesses along 42nd Street sold discount clothing and electronics, not porn—but all small businesses, regardless of wares, were being displaced by giant corporations hungry for the valuable real estate.

To fight the proposed amendment, seventy-seven adult business owners joined together to form a legal front, the Coalition for Free Expression,
hiring the noted First-Amendment lawyer Herald Price Fahringer (Show
World's longtime counsel) as their lead counsel. Fahringer pointed out that
the bill offered no real alternatives for relocation. "In midtown Manhattan,
there are forty-seven of these establishments. Under this plan, only four
would survive. That's not reasonable."[36] He told the *New York Times*, "It's
almost unthinkable, from a constitutional standpoint, to wipe out a significant branch of New York's entertainment industry that enjoys such large
support from the public."[37]

In addition to the sex shop owners, several other groups also opposed
the bill, for a variety of reasons. The ACLU argued that the 60-40 law was
unconstitutional because the proposed adult zones were so far away from
public transportation and commercial areas that it infringed on the right of
the consumer to purchase legal material.[38] Gay consumers and activists suspected the 60-40 law could be erroneously applied to gay businesses, even
if they were not adult establishments, because of the lingering stereotype
of homosexuality as perversion. They worried that businesses that had sur-
vived the 1985 bathhouse closures and the terrible impact of AIDS would
be eliminated by rezoning, leaving virtually no gay-oriented businesses in
historically gay neighborhoods such as Chelsea and the West Village. There
was also the question of safety. For a population constantly wary of bias
attacks, said Richard Dadey, the president of the statewide gay advocacy
group Empire State Pride Agenda, "moving these establishments to the
dark, isolated outskirts of each borough…[would cause] substantial safety
concerns for those who frequent or work for adult establishments."[39]

In an alliance that recalled the bizarre pact between anti-porn feminists and Christian fundamentalists in the early eighties, outer-borough
residents whom Giuliani had originally wanted to protect from the adult
establishments' presence allied with porn barons against the 60-40 law. At
one sweltering public hearing at a school in July 1995, residents of Bay
Ridge, Brooklyn complained that the law would disperse the shops from
Times Square and push them into their residential neighborhood. Howard Golden, then the Brooklyn Borough President, claimed Giuliani's plan

would "clean up Times Square by creating a new sex industry in the work-ing-class neighborhoods of our city. This is totally unacceptable." A pastor at a local Catholic Church reported than the plan was "very, very unpopu-lar" with his constituents.[40]

Despite the outcry, many outer-borough residents didn't care one way or the other about the proposed amendment, as adult businesses had been part of their neighborhoods for a long time, without causing any problems. For example, Honey's, a topless bar in Woodside, Queens, had been up and running for years without incident, long enough to become a harm-less part of the social fabric of the community. According to the *New York Times*, five adjacent merchants claimed that Honey's "never produced any crime, loss of business, or any significant problems other than the occasional double-parking by patrons." The reporter interviewed merchants in similar situations throughout Queens and received exactly the same answer.[41] Resi-dents said that the older topless clubs like Honey's, in contrast to newer, flashier tourist-oriented nightclubs, did not upset the quality of life in their neighborhoods because they drew a more mature, local clientele and didn't advertise with flashing neon breasts or lewd signs.

COMPROMISE

On March 13, 1995, Giuliani and the City Council reached a compromise on the zoning amendment, which muted some of the harsher restrictions for Manhattan and allayed some Council members' fears of a sudden in-flux of sex shops in the outer boroughs. The amendment now needed to be formally passed by the City Council and delivered to the city's fifty-nine community boards and its five borough presidents for approval. It would also need authorization from the City Planning Commission in time for its planned implementation in November 1995 to coincide with the end of the moratorium on new sex businesses in the city.[42]

Momentum was in the 60-40 law's favor. On October 25, 1995, City Council members overwhelmingly passed the amendment into law by a vote of forty-one to nine, with one member absent.[43] Jubilant, Giuliani shouted down critics of the legislation and hoped that the new rules could be implemented within a week. He confidently announced that the bill was legally sound, based on similar statutes approved in Renton, Washington and other cities. Councilman Walter McCaffrey backed up the mayor. "This ultimately will improve the quality of life for everyone," he said, reiterating that the stores were not being censored for their content or merchandise. When the 60-40 law went into effect, Giuliani claimed, only twenty to thirty out of 177 adult businesses in New York City would survive unscathed. "Politicians run the city," complained *Screw* publisher Al Goldstein. "They give real prostitutes a bad name."[44]

Despite the favorable vote in the city council, there were still pockets of opposition to the amendment. Six dissenting Council members from Brooklyn and Queens were still of the belief that the bill would speed up the migration of sex shops out of midtown Manhattan and into their neighborhoods, while one Manhattan Councilwoman insisted that the law would unfairly hurt gay and lesbian bookstores and bars. "This zoning will eliminate predominantly gay and lesbian businesses that have peacefully existed for years," concurred Richard Dadey of the Empire State Pride Agenda.[45] Feminist groups were unusually silent on the whole matter, which was surprising, considering their vociferous opposition to Times Square porn in the seventies.

Meanwhile, adult business owners readied challenges to prevent the law from going into effect. "Any time the government is going to limit any kind of expression—especially pleasurable expression—you get a censored city," complained Richard Kunis, owner of Manhattan Video in midtown.[46] The ACLU's Norman Siegel (representing consumers) and the Coalition for Free Expression's Herald Price Fahringer (representing the adult store owners) filed their first appeal on February 27, 1996, claiming that the law "would violate constitutional guarantees of free speech, unlawfully restrict consumer access and eliminate 85 percent of the city's adult entertainment industry."[47] As lawyers argued the appeal for the next year, many sex shop owners, aware that it was just a matter of time until the law was passed and their businesses were gone, decided to get out before it was too late. Several small-time proprietors voluntarily relocated to the designated red-light zones in the outer boroughs. Richard Basciano, the elusive potentate of Show World Center, generously sold a lucrative parcel of his porn empire located next to the New Amsterdam Theater, in mock deference to the Disney Corporation (he held on to many more properties, including the building housing Show World).[48]

Elsewhere in the neighborhood, electric signs advertising a wholly different product were being mounted in the brightening night sky. Three major corporations who had leased the property north of Times Square while the city's deal with Disney was being negotiated were now moving into their new digs. With $15 million in tax breaks from the city, Viacom signed a lease for 1515 Broadway, the former site of the Hotel Astor, in 1990 and moved its studios into the space over the next four years. In March 1992, the German entertainment conglomerate Bertelsmann A.G. bought a vacant building at 1540 Broadway at 46th Street for its North American headquarters; it opened the world's largest music retail outlet, the Virgin Megastore, on the ground floor in April 1996. The brokerage firm Morgan Stanley bought 1585 Broadway between 47th and 48th Streets in August 1993, and 750 Seventh Avenue in March 1994. The company installed a colossal stock ticker on the latter's façade (in keeping with the "razzle-dazzle" aesthetic of the 42nd Street Now! project) in March 1995.[49] However, the frenzy of construction had yet to reach its zenith, as the sex shops obstinately refused to budge as long as they had a case winding through the court system, however dim their chances may have looked.

On October 23, 1996, almost a year to the day after the 60-40 law had passed the City Council, the New York State Supreme Court ruled it legal. Judges believed that the law did not infringe upon the First Amendment, as there were suitable sites in the new adult-use zones for businesses to relocate to. Justice Marylin Diamond told the lawyers sarcastically, "those seeking to patronize adult establishments will be able to continue to beat a path to their doors."[50] Owners of established sex businesses expressed dismay and irritation. "I love people who don't know what it's really like to open and run a business, telling us we should just move," snorted the owner of the strip club Wiggles. "After putting so much money into this club, to just pick up and move is crazy." The owner of Playground, across the street from the Port Authority Bus Terminal, was circumspect. "[We're] going to make [our] money, no matter what happens." On the other hand, Norman

Siegel vowed, "this decision reflects a new New York which is hostile to sexual expression and where 'quality of life' trumps freedom of expression principles and values. We will vigorously fight to reverse this."[51] Two days after the State Supreme Court's decision, as the city readied eviction notices for improperly-zoned sex shops, Herald Price Fahringer managed to obtain an injunction against enforcement of the law from the Appellate Division of State Supreme Court. Councilman Walter McCaffrey was nonplussed. "The [sex shop] owners are desperately clinging to a belief that the courts will save them, but eventually they'll have to come to terms with the fact that this law is constitutional."[52]

"YOU HAVE TO HAVE MURDER AND HORROR TO MAKE THE PLEASURE LEGAL"

While pro- and anti-zoning forces awaited the Appellate Court's decision, on April 2, 1997, Disney and a triumphant Giuliani unveiled the sparkling New Amsterdam Theater after its multi-million dollar, city-subsidized facelift. The mayor called the refurbishment of the theater the "turning point" in the saga of Times Square's rebirth, perhaps oblivious to the irony of Disney's presence on what was still a desolate swath of construction sites and side-street sex shops. Nevertheless, Disney's Michael Eisner used the photo-op to announce that the world premier of Disney's new animated children's film, *Hercules*, would take place at the New Amsterdam, complete with a $500,000 celebratory parade from 42nd Street to 66th Street.[53]

On July 10, 1997, Siegel and Fahringer lost their appeal in the Appellate Division of the State Supreme Court. They followed up by filing an immediate appeal with the state's highest court, the State Court of Appeals, which again prevented enforcement of the 60-40 law. The city, however, maintained that the 60-40 law had won its challenge in court, and could now be enforced. "This is a major victory not only for the Giuliani administration but for the many parents who were sick and tired of seeing their kids exposed to sex shops right in their neighborhoods," gloated Deputy Mayor Randy Mastro.

On September 19, 1997, Giuliani applied the 60-40 law to the Video Warehouse Outlet, the first adult business to have opened in a now off-limits zone (in this case, Maurice Avenue in Maspeth, Queens). Flanked by police officers, officials from the Department of Buildings, and city lawyers, Giuliani personally padlocked the store as cameras flashed and reporters scribbled, evoking La Guardia's staged sledge-hammering of slot machines (a similarity that was surely not a coincidence). "Our adult-use zoning regulations not only mean that valuable commercial areas like Times Square will be cleaned up, but that sex shops will no longer be allowed to destroy the quality of life in residential neighborhoods," the mayor reiterated, as if repeating the idea would make it true.[54] Though the injunction against such enforcement, granted to Siegel and Fahringer by the Appellate Division of the State Supreme Court, was still in place pending the ruling by the State Court of Appeals, the city argued that it only applied to businesses that had been in operation when the law was passed back in 1995. Video Warehouse Outlet, unfortunately, had opened in 1996.

As it so happened, the State Court of Appeals threw out Siegel and Fahringer's appeal on February 24, 1998, clearing the way for full implementation of the 60-40 law. Giuliani was elated and vowed to begin closing procedures for 138 of the 155 sex businesses then extant, leaving only seventeen in all the five boroughs.[55] Long-time sex shop owners were dumbfounded. A manager at the twenty-year-old topless club Gallagher's expected the club to be grandfathered in after the passage of the law, but it turned out that no sex business in an off-limits zone would be exempt. Civic organizations in the new red-light zones braced for a flood of porn from Manhattan.

Fahringer again appealed the case, this time to a Federal judge. Just three days after the 60-40 law was upheld, on February 27, 1998, Federal district judge Miriam Goldman Cedarbaum blocked enforcement of the law based on Fahringer's argument that it was so restrictive as to violate the owners' right to free expression: by forcing them to relocate to unprofitable sites, the law would effectively put them out of business. While Cedarbaum evaluated Fahringer's claim, sex shops again earned a reprieve from the chopping block, though few owners expected the Federal judge to rule in their favor. "At the present time we are [buying] stuff that will make us legal," said one owner, to add to his huge stock of "pleasure movies." "You have to have murder and horror to make the pleasure legal," he pointed out.[56]

Cedarbaum handed the Fahringer team a disappointing verdict when she lifted the stay on enforcement on March 7, 1998, ruling that the city had provided suitable sites for the relocation after all. Owners vehemently disagreed. "[Giuliani] can take our businesses and turn them upside down whenever he chooses to, and put everybody out of work," fumed one bar owner. Fahringer argued it was totally impractical for, say, a gay bookstore in Greenwich Village, having spent years building a local customer base, to be forced to move to the outer edges of Brooklyn. Cedarbaum's ruling allowed Fahringer one last appeal, however, and the Federal court once more issued a stay of enforcement on March 18.

As both sides waited for the long-sought Federal appeals court ruling, a group of sex industry workers loudly protested outside City Hall on April 21 in full striptease regalia, another moment of déjà-vu recalling La Guardia's battled against burlesque acts. Giuliani responded by suggesting that citizens could shame the sex shop customers and workers by photographing them entering and leaving stores. "This is clear evidence that the mayor's effort to regulate adult businesses is, in reality, a morality crusade," spat a spokesman for a group called New Yorkers for Free Expression.[57]

Finally, on June 3, 1998, the appeals court ruled in favor of the 60-40 law. As a last resort, Fahringer asked the United States Supreme Court to grant an injunction preventing the law from being enforced, but the Justices refused to hear the case. Deputy Mayor Randy Mastro announced the decision to reporters while symbolically wielding a baseball bat.[58] The first four victims of the now-enforceable law, raided on August 1, 1998, were Show World (a symbolic target), Wiggles in Brooklyn, El Coche in the Bronx and Sharks Go-Go in Staten Island. According to an account in the *New York Times* quoting Steven M. Fishner, the mayor's Criminal Justice Coordinator, "Officers burst into three clubs and, with dancers gyrating and patrons ogling, shouted, 'Police! Nobody move!'...city inspectors had visited the clubs as customers and had seen the women 'simulating sexual intercourse' as they danced." No one was arrested in the raids—after all, "simulating sexual intercourse" was not an illegal act and certainly not the stated reason behind the 60-40 law—but the strip clubs were padlocked until further notice (only Show World escaped closure).[59] One wondered why the raids were necessary to begin with, considering that it was not originally the content of the shops that Giuliani's zoning amendment condemned, but the secondary effects of said shops. But Giuliani loved a good photo op.

The *Times*, eerily prescient, noted Giuliani's broader political goals, beyond the 60-40 fight. "A successful crusade against pornographers would provide a crucial conservative credential for Mr. Giuliani as he works Republican audiences throughout the country," leading one to infer that the quality of life campaign, as it applied to sex shops, was but a strategic stepping-stone to a run for higher political office. In such a bald effort to curry favor with conservative Republican Party leaders, it appeared that the livelihoods and civil rights of the store owners, employees, and fellow New Yorkers were casually sacrificed.

While Giuliani may have gained conservative credibility with the 60-40 victory, in the end, what did the city gain from his strategy? "Niketown, the Gap, Starbucks, Banana Republic and the Body Shop—these are now the wholesome storefronts that increasingly set the city's tone… they have nothing essential to do with [New York] and all sell precisely the same demographically correct and scientifically test-marketed designs that appear in malls across America," lamented journalist Elizabeth Kolbert in the *Times*. "One thing to be said for Peepland, with the unblinking neon eye on its marquee, is that at least you had to come to 42nd Street to see it."[60]

NOT "ONLY IN NEW YORK" ANYMORE

The decline of what remained of New York's sexual culture continued at a fast pace in the late nineties. Once it became known that Disney, the most recognizable family-friendly brand in the world, had faith in the rebirth of the city, corporate investment flowed into the empty lots left behind by the demolished adult theaters and peepshows. In August 1996, the Durst Organization, one of the giants of New York real estate development, signed on to finally build one of the four office towers that had originally been planned back in the early eighties. Located at 4 Times Square, the skyscraper would become the headquarters of the Condé Nast magazine group (for which the company received $10.75 million in tax exemptions) and anchor the eastern end of the 42nd Street strip when it opened in October 1999.[61]

The Rudin development company acquired the second of the four tower sites for the headquarters of media giant Reuters in August 1997; the Giuliani administration gave the corporation $25 million in tax breaks and incentives just for moving in.[62] On the southwest corner of 42nd Street and Seventh Avenue, the accounting firm of Ernst & Young agreed to build its new headquarters for a $20 million package of tax breaks. The fate of the remaining tower site from the original 42DP scheme has yet to be determined.

On the south side of 42nd Street, Forest City Ratner Companies agreed to develop a tourist-friendly retail and attractions complex, featuring a twenty-five-screen AMC movie theater occupying the former Empire, né Eltinge, Theater, a 444-room Hilton hotel, and Madame Tussaud's Wax Museum, on the spot where the Peepland edifice once stood. The complex would abut the Candler Building, the only property on 42nd Street left unaffected by development, which was next to Disney's New Amsterdam Theater. Across the street, the awkwardly named E-Walk On The New 42nd Street, containing another thirteen-screen multiplex, several chain restaurants, and retail shops, supported the Westin New York at Times Square hotel (opened in 2002), all developed by Tishman Real Estate Services.

With big-name developers came corporate sponsorships and the naming of theaters, previously anathema on Broadway. Disney's refurbished New Amsterdam, also developed by Tishman, became the home of Disney On Broadway in 1997. The Lyric and Apollo Theaters were incorporated into the Ford Center for the Performing Arts, and then renamed the Hilton Theater. The American Airlines Theater (formerly the Selwyn) was renovated and opened in 2000.

Times Square's famous and infamous landmarks were also retrofitted to blend in with the new wholesomeness. The Paramount building, the grandest theater in the early days of cinema, was turned first into a World Wrestling Federation-themed restaurant complex and then into a Hard Rock Café. The X-rated Adonis Theater became a Blockbuster video store. The Eros I and Venus gay cinemas were transformed into Broadway-themed restaurants. The site of the New World Theater, where *Deep Throat* premiered in 1972, was turned into the upscale Asian eatery Ruby Foo's.

The transformation of Times Square did succeed in creating thousands of jobs in the Broadway theaters, amusement sites and restaurants. As a result, many more people were living and working in the Square in the early years of the twenty-first century than had been back in the seventies and eighties. The Times Square BID counted 158,654 workers by 2003, and projected an increase to 237,445 by 2020, due to plans to triple the amount of office space in the area to almost twenty million square feet.[63] Pedestrian traffic also swelled. During a given afternoon weekday rush hour in 1982, less than 500 people traversed the south side of the 42nd Street strip; by 1996, the count was about 1,200. With the addition of hundreds of commercial businesses and residences, sidewalk traffic could increase to nearly 2,500 by 2030.[64]

Tourism contributed to the boom as well. In 1998, approximately thirty-three million domestic and international tourists made their way to Manhattan; that number had risen to almost forty-four million by 2006. The Times Square BID estimated that 80 percent of tourists who come to New York City make a point of visiting Times Square—meaning that thirty-five million tourists were walking five abreast on the sidewalks, stopping to gaze at subway maps and crowding the TKTS booth, in addition to the two hundred thousand or so residents and workers of Times Square. And all of those tourists spent money on hotel rooms (average price: $213.97 per night) and Broadway shows (average ticket price: seventy-three dollars)—both key indicators of the health of the Times Square economy.

By extrapolating the demographic information compiled by two publications geared to Broadway theatergoers—*Playbill* and *Broadway*—a clear picture of the modern Times Square tourist emerges. She (65 percent of theatergoers were female) is in her forties and middle to upper-middle class with a household income of at least one hundred thousand a year. She is also well-educated and definitely likes to shop—she might spend 750 dollars during her trip to New York.[65] Finally, she is married, probably has one or more children, and most likely hails from another U.S. state or the United Kingdom, Canada, Germany, Scandinavia, Italy or France.

At the turn of the twenty-first century, only the stubborn strip of Eighth Avenue from 42nd to 44th Street preserves the area's timeworn traditions. One such relic, PeepWorld was squashed between the stalwart Show World and the garish marquee of the Playpen strip club, featuring a Manhattan skyline in rainbow neon. PeepWorld's beckoning sign was nothing more than a lit-up billboard with a string of on-and-off electric bulbs. Owner Frank Mastrangelo correctly sensed that he was on borrowed time, but still hoped for the best. "If you own a sex-oriented business, and it's a ten, twelve, thirteen billion dollars-a-year industry, what's gonna happen? Politicians are going to eradicate something that big?" he snorted. "I can say straight out: when all else fails, sex prevails. Sex sells no matter what."[66]

EPILOGUE

THE "WICKEDEST CITY"

While architect Robert Stern's vision of "vulgar heterogeneity"—glitz and glamour at all costs—was finally realized in Times Square, and Mayor Giuliani was vindicated in his bitter fight to improve the quality of life in New York, questions still remain, including: exactly whose quality of life was improved? That of residents in rapidly-gentrifying neighborhoods and formerly crime-ridden pockets of the city, certainly; but what of the people and businesses displaced by Giuliani's sweeping initiatives? In the long run, will the masses benefit from the turn toward wholesome family-friendliness, as Giuliani insisted? In ridding the city of adult businesses, have New Yorkers given up a bit of the edge and sleaze, the ironic sophistication and savoir-faire, that made them unique among humans?

A safer city is a good thing, but as the critic Kurt Andersen notes, "Preservationism can also tend toward the prissy, the anal and the monomaniacal and become a kind of by-the-book undertaker's approach that makes dead and dying downtowns prettier but not quite alive."[1] In the forced revitalization of organically-composed urban areas, "the goal is not a 'themed' simulacrum of honky-tonk diversity but the real thing," Andersen writes. "Such a splendidly oxymoronic turn: a municipal code for discouraging tastefulness, a quarter-billion dollars spent to conjure a trashy Damon Runyon spirit." Which begs the question: why change Times Square, or New York City, at all? But, the old Times Square would never have attracted the barnacles of such crowd-pleasing faux-authenticity as McDonald's franchises, Gap stores, and Red Lobsters.

New York, sadly, does not seem to love contradiction as much as it once did. Its place as the world's cultural capital and prime incubator for subversive thought and action is not as secure as it was in, say, the late nineteenth century. This is perhaps an indication that, in the war between "good" (moral, traditional, orderly) and "evil" (provocative, futuristic, sexual), "good" has won. But, as I have shown, this war is ever on-going. Good's victory will be temporary, though we do not know when evil will again pose enough challenge to alter the status quo.

Ultimately, New York has inspired much of the sexual expression and boundary pushing in the United States over the past 135 years. Today, however, sexual commerce is more global than ever, and the internet arguably negates the need for localized, individualistic, homegrown sex industries. Yet the symbiotic relationship between the purveyors and consumers of sexuality and disapproving municipal bodies clearly continues. The "wickedest city" in the country is still home to "the best and brightest" of New Yorkers, as James McCabe insisted over a century ago: Though Giuliani's zeal for zoning scattered the now-minimal number of strip clubs to the outer boroughs, new adult video stores (carrying the requisite 60 percent non-adult material) have since opened on major avenues in Chelsea, the East Village and other neighborhoods. Good must always beware, as evil always lurks in the shadows, ready to strike again.

I began my narrative for *The Forbidden Apple* in the early 1870s, at a turning point of moral and civic discourse in New York's history. Today, after the horrors of September 11, and the transformation of the city into a capital of wealth, New York faces a similar moment of soul searching, moral evaluation and physical change. If the city's erotic history is any guide, we can still look forward to another few centuries of sexual revolution.

ACKNOWLEDGMENTS

This book could not have been written without the constant encouragement and support from many people. I first want to thank Robert Lasner and Elizabeth Clementson of Ig Publishing, who found me at exactly the right time. They have both shown incredible enthusiasm for *The Forbidden Apple* and gave me a huge dose of confidence in its worth as a scholarly history. Not only have they allowed me the chance to finally publish the book after seven years' effort; they worked tirelessly to read, edit, suggest improvements, and deliver it to the public.

Many scholars in the history field have offered me advice and encouragement during the researching and writing process. I'm particularly indebted to Timothy R. Gilfoyle and Kevin Baker, two amazingly generous and astute historians, for their time in reading and assessing this newbie's first book. And because most of the idiosyncratic documents and ephemera of New York's sex life were found at the New York Public Library's Humanities and Social Sciences branch, I'm grateful for the staff's guidance.

Most importantly, I want to thank my friends and especially my family for putting up with me during the seven years of this project. I often forgot to respond to emails and return calls, but they never failed to ask, "So how's the book going?" None of this book would have been possible, though, without the love and inspiration of Shannon Leigh O'Neil.

NOTES

INTRODUCTION

1. James D. McCabe Jr., *New York by Gaslight*, Facsimile of 1882 Edition (New York: Greenwich House, 1984), 59-60.
2. Edwin G. Burrows and Mike Wallace, *Gotham: A History of New York City to 1898* (New York: Oxford University Press, 2000), 146, 185.
3. McCabe Jr., *New York by Gaslight*, 59-60.
4. Quoted in Samuel F. Delany, *Times Square Red, Times Square Blue* (New York: New York University Press, 1999), 14.

1. THE DASTARDLY DO-GOODERS

1. *New York Times*, "The Assault on Mr. Anthony Comstock," November 3, 1874.
2. Anthony Comstock, personal journal. Quoted in Heywood Broun and Margaret Leech, *Anthony Comstock: Roundsman of the Lord* (New York: Albert and Charles Boni, 1927), 33.
3. Broun and Leech, *Anthony Comstock: Roundsman of the Lord*, 72.
4. McCabe Jr., *New York by Gaslight*, Introduction.
5. Broun and Leech, *Anthony Comstock: Roundsman of the Lord*, 75.
6. McCabe Jr., *New York by Gaslight*, 123.
7. George J. Lankevich, *American Metropolis: A History of New York City* (New York: New York University Press, 1998), 122.
8. McCabe Jr., *New York by Gaslight*. 33.
9. McCabe Jr., *New York by Gaslight*. 33.
10. Lankevich, *American Metropolis*, 128.
11. McCabe Jr., *New York by Gaslight*, 559.
12. Jacob Riis, *How the Other Half Lives* (New York: Penguin Classics, 1997), 135.
13. *New York Tribune*, "Frightful Conditions," March 8, 1903.
14. McCabe Jr., *New York by Gaslight*, 154.
15. Charles Loring Brace, *The Dangerous Classes of New York; and Twenty Yearsí Work Among Them* (New York: Wynkoop and Hallenbeck, 1872), 114-19.
16. Timothy Gilfoyle, "From Soubrette Row to Show World: The Contested Sexualities of Times Square, 1880-1995," in *Policing Public Sex: Queer Politics and the Future of AIDS Activism*, ed. Dangerous Bedfellows (Ephen Glenn Coulter, Wayne Hoffman, Eva Pendleton, Alison Redick, David Serlin) (Boston: South End Press, 1996), 263-94.
17. McCabe Jr., *New York by Gaslight*. 479.
18. Gilfoyle, "From Soubrette Row to Show World," *Policing Public Sex*, 263-94.

19. Gilfoyle, "From Soubrette Row to Show World," *Policing Public Sex*, 263-94.

20. Stephen Crane, *Maggie: A Girl of the Streets and Other New York Writings* (New York: Modern Library, 2001), 153.

21. James D. McCabe Jr., *Lights and Shadows of New York Life; Or, The Sights and Sensations of the Great City*, Facsimile edition (New York: Farrar, Straus and Giroux, 1970), 190.

22. George Chauncey, *Gay New York: Gender, Urban Culture, and the Making of the Gay Male World, 1890-1940* (New York: Basic Books, 1994), 37.

23. Luc Sante, *Low Life: Lures and Snares of Old New York* (New York: Vintage, 1991), 285.

24. Quoted in Jonathan Ned Katz, *Gay American History: Lesbians and Gay Men in the USA*, revised edition (New York: Meridian, 1976, 1972), 46-7.

25. Quoted in Katz, *Gay American History*, 366-367.

26. *New York Times*, "Nip Plot to Bring Strong Opium Here," March 4, 1914.

27. Sante, *Low Life*, 151.

28. YMCA memorandum, 1866. Quoted in Broun and Leech, *Anthony Comstock: Roundsman of the Lord*, 78.

29. Broun and Leech, *Anthony Comstock: Roundsman of the Lord*, 80.

30. New York Society for the Suppression of Vice, *Second Annual Report*, 1876, 5. Quoted in Nicola Beisel, *Imperiled Innocents: Anthony Comstock and Family Reproduction in Victorian America* (Princeton, NJ: Princeton University Press, 1997), 40.

31. Anthony Comstock, personal journal. Quoted in Broun and Leech, *Anthony Comstock: Roundsman of the Lord*, 131.

32. *Act of the Suppression of Trade in, and Circulation of, Obscene Literature and Articles of Immoral Use of 1873* (17 Stat. 599).

33. Beisel, *Imperiled Innocents*, 53.

34. Confidential YMCA pamphlet, January 1874. Quoted in Broun and Leech, *Anthony Comstock: Roundsman of the Lord*, 153.

35. *New York Sun*. Quoted in Broun and Leech, *Anthony Comstock: Roundsman of the Lord*, 157.

36. Anthony Comstock, personal journal. Quoted in Broun and Leech, *Anthony Comstock: Roundsman of the Lord*, 167.

37. *New York Times*, Obituary of Charles H. Parkhurst, September 9, 1933.

38 Charles W. Gardner, *The Doctor and the Devil, or, Midnight Adventures of Dr. Parkhurst* (New York: Gardner, 1894), 53.

39. Sante, *Low Life*, 285.

40. *New York Times*, "Dr. Parkhurst Speaks Out; Another Scathing Arraignment of City Officials," March 14, 1892.

41. *New York Times*, "The Jury Did Not Agree; Hattie Adams May Remain in Her House," April 8, 1892.

42. *New York Times*, "Nine Months for Hattie Adams; Judge Fitzgerald Little Impressed by Her Plea for Mercy," May 13, 1892.

43. New York State Senate, *Report and Proceedings of the Senate Committee Appointed to Investigate the Police Department of the City of New York, Vol. III, January 18, 1895* ("Lexow Report") (Albany, NY: James B. Lyon, State Printer, 1895), 2744, 1753.

44. Augustine Costello, *Our Police Protectors, History of the New York Police, Published for the benefit of the Police Pension Fund* (n.p.: published by author, 1885), http://www.usgennet.org/usa/ny/state/police/ch13pt1.html (accessed November 21, 2006).

45. *New York Times*, "Without Fear or Favor; Superintendent Byrnes Tells How He Would Enforce Laws," May 25, 1892.

46. Thomas C. Mackey, *Pursuing Johns: Criminal Law Reform, Defending Character, and New York City's Committee of Fourteen, 1920-1930* (Columbus, OH: Ohio State University Press, 2005), http://www.ohiostatepress.org/Books/Book%20PDFs/Mackey%20Pursuing.pdf (accessed November 26, 2006).

47. Mara L. Keire, "The Committee of Fourteen and Saloon Reform in New York City, 1905-1920," *Business and Economic History* 26, no. 2 (1997): 575, http://www.h-net.org/~business/bhcweb/publications/BEHprint/v026n2/p0573-p0583.pdf (accessed November 26, 2006).

48. *New York Tribune*, "Raines Law Hotels," April 10, 1905.

49. Keire, "The Committee of Fourteen," 576.

50. Marc Eliot, *Down 42nd Street: Sex, Money, Culture and Politics at the Crossroads of the World* (New York: Warner Books, 2002), 21.

51. Andrea Friedman, *Prurient Interests: Gender, Democracy, and Obscenity in New York City, 1909-1945* (New York: Columbia University Press, 2000), 43-4.

52. Sante, *Low Life*, 101.

53. Friedman, *Prurient Interests*, 44.

54. Friedman, *Prurient Interests*, 44.

55. *New York Times*, "Find Moving Picture Evils; Children's Society Says 'Guardians' Are Hired," April 28, 1913.

56. Friedman, *Prurient Interests*, 47.

57. James R. Petersen and Hugh M. Hefner, *The Century of Sex: Playboy's History of the Sexual Revolution, 1900-1999* (New York: Grove Press, 1999), 52.

58. *New York Times*, "White Slavery on Film; Audience Sees Various Alleged Methods of the Traffickers," December 9, 1913.

59. *New York Times*, "Upholds White Slave Film; Magistrate Dismisses Charge Against Manager of Park Theatre," December 17, 1913.

60. *New York Times*, "Film Show Raided at Park Theatre," December 20, 1913.

61. *New York Times*, "Film Show Raided..."

62. *New York Times*, "Show Films Under New Court Order," December 27, 1913.

63. *New York Times*, "Park Theatre Shut ..."

64. Friedman, *Prurient Interests*, 48.

65. Friedman, *Prurient Interests*, 49.
66. Salvato, Richard and Myers, Cherie. "National Board of Review of Motion Pictures Records, 1907-1971." The New York Public Library, Humanities and Social Sciences Library, Manuscripts and Archives Division, 1984. 14-5.
67. Letter from Assistant Secretary to Samuel London. Quoted in Friedman, *Prurient Interests*, 49.
68. Margaret Sanger, *What Every Girl Should Know* (Girard, KS: Haldeman-Julius Company, 1922), 3, http://archive.lib.msu.edu/AFS/dmc?radicalism/public/all/whateverygirl1922/AEZ.pdf?FID=577301&CFTOKEN=48590189 (accessed December 2, 2006).
69. Sanger, *What Every Girl Should Know*, 63.
70. Margaret Sanger, "The Aim," *The Woman Rebel* 1, no. 1 (1914): 1, http://adh.sc.edu/dynweb/MEP/ms/@ebtlink;td=2;hf=0?target=%25N%15_485 34_START_RESTART_N%25#X (accessed December 2, 2006).
71. Sanger, "The Aim," In *The Woman Rebel*, 1.
72. Margaret Sanger, "The Case for Birth Control," *The Woman Citizen* 8 (1924): 17-8, http://womenshistory.about.com/library/etext/bl_sanger_1924.htm (accessed December 2, 2006).
73. Christine Stansell, *American Moderns: Bohemian New York and the Creation of a New Century* (New York: Metropolitan Books, 2000), 236-7.
74. Stansell, *American Moderns*, 236.
75. *New York Times*, "Disorder in Court as Sanger is Fined," September 11, 1915.
76. *New York Times*, "Disorder in Court..."
77. Clinic flyer, Sophia Smith Collection, Smith College.
78. "The Wreck of Commercialized Vice," *The Survey*, February 5, 1916, 532-33.
79. "The Wreck of Commercialized Vice."
80. Allan M. Brandt, *No Magic Bullet: A Social History of Venereal Disease in the United States Since 1880*, expanded edition (New York: Oxford University Press, 1987), 12.
81. "Men, Women, Children and Venereal Disease," *The Survey*, May 29, 1915, 192.
82. Brandt, *No Magic Bullet*, 59.
83. Brandt, *No Magic Bullet*, 36-7.
84. Prince A. Morrow, "Sanitary Aspects of Clause 79 of the Page Law," *Social Diseases* 1 (1910): 8, 15. Quoted in Brandt, *No Magic Bullet*, 37.
85. Brandt, *No Magic Bullet*, 38.
86. Bureau of Social Hygiene, *Commercialized Prostitution in New York City: A Comparison Between 1912, 1915, 1916 and 1917* (New York: The Century Company, 1917): frontispiece, http://pds.harvard.edu:8080/pdx/servlet/pds?id=2581290 (accessed February 18, 2007).
87. Bureau of Social Hygiene, *Commercialized Prostitution*, frontispiece.
88. Bureau of Social Hygiene, *Commercialized Prostitution*, 14-5.
89. Bureau of Social Hygiene, *Commercialized Prostitution*, 16.

2. MODERN MADNESS

1. United States Bureau of the Census, "Population by Age, for the United States and Urban and Rural Population, 1920 and 1910," *Fourteenth Decennial Census* (1920), www2.census.gov/prod2/decennial/documents/41084484v3ch01.pdf (accessed October 9, 2007).

2. United States Bureau of the Census, "State Compendium, New York, 'Composition and Characteristics by Age, for Cities of 10,000 or More, 1920,'" *Fourteenth Decennial Census* (1920), www2.census.gov/prod2/decennial/documents/06229686v26-31ch5.pdf (accessed October 9, 2007).

3. Frederick Lewis Allen, *Only Yesterday: An Informal History of the 1920ís* (New York: Harper & Row, 1931), 82.

4. Allen, *Only Yesterday*, 87.

5. Allen, *Only Yesterday*, 214.

6. United States Constitution, Eighteenth Amendment, Sec. 1.

7. *New York Times*, "John Barleycorn Died Peacefully at the Toll of 12," January 17, 1920.

8. *New York Times*, "John Barleycorn Died Peacefully..."

9. *New York Times*, "John Barleycorn Died Peacefully..."

10. *New York Times*, "Prohibition's Effect on Meals and Movies," January 19, 1919.

11. Mark McCloskey, "Prohibition in Chelsea," *The Survey*, August 15, 1924. 545-6.

12. American Social Hygiene Association, *Keeping Fit to Fight* (Washington, D.C.: The War Department Commission on Training Camp Activities, n.d.), 44, 8.

13. Marie Stopes, *Married Love*, ed. Ross McKibbin (New York: Oxford University Classics, 2004), 31.

14. Margaret Sanger, *Woman and the New Race* (New York: Brentano's, 1920; Bartleby.com, 2000), http://www.bartleby.com/1013/ (accessed November 4, 2006).

15. Emily Post, *Etiquette in Society, in Business, in Politics, and at Home* (New York: Funk & Wagnalls, 1922; Bartleby.com, 2000), http://www.bartleby.com/95/ (accessed November 4, 2006).

16. Federal Writers Project, *The WPA Guide to New York City: A Comprehensive Guide to the Five Boroughs of the Metropolis—Manhattan, Brooklyn, the Bronx, Queens, and Richmond—Prepared by the Federal Writers' Project of the Works Progress Administration in New York City* (New York: Random House, 1939), 124.

17. Stansell, *American Moderns*, 273.

18. P.W. Wilson, "Newest Woman Emerges in Full Glory," *New York Times*, October 4, 1925.

19. Allen, *Only Yesterday*, 89.

20. Allen, *Only Yesterday*, 92.

21. Wilson, "Newest Woman..."

22. Allen, *Only Yesterday*, 86.

23. Allen, *Only Yesterday*, 94.

24. Max Ewing. Quoted in Steven Watson, *The Harlem Renaissance: Hub of African-American Culture, 1920-1930* (New York: Pantheon Books, 1995), 124.

25. David Levering Lewis, ed., *The Portable Harlem Renaissance Reader* (New York: Viking, 1994), introduction.

26. Watson, *The Harlem Renaissance*, 127.

27. Watson, *The Harlem Renaissance* 126.

28. Elizabeth Frazer, "Let's Go to a Cabaret," *The Saturday Evening Post*, July 19, 1924.

29. Watson, *The Harlem Renaissance*, 131.

30. Eric Garber, "A Spectacle in Color: The Lesbian and Gay Subculture of Jazz Age Harlem," in *Hidden From History: Reclaiming the Gay and Lesbian Past*, ed. Martin Bauml Duberman, Martha Vicinus, George Chauncey Jr. (New York: New American Library, 1989), 318-331.

31. Ruby Smith. Quoted in Garber, "A Spectacle in Color," *Hidden From History*, 318-331.

32. Garber, "A Spectacle in Color," *Hidden From History*, 318-31.

33. Andrea Barnet, *All Night Party: The Women of Bohemian Greenwich Village and Harlem, 1913-1930* (Chapel Hill, NC: Algonquin Books, 2004), 147.

34. Richard Bruce Nugent, "You See, I Am a Homosexual," in *Gay Rebel of the Harlem Renaissance,* ed. Thomas H. Wirth (Durham, NC: Duke University Press, 2002), 268.

35. Ann Douglas, *Terrible Honesty: Mongrel Manhattan in the 1920's* (New York: Farrar, Straus and Giroux, 1995), 399.

36. Ma Rainey, "Prove It on Me Blues," quoted in *The Queer Encyclopedia of Music, Dance and Musical Theater*, ed. Claude J. Summers (San Francisco: Cleis Press, 2004), 213.

37. Eslanda Robeson. Quoted in Garber, "A Spectacle in Color," *Hidden From History,* 324.

38. *New York Times*, "Enright Lectures Vice Squad; Thinks Some are Grafting," February 26, 1924.

39. *New York Times*, "Belton Says Public Hampers Dry Work," January 11, 1925.

40. *New York Times*, "Belton Says Public..."

41. Lankevich, *American Metropolis*, 157.

42. James Walker. Quoted in Eliot, *Down 42ⁿᵈ Street*, 27.

43. *New York Times*, "Night Clubs Found Chief Vice Centres; Committee of Fourteen, it its Annual Survey, Reports Harlem Conditions Worst," October 14, 1929.

44. *New York Times*, "City Vice Conditions Worst in 20 Years, Survey Declares," July 9, 1928.

45. *New York Times,* "Calls Night Clubs Rendezvous of Vice," *New York Times,* July 15, 1927.

46. *New York Times,* "Calls Night Clubs..."

47. *New York Times,* "City Vice Conditions..."

48. Anonymous, "Worse than the Raines Law," letter to the editor, *New York Times,* July 10, 1928.

49. *New York Times,* "Whalen Says City Has 32,000 Speakeasies and Lays Crime Increase to Prohibition," April 5, 1929.

50. *New York Times,* "Night Clubs Found..."

51. *New York Times,* "Night Clubs Found..."

52. Adam Clayton Powell, *Against the Tide: An Autobiography,* reprint edition (New York: Arno Press, 1980), 217.

53. Powell, *Against the Tide,* 212.

54. Powell, *Against the Tide,* 214.

55. Langston Hughes, "When the Negro was in Vogue," in *History Resource Center,* ed. Gale Research, galenet.galegroup.com/servlet/HistRC/ (accessed June 10, 2008).

56. *New York Times,* "Stocks Collapse in 16,410,000-Share Day, but Rally at Close Cheers Brokers," October 29, 1929.

57. *New York Times,* "Stocks Collapse in..."

3. BURLESQUE AND THE BISHOP

1. Robert A. Caro, *The Power Broker: Robert Moses and the Fall of New York* (New York: Vintage, 1974), 323.

2. Caro, *The Power Broker,* 323-6.

3. Mark Caldwell, *New York Night: The Mystique and its History* (New York: Scribner, 2005), 254.

4. *New York Times,* "Slump Has Restored Family Life, Social Workers Report at Parley," January 24, 1932.

5. *New York Times,* "Increase in Vice Laid to Depression," October 28, 1932.

6. *New York Times,* "Increase in Vice..."

7. Federal Writers Project, *The WPA Guide,* 175.

8. Brooks Atkinson, "Broadway Side-Show: Flea Circus and Two Burlesque Academies on the Shady Side of Times Square," *New York Times,* April 24, 1932.

9. *New York Times,* "Civic Groups Rush 42d St. Clean-Up," April 26, 1932.

10. *New York Times,* "Civic Groups Rush..."

11. *New York Times,* "Cardinal Censures 42d. St. Burlesque," May 3, 1932.

12. *New York Times,* "Cardinal Censures..."

13. *New York Times,* "McKee Closes Two Burlesques in 42d St.; Not a 'Reformer' but Demands Clean Stage," September 20, 1932.

14. *New York Times,* "McKee Closes Two..."

15. *New York Times,* "McKee Closes Two..."

16. *New York Times*, "Burlesque Houses Will Reopen Today," October 12, 1932.

17. *New York Times*, "Burlesque Houses Will..."

18. *New York Times*, "City Toasts New Era," December 6, 1933.

19. Lankevich, *American Metropolis*, 165.

20. Lankevich, *American Metropolis*, 172.

21. *New York Times*, "City Clergy to Widen Film Drive to Clean Up Stage, Dance Halls," July 9, 1934.

22. John D'Emilio and Estelle B. Freedman, *Intimate Matters: A History of Sexuality in America* (New York: Harper & Row, 1988), 281.

23. *New York Times*, "Cardinal Declares War on 'Evil' Films," July 13, 1934.

24. *New York Times*, "Broadway 'Filth' Fought by Priest," February 12, 1934.

25. *New York Times*, "Broadway 'Filth' Fought ..."

26. *New York Times*, "Book Censorship by Licenses in Urged," February 14, 1934.

27. Charles Garrett, *The La Guardia Years: Machine and Reform Politics in New York City* (New Brunswick, NJ: Rutgers University Press, 1961), 154.

28. Frederick Lewis Allen, *Since Yesterday: The 1930s in America, September 3, 1929-September 3, 1939* (New York: Harper & Row, 1939, 1940), 184.

29. Garrett, *The La Guardia Years*, 160.

30. Garrett, *The La Guardia Years*, 161-2.

31. *New York Times*, "Prey of Vice Ring Tells of Beatings," May 16, 1936.

32. *New York Times*, "Lucania is Named Again as Vice Chief," May 23, 1936.

33. *New York Times*, "Lucania Convicted with 8 in Vice Ring on 62 Counts Each," June 8, 1936.

34. *New York Times*, "Vice Group Gloomy on City's Morals," April 25, 1935.

35. *New York Times*, "State Board to protect Marriage Urged in Report to Gov. Lehman," October 29, 1935.

36. *New York Times*, "Wider Drive Urged on Social Disease," January 16, 1936.

37. Chauncey, *Gay New York*, 308.

38. *New York Herald Tribune*, "Clubs Raided," January 29, 1931. Quoted in Chauncey, *Gay New York*, 332.

39. Chauncey, *Gay New York*, 333.

40. Chauncey, *Gay New York*, 337.

41. Chauncey, *Gay New York*, 341.

42. Donald Vining, *How Can You Come Out if You've Never Been In?: Essays on Gay Life and Relationships* (Trumansburg, NY: The Crossing Press, 1986), 54, 59.

43. *New York Times*, "Strip Tease Held Indecent by Court," April 9, 1937.

44. *New York Times*, "Burlesque House Loses its License," April 16, 1937.

45. *New York Times*, "Churches Demand End of Burlesque," April 29, 1937.

46. *New York Times*, "Churches Demand End..."

47. *New York Times*, "Churches Demand End..."

48. *New York Times,* "Moss Weighs Ban on 14 Burlesques," April 30, 1937.

49. *New York Times,* "Moss Weighs Ban..."

50. *New York Times,* "5 Tons of Books Seized in Vice War," May 6, 1937.

51. *New York Times,* "Moss Weighs Ban..."

52. *New York Times,* "Burlesque Shows of City are Shut as Public Menace," May 2, 1937.

53. *New York Times,* "La Guardia Backs Ban," May 3, 1937.

54. *New York Times,* "Burlesque Shows of City..."

55. *New York Times,* "Police Clean-up of Pitfalls is On," April 29, 1939.

56. Stanley Appelbaum, *The New York World's Fair 1939/1940 in 155 Photographs by Richard Wurts and Others* (New York: Dover Publications, Inc., 1977), introduction.

57. Appelbaum, *The New York World's Fair,* introduction.

58. Appelbaum, *The New York World's Fair,* 142.

59. *New York Times,* "Fair Credit to City, Vice Survey Finds," April 23, 1940.

4. THE UNDESIRABLES

1. *New York Times,* "Young Girls Found Menace to Troops," February 4, 1942.

2. *Time,* "VD Among the Amateurs" (March 29, 1943), http://www.time.com/time/magazine/article/0,9171,790841,00.html (accessed March 15, 2007).

3. *Time,* "VD Among the Amateurs."

4. *New York Times,* "800 Arrested in Drive on Vice, Hogan Says," July 26, 1942.

5. *New York Times,* "Army, Navy Spur Vice Drive Here," August 11, 1952.

6. Special to the *New York Times,* "Police War Urged on the Pick-Up Girl," July 27, 1944.

7. Marguerite Marsh, "Prostitutes in New York City: Their Apprehension, Trial, and Treatment, June 1939-June 1940" (New York: Research Bureau, Welfare Council of New York City, 1941), n.p.

8. Martin Goodkin. Quoted in Chauncey, *Gay New York,* 201.

9. George W. Henry, M.D., *All the Sexes: A Study of Masculinity and Femininity* (New York: Rinehart and Co., Inc., 1955), 371.

10. John Rechy, *City of Night* (New York: Grove Press, 1963), 34-5.

11. Laud Humphreys, "Tearoom Trade: Impersonal Sex in Public Places," in *Public Sex/Gay Space,* ed. William L. Leap (New York: Columbia University Press, 1999), 24-54.

12. Chauncey, *Gay New York,* 198.

13. Rechy, *City of Night,* 25.

14. Louis E. Quoted in George W. Henry, M.D., *Sex Variants* (New York: Paul B. Hoeber, 1941), 199-200.

15. Rechy, *City of Night,* 25.

16. Chauncey, *Gay New York,* 218.

17. United States Bureau of the Census, *U.S. Census of Population 1940,* vol. 2,

part 5: New York-Oregon (Washington, D.C.: Government Printing Office, 1943).

18. United States Bureau of the Census, *U.S. Census of Population 1950*, vol. 2, part 32: New York (Washington, D.C.: Government Printing Office, 1952).

19. United States Bureau of the Census, *U.S. Census of Population, 1960*, vol. 1, part 34: New York (Washington, D.C.: Government Printing Office, 1963).

20. United States Bureau of the Census, "Puerto Ricans in Continental United States," *U.S. Census of Population 1950*, vol. 4, part 3 (Washington, D.C.: Government Printing Office, 1953).

21. Caro, *The Power Broker*, 318-9.

22. Caro, *The Power Broker*, 1014.

23. John Cooney, *The American Pope: The Life and Times of Francis Cardinal Spellman* (New York: Times Books, 1984), 202.

24. Francis Cardinal Spellman. Quoted in Cooney, *The American Pope*, 201.

25. Marjorie Heins, "*The Miracle*: Film Censorship and the Entanglement of Church and State" (lecture, University of Virginia, Charlottesville, VA, October 28, 2002).

26. Richard Parke, "Rossellini Film is Halted by City, 'The Miracle' Held 'Blasphemous'," *New York Times*, December 24, 1950.

27. *Burstyn v. Wilson*, 343 U.S. 495 (1952).

28. *New York Times*, "Perverts Called Government Peril," April 19, 1950.

29. James A. Hagerty, "Truman 'Faro Deal' Derided by Dewey," *New York Times*, May 5, 1950.

30. Max Lerner, column, *New York Post*, July 17, 1950. Quoted in Katz, *Gay American History*, 95.

31. *New York Times*, "Federal Vigilance on Perverts Asked," December 16, 1950.

32. *New York Times*, "New York's Crime Problem," Editorial, August 19, 1953.

33. *New York Times*, "While Crime Rises," Editorial, September 18, 1952.

34. New York State Youth Commission, "Blueprint for Delinquency Prevention" (state government report, Albany, NY: 1953), 3.

35. Temporary State Commission on Youth and Delinquency, "Report" (state government memorandum, New York, NY: 1955), 18.

36. Ira Henry Freeman, "The Making of a Boy Killer," *New York Times Magazine*, February 18, 1962.

37. James Traub, *The Devil's Playground: A Century of Pleasure and Profit in Times Square* (New York: Random House, 2004), 114.

38. Guy D'Aulby, "Midtown Teen-Age Loiterers," letter to the editor, *New York Times*, February 8, 1954.

39. John Clellon Holmes, "This is the Beat Generation," *New York Times Magazine*, November 16, 1952.

40. Henry, *All the Sexes*, 395.

41. Henry, *All the Sexes*, 313-4.

42. Henry, *All the Sexes*, 397.

43. *New York Times*, "125 Seized in Times Square In a Drive on Undesirables," July 31, 1954.

44. *New York Times*, "23 More Undesirables Are Seized in Times Square as Round-up Spreads," August 1, 1954.

45. *New York Times*, "125 Seized..."

46. Milton Bracker, "Mayor Backs Plea for More Police; Pledges Other Aid," *New York Times*, August 2, 1954.

47. *New York Times*, "Drive on Riffraff Sets Arrest Mark," August 30, 1954.

48. *New York Times*, "Times Sq. a Midway, Zone Backers Say," April 19, 1952.

49. *New York Times*, "Pastor Condemns Times Square 'Nudity' In 'Shocking' Movie Ads and Book Shops," February 1, 1954.

50. Milton Bracker, "Life on W. 42nd St. A Study in Decay," *New York Times*, March 14, 1960.

51. Charles G. Bennett, "Plea to Remove Times Sq. Dross by Rezoning is Joined by Priest," *New York Times*, November 26, 1953.

52. Gilbert Millstein, "'Family-Type' Burlesque," *New York Times*, May 29, 1955.

53. *New York Times*, "Burlesque a Dirty Word to Public, Objectors Say at License Hearing," March 30, 1955.

54. Millstein, "'Family-Type' Burlesque."

55. *New York Times*, "Burlesque a Dirty Word..."

56. *New York Times*, "Pastor Condemns Times Square..."

57. Charles G. Bennett, "Burlesque Plan Grinds to a Halt," *New York Times*, April 21, 1955.

58. *New York Times*, "Return of Burlesque Sanctioned by Court," May 20, 1955.

59. *New York Times*, "Burlesque Going on Marquee Again," December 22, 1955.

5. PRURIENT INTERESTS

1. Elizabeth Siegel Watkins, *On The Pill: A Social History of Oral Contraceptives, 1950-1970* (Baltimore, MD: Johns Hopkins University Press, 1998), 10.

2. Robert Coughlin, "Changing Roles in Modern Marriage," *Life*, December 24, 1956.

3. Bernard Asbell, *The Pill: A Biography of the Drug that Changed the World* (New York: Random House, 1995), 9.

4. Loretta McLaughlin, *The Pill, John Rock, and The Church: The Biography of a Revolution* (New York: Little, Brown and Company, 1982), 132.

5. Asbell, *The Pill*, 161-7.

6. McLaughlin, *The Pill, John Rock, and The Church*, 208.

7. Asbell, *The Pill*, 175.

8. Ervin Drake, "The Second Sexual Revolution," *Time*, January 24, 1964.

9. *New York Times*, "Smut Held Cause of Delinquency," June 1, 1955.

10. Gay Talese, *Thy Neighbor's Wife* (Garden City, NY: Doubleday and Co., 1980), 95.

11. Edward De Grazia, "I'm Just Going to Feed Adolphe," *Cardozo Studies in Law and Literature* 3, no. 1 (1991): 127-51.

12. *New York Times*, "Joyce Testimony on 'Ulysses' Here," May 20, 1928.

13. Talese, *Thy Neighbor's Wife*, 96.

14. *New York Times*, "Seize 3,000 Books as 'Indecent' Writing," October 5, 1929.

15. *Venus and Tannhäuser*. Quoted in De Grazia, "I'm Just Going to Feed Adolphe," 127-51.

16. *Samuel Roth vs. the United States of America*, 354 U.S. 476 (1957).

17. Edward De Grazia, "How Justice Brennan Freed Novels and Movies During the Sixties," *Cardozo Studies in Law and Literature* 8, no. 2 (1996): 259-65.

18. Charles Rembar, *The End of Obscenity: The Trials of Lady Chatterley, Tropic of Cancer, and Fanny Hill* (New York: Random House, 1968), 134-5.

19. Harry T. Moore, "From Under the Counter to Front Shelf," *New York Times Magazine*, June 18, 1961.

20. Rembar, *The End of Obscenity*, 207.

21. *New York Times*, "Court Voids Ban on 'Tropic' Book," June 22, 1964.

22. Raymond Walters, Jr., "There's Something for Everyone," *New York Times*, January 17, 1960.

23. Walters, Jr., "There's Something for Everyone."

24. Barry Devlin, *Forbidden Pleasures*, cover. Quoted in Susan Stryker, *Queer Pulp: Perverted Passions from the Golden Age of the Paperback* (San Francisco: Chronicle Books, 2001), 31.

25. Lee Mortimer, *Women Confidential*, cover. Quoted in Stryker, *Queer Pulp*, 60.

26. Lilyan Brock, *Queer Patterns*, cover. Quoted in Stryker, *Queer Pulp*, 53.

27. Paul L. Montgomery, "Pulp Sex Novels Thrive as Trade Comes into Open," *New York Times*, September 5, 1965.

28. Montgomery, "Pulp Sex Novels Thrive..."

29. Paul L. Montgomery, "Panic in 'Dirty Books'," *New York Times Magazine*, March 27, 1966.

30. Lou Morgan, *Hangout for Queers*, cover. Quoted in Stryker, *Queer Pulp*, 37.

31. Sheldon Lord, *69 Barrow Street*, cover. Quoted in Stryker, *Queer Pulp*, 68.

32. Sheldon Lord, *21 Gay Street* (New York: Tower Publications, 1960), cover.

33. Howard Thompson, "Mini Movie Houses Are Flourishing," *New York Times*, October 22, 1969.

34. *Washington Post*, "Amazon Nudity in Film Upheld," March 9, 1957.

35. Chuck Smith, interview with author, February 2002.

36. Chuck Smith, interview with author, February 2002.

37. *Bad Girls Go To Hell*, promotional trailer, directed by Doris Wishman (1965; Juri Productions), http://www.youtube.com/watch?v=hgn0AXpQbHI) (accessed May 5, 2007).

38. Letter. Quoted in Anthony Bianco, *Ghosts of 42nd Street: A History of America's Most Infamous Block* (New York: William Morrow, 2004), 162.

39. Bianco, *Ghosts of 42nd Street*, 163.

40. Josh Alan Friedman, *Tales of Times Square* (Portland, OR: Feral House, 1993), 76.

41. Richard F. Shepard, "Peep Shows Have New Nude Look," New York Times, June 9, 1969.

42. Shepard, "Peep Shows Have..."

43. Friedman, *Tales of Times Square*, 78.

44. Friedman, *Tales of Times Square*, 76.

45. Charles Peden, "Times Square Jetsam," letter to the editor, *New York Times*, March 21, 1969.

46. George Dugan, "Jesuit Begins Fast to Protest Pornography Sales to Children," *New York Times*, October 28, 1963.

47. McCandlish Phillips, "City Opens Drive on Pornography," *New York Times*, October 29, 1963.

48. Philip Benjamin, "City Calls Parley on Sale of Smut," *New York Times*, October 30, 1963.

49. Montgomery, "Pulp Sex Novels Thrive..."

50. Charles G. Bennet, "New Smut Drive Planned by City," *New York Times*, August 7, 1964.

51. Edward De Grazia, *Girls Lean Back Everywhere: The Law of Obscenity and the Assault on Genius* (New York: Random House, 1992), 435.

52. Charles G. Bennett, "City's Smut Drive Will Try Suasion," *New York Times*, December 5, 1964.

53. Alfred E. Clark, "City Starts Drive on Subway Smut," *New York Times*, March 27, 1965.

54. Morris Kaplan, "Di Carlo to Fight Newsstand Smut," *New York Times*, April 13, 1965.

55. Ralph Ginzburg, *An Unhurried View of Erotica* (New York: Ace Books, 1958), author biography.

56. Ralph Ginzburg, "Eros Unbound," 1999, http://www.evesmag.com/ginzburg.htm (accessed May 1, 2007).

57. Fred C. Graham, "Publisher of Erotica: Ralph Ginzburg," *New York Times*, March 22, 1966.

58. Graham, "Publisher of Erotica: Ralph Ginzburg."

59. Richard Corliss, "My Favorite Pornographer," *Time*, July 15, 2006, http://www.time.com/time/arts/article/0,8599,1214094,00.html (accessed May 12, 2007).

60. Corliss, "My Favorite Pornographer."

61. Phillips, "City Opens Drive..."

62. Fred C. Graham, "High Court Rules Ads Can be Proof of Obscene Work," *New York Times*, March 22, 1966.

63. Ginzburg, "Eros Unbound."

64. Graham, "High Court Rules Ads..."

65. *Ginzburg. V. United States, 383 U.S. 463 (1966)*

66. *Ginzburg. V. United States, 383 U.S. 463 (1966)*

67. Victor Jay, *AC/DC Lover*, cover. Quoted in Stryker, *Queer Pulp*, 38.

68. Paul L. Montgomery, "Booksellers Here Staging a Cleanup," *New York Times*, March 23, 1966.

69. *New York Times*, "Six Suspects Seized in Smut Film Raids," March 17, 1967.

70. *New York Times*, "42nd Street Shop Raided on Smut," December 6, 1968.

71. Montgomery, "Booksellers Here Staging..."

72. Ralph Ginzburg, "Castrated: My Eight Months in Prison," *New York Times Magazine*, December 3, 1972.

73. Ginzburg, "Castrated..."

6. YOUR MOST FANTASTIC FANTASIES

1. Robert C. Doty, "Growth of Overt Homosexuality in City Provokes Wide Concern," *New York Times*, December 17, 1963.

2. Doty, "Growth of Overt Homosexuality..."

3. Doty, "Growth of Overt Homosexuality..."

4. Doty, "Growth of Overt Homosexuality..."

5. Doty, "Growth of Overt Homosexuality..."

6. Enid Nemy, "The Woman Homosexual: More Assertive, Less Willing to Hide," *New York Times*, November 17, 1969.

7. Nemy, "The Woman Homosexual..."

8. Webster Schott, "Civil Rights for the Homosexual: A 4-Million Minority Asks for Equal Rights, Some Sex-Law Reformers are Asking for the Moon," *New York Times Magazine*, November 12, 1967.

9. Doty, "Growth of Overt Homosexuality..."

10. Martin Duberman, *Stonewall* (New York: Plume, 1993), 181-5.

11. Duberman, *Stonewall*, 181.

12. Howard Smith, "Full Moon Over the Stonewall," *Village Voice*, July 3, 1969.

13. Duberman, *Stonewall*, 185.

14. Duberman, *Stonewall*, 195.

15. Lucian Truscott IV, "Gay Power Comes to Sheridan Square," *Village Voice*, July 3, 1969.

16. Truscott IV, "Gay Power Comes to..."

17. Truscott IV, "Gay Power Comes to..."

18. Smith, "Full Moon Over Stonewall."

19. *New York Times*, "4 Policemen Hurt in 'Village' Raid," June 29, 1969.

20. Truscott IV, "Gay Power Comes to..."

21. Truscott IV, "Gay Power Comes to..."

22. National Organization for Women, "1966 Statement of Purpose," http://www.now.org/history/purpose66.html (accessed November 28, 2007).

23. Betty Friedan, *Life So Far: A Memoir* (New York: Simon & Schuster, 2000), 239.

24. David Allyn, *Make Love, Not War: The Sexual Revolution: An Unfettered History* (New York: Little, Brown and Co., 2000), 250.

25. Lois Hart, untitled letter to the editor, *New York Times*, April 5, 1970.

26. *Time*, "Women's Lib: A Second Look," December 14, 1970, http://www.time.com/time/magazine/article/0,9171,944216,00.html (accessed November 28, 2007).

27. *Time*, "People" column, December 28, 1970, http://www.time.com/time/magazine/article/0,9171,944258,00.html (accessed December 6, 2007).

28. Al Goldstein and Josh Alan Friedman, *I, Goldstein: My Screwed Life* (New York: Thunder's Mouth Press, 2006), 87.

29. Goldstein and Friedman, *I, Goldstein*, 88.

30. Goldstein and Friedman, *I, Goldstein*, 90.

31. Al Goldstein, "Screw Goes to Market," *Screw* no. 1, November 4, 1968, n.p.

32. *Inside Deep Throat*, DVD, directed by Fenton Bailey and Randy Barbato (2005; Hollywood, CA: World of Wonder, Imagine Entertainment).

33. Linda Lovelace with Mike McGrady, *Ordeal: An Autobiography* (New York: Bell Publishing, 1980), 103.

34. Lovelace and McGrady, *Ordeal*, 113.

35. *Deep Throat*, videocassette, directed by Gerard Damiano (1972; P.D., Inc./Aquarius Releasing, Inc.)

36. Ralph Blumenthal, "Porno Chic: 'Hard-core' grows fashionable—and very profitable," *New York Times Magazine*, January 21, 1973.

37. Luke Ford, *A History of X: 100 Years of Sex in Film* (Amherst, NY: Prometheus Books, 1999), 49.

38. *Deep Throat*.

39. *Inside Deep Throat*.

40. *Newsweek*, "The 'Throat' Case," January 15, 1973.

41. Blumenthal, "Porno Chic."

42. Paul L. Montgomery, "Psychiatrist Testifies that 'Deep Throat' Could be Harmful to a Normal Man by Clouding Female Sexuality," *New York Times*, December 27, 1972.

43. Paul L. Montgomery, "'Throat' Obscene, Judge Rules Here," *New York Times*, March 2, 1973.

44. Montgomery, "'Throat' Obscene..."

45. *Miller v. California*, 413 U.S. 15 (1973).

46. Larry Kramer, interview by Maer Roshan, "Queer Conscience," *New York*, April 6, 1998.

47. Allan Bérubé, "A History of the Gay Bathhouses," in *Policing Public Sex*, 187-220.

48. Bérubé, "A History...," in *Policing Public Sex*, 187-220.

49. Bérubé, "A History...," in *Policing Public Sex*, 187-220.

50. *Saturday Night at the Baths*, DVD, directed by David Buckley (1975; Charlottesville, VA: Water Bearer DVD, 2006).

51. *New York Times*, "Screen: 'At the Baths,'" June 12, 1975.

52. "Carol" and "Tim," *The Swinger's Handbook: The Definitive How-To Guide to Group Sex* (New York: Pocket Books, 1974), back cover.

53. "Carol" and "Tim," *The Swinger's Handbook:*, 13.

54. "Carol" and "Tim," *The Swinger's Handbook*, 58.

55. "Carol" and "Tim," *The Swinger's Handbook*, 53.

56. Allyn, *Make Love Not War*, 209.

57. Judy Bachrach, "The Romans Did it, and Now...," *Washington Post*, February 23, 1978.

58. Friedman, *Tales of Times Square*, 108.

59. Friedman, *Tales of Times Square*, 107.

60. Friedman, *Tales of Times Square*, 120.

61. *Newsweek*, "Pornography Goes Public," December 21, 1970.

62. Murray Schumach, "Sex Exploitation Spreading Here," *New York Times*, July 11, 1971.

63. Shumach, "Sex Exploitation..."

64. Richard Halloran, "A Federal Panel Asks Relaxation of Curbs on Smut," *New York Times*, October 1, 1970.

65. Morton A. Hill, S.J. and Winfrey C. Link, "Report," in *The Report of the Commission on Obscenity and Pornography* (New York: Bantam, 1970), 456-505.

66. Lee Dembart, "Along Eighth Avenue, Where Leer is King...," *New York Times*, November 12, 1976.

67. Tom Goldstein, "Landlord Shuts Sex Parlor by Hiring 3 to Buy and Tell," *New York Times*, November 16, 1976.

68. Goldstein, "Landlord Shuts Sex Parlor..."

69. Charles Kaiser, "New Zoning to Curb Pornography Places Submitted by Beame," *New York Times*, November 12, 1976.

70. Tom Goldstein, "Will Pornography Zoning Stand Up in Court?" *New York Times*, January 30, 1977.

71. Ronald Smothers, "Zoning Threat Fails to Faze Proprietors of Sex Shops," *New York Times*, November 13, 1976.

72. Anna Quindlen, "Mayor Gets Some Bad Notices After 2nd Raid on Times Sq. Show," *New York Times*, March 26, 1977.

73. Andrea Dworkin, "The Root Cause," in Andrea Dworkin, *Our Blood: Prophecies and Discourses on Sexual Politics* (New York: Harper & Row, 1976), 104.

74. Dworkin, "The Root Cause," 107.

75. *Miller v. California*, 413 U.S. 15 (1973).

76. Susan Brownmiller, "Let's Put Pornography Back in the Closet," http://

www.susanbrownmiller.com/html/antiporno.html (accessed July 22, 2006).

77. Susan Brownmiller, *In Our Time: Memoir of a Revolution* (New York: Dial Press, 1999), 302.

78. Georgia Dullea, "In Feminists'Antipornography Drive, 42nd Street is the Target," *New York Times*, July 6, 1979.

79. Dullea, "In Feminists'Antipornography Drive..."

80. Dullea, "In Feminists'Antipornography Drive..."

81. Leslie Bennetts, "Conference Examines Pornography as a Feminist Issue," *New York Times*, September 17, 1979.

82. Barbara Basler, "5,000 Join Feminist group's Rally in Times Sq. Against Pornography," *New York Times*, October 21, 1979.

83. Andrea Dworkin, "The Lie," in Andrea Dworkin, *Letters from a War Zone: Writings 1976-1989* (Chicago: Lawrence Hill Books, 1993),http://www.nostatusquo.com/ACLU/dworkin/WarZoneChaptIa.html (accessed July 23, 2006).

84. Brownmiller, *In Our Time*, 306-7.

85. Lovelace, *Ordeal*, 129.

7. RISE AND FALL

1. Nathaniel Sheppard, Jr., "V.D. Found Rising in Homosexuals," *New York Times*, July 26, 1976.

2. John Leo, "The New Scarlet Letter,"*Time*, August 2, 1982.

3. Leo, "The New Scarlet Letter."

4. *Time*, "Herpes: The New Sexual Leprosy," July 28, 1980.

5. American Social Health Association, "ASHA Background," http://www.ashastd.org/about/about_history.cfm (accessed July 13, 2007).

6. Leo, "The New Scarlet Letter."

7. Clyde Haberman, "Health Officials Test Prostitutes for Gonorrhea," *New York Times*, March 5, 1982.

8. Doug Ireland, "Rendezvous in the Ramble," *New York*, July 24, 1978.

9. Charles Kaiser, *The Gay Metropolis: 1940-1996* (New York: Houghton-Mifflin, 1997), 246.

10. Larry Kramer, interview by Maer Roshan, "Queer Conscience."

11. Lawrence K. Altman, "Rare Cancer Seen in 41 Homosexuals," *New York Times*, July 3, 1981.

12. Matt Clark with Mariana Gosnell, "Diseases that Plague Gays," *Newsweek*, December 21, 1981.

13. Clark with Gosnell, "Diseases the Plague Gays."

14. Robin Herman, "A Disease's Spread Provokes Anxiety," *New York Times*, August 8, 1982.

15. Glenn Collins, "Facing the Emotional Anguish of AIDS," *New York Times*, May 30, 1983.

16. Glenn Collins, "Impact of AIDS: Patterns of Homosexual Life Changing," *New York Times*, July 22, 1985.

17. "Impact of AIDS..."
18. Larry Kramer, "A Personal Appeal," in Larry Kramer, *Reports from the Holocaust: The Story of an AIDS Activist* (New York: St. Martin's Press, 1994), 8-9.
19. Kramer, "A Personal Appeal."
20. Larry Kramer, "Where Are We Now?" in *Reports from the Holocaust,* 22-32.
21. Larry Kramer, "1,112 and Counting," *New York Native,* March 14, 1983.
22. Kramer, "1,112 and Counting."
23. David Wojnarowicz, "The Seven Deadly Sins Fact Sheet," in David Wojnarowicz, *Close to the Knives* (New York: Serpent's Tail, 1991), 124-31.
24. Eric Pace, "Broader Medical View Urged for Homosexuals," *New York Times,* June 18, 1984.
25. Larry Kramer, "2,339 and Counting," in *Reports from the Holocaust,* 68-74.
26. Frank Lynn, "McGrath Proposes Closing Homosexuals' Bathhouses," *New York Times,* October 4, 1985.
27. Robert D. McFadden, "Cuomo and Koch Reconsidering Their Opposition to Closing of Bathhouses," *New York Times,* October 5, 1985.
28. McFadden, "Cuomo and Koch Reconsidering..."
29. Lynn, "McGrath Proposes..."
30. *New York Times,* "Morality, AIDS and the Bathhouses," October 19, 1985.
31. Maurice Carroll, "State May Shut Bathhouses in a Drive to Combat AIDS," *New York Times,* October 25, 1985.
32. Joyce Purnick, "AIDS and the State," *New York Times,* October 30, 1985.
33. McFadden, "Cuomo and Koch Reconsidering..."
34. Maurice Carroll, "State Permits Closing of Bathhouses to Cut AIDS," *New York Times,* October 26, 1985.
35. Lenny Waller, interview with author, March 2002.
36. Carroll, "State Permits Closing..."
37. Ralph Blumenthal, "At Homosexual Establishments, a New Climate of Caution," *New York Times,* November 9, 1985.
38. Jane Gross, "Bathhouses Reflect AIDS Concerns," *New York Times,* October 14, 1985.
39. Bruce Mailman, "The Battle for Safe Sex in the Baths," editorial, *New York Times,* December 5, 1985.
40. Joyce Purnick, "Koch Says City Will Now Enforce New State Rules to Combat AIDS," *New York Times,* October 31, 1985.
41. Joyce Purnick, "City Closes Bar Frequented by Homosexuals, Citing Sexual Activity Linked to AIDS," *New York Times,* November 8, 1985.
42. Lenny Waller, interview with author, March 2002.
43. Lenny Waller, interview with author, March 2002.
44. Blumenthal, "At Homosexual Establishments..."
45. Blumenthal, "At Homosexual Establishments..."
46. Erik Eckholm, "Prostitutes Impact on Spread of AIDS is Debated," *New York Times,* November 5, 1985.

47. Suzanne Golubski and Bob Kappstatter, "Swinging Doors Shut, City Probe KOs Plato's," *New York Daily News*, January 1, 1986.

48. New York City Department of Health and Mental Hygiene, "New York City HIV/AIDS Annual Surveillance Statistics" (updated December 4, 2006), http://www.nyc.gov/html/doh/html/ah/hivtables.shtml (accessed July 12, 2006).

49. Kramer, "1,112 and Counting."

50. Larry Kramer, commentary on "The AIDS Network Letter to Mayor Koch," in *Reports From the Holocaust*, 52-9.

51. Larry Kramer, "The Beginning of ACTing UP (1987)," in *Reports from the Holocaust*, 127-36.

52. AIDS Coalition to Unleash Power (ACT UP), "Reagan's AIDSgate," http://www.actupny.org/reports/reagan.html (accessed August 18, 2006).

53. Bruce Lambert, "3,000 Assailing Policy on AIDS Ring City Hall," *New York Times*, March 29, 1989.

54. AIDS Coalition to Unleash Power (ACT UP), first demonstration flyer, http://www.actupny.org/documents/1stFlyer.html (accessed July 28, 2007).

55. J. Levine, "The Toughest Virus of All," *Time*, November 3, 1986.

56. *New York Times*, photo caption, March 25, 1987.

57. Peter Steinfels, "Death of a Cardinal; Cardinal O' Connor, 80, Dies; Forceful Voice for Vatican," obituary, *New York Times*, May 4, 2000.

58. *New York Times*, "O'Connor Defends AIDS Panel Role," July 31, 1987.

59. Wojnarowicz, "The Seven Deadly Sins Fact Sheet."

60. Thomas L. Waite, "New York Shuts 2 Gay Theaters as AIDS Threats," *New York Times*, February 12, 1989.

61. Jason DeParle, "111 Held in St. Patrick's AIDS Protest," *New York Times*, December 11, 1989.

62. Tom Keane, "Cardinal Sin," *Poz*, December 2000.

63. Kaiser, *The Gay Metropolis*, 323.

64. Todd S. Purdum, "Cardinal Says He Won't Yield to Protests," *New York Times*, December 12, 1989.

65. DeParle, "111 Held..."

66. Purdum, "Cardinal Says..."

67. Purdum, "Cardinal Says..."

68. ACT UP activist. Quoted in Susan M. Chambré, *Fighting for Our Lives: New York's AIDS Community and the Politics of Disease* (New Brunswick, NJ: Rutgers University Press, 2006), 128.

69. Ed Magnuson, "In a Rage Over AIDS," *Time*, December 25, 1989, http://www.time.com/time/magazine/article/0,9171,959419,00.html (accessed July 30, 2007).

70. Richard J. Meislin, "Carey Signs Bill Raising Sentences for Pimps and Prostitutes' Patrons," *New York Times*, July 29, 1978.

71. Dena Kleiman, "Drive Against 'Massage Parlors' in New York is Gaining Strength," *New York Times*, November 19, 1978.

72. Arnold H. Lubasch, "A U.S. Judge Upholds City's Ban on Opening of New Massage Sites," *New York Times*, December 29, 1979.

73. Lynne B. Sagalyn, *Times Square Roulette: Remaking the City Icon* (Cambridge, MA: MIT Press, 2001), 595.

74. Paul Goldberger, "Portman Hotel's Plan Seems to Assure Mall on Broadway," *New York Times*, January 17, 1982.

75. Alexander Reichl, *Reconstructing Times Square: Politics and Culture in Urban Development* (Lawrence, KS: University Press of Kansas, 1999), 79.

76. Sagalyn, *Times Square Roulette*, 595.

77. Reichl, *Reconstructing Times Square*, 79.

78. William Kornblum and Terry Williams, "West 42nd Street: The Bright Lights Zone," unpublished study, City University of New York Graduate Center, 1978, 1.

79. "A Talk with William Kornblum," *Folio: Highlighting Research and Scholarship at the Graduate Center* (Spring 2003), http://www.gc.cuny.edu/faculty/folio/spring2003/Kornblum.htm (accessed December 3, 2008)

80. Kornblum and Williams, "The Bright Lights Zone," 1.

81. Kornblum and Williams, "The Bright Lights Zone," acknowledgments.

82. Kornblum and Williams, "The Bright Lights Zone," 135.

83. Kornblum and Williams, "The Bright Lights Zone," 143.

84. Kornblum and Williams, "The Bright Lights Zone," 143-4.

85. Kornblum and Williams, "The Bright Lights Zone," 118-9.

86. William Serrin, "Sex is a Growing Multibillion Business," *New York Times*, February 9, 1981.

87. William Serrin, "Opponents of Flourishing Sex Industry Hindered by its Open Public Acceptance," *New York Times*, February 10, 1981.

88. Kornblum and Williams, "The Bright Lights Zone," 37.

89. Sagalyn, *Times Square Roulette*, 595.

90. Sagalyn, *Times Square Roulette*, 63.

91. Sagalyn, *Times Square Roulette*, 63.

92. Reichl, *Reconstructing Times Square*, 86.

93. Sagalyn, *Times Square Roulette*, 63.

94. Sagalyn, *Times Square Roulette*, 64, 66.

95. Carl Weisbrod, "Transforming Times Square," in *New York Comes Back: The Mayoralty of Edward I. Koch*, ed. Michael Goodwin (New York: powerhouse Books, in association with the Museum of the City of New York, 2005), 76-80.

96. Sagalyn, *Times Square Roulette*, 64.

97. Lesley Oelsner, "'New' Times Square Waiting in the Wings," *New York Times*, November 14, 1978.

98. Weisbrod, "Transforming Times Square."

99. Sagalyn, *Times Square Roulette*, 66.

100. Reichl, *Reconstructing Times Square*, 30.

101. Phillip Lopate, "42d Street, You Ain't No Sodom," op-ed, *New York Times*,

March 8, 1979.

102. Ralph Blumenthal, "A Times Square Revival?," *New York Times*, December 27, 1981.

103. Martin Gottlieb, "Study of Project in Times Square Sees Rise in Jobs," *New York Times*, January 26, 1984.

104. Sagalyn, *Times Square Roulette*, 99.

105. Carter Wiseman, "Brave New Times Square," *New York*, April 2, 1984.

106. Reichl, *Reconstructing Times Square*, 95.

107. Wiseman, "Brave New Times Square."

108. Gottlieb, "Study of Project..."

109. Gottlieb, "Study of Project..."

110. Martin Gottlieb, "Development Plan for Times Sq. Wins Unanimous Backing of Estimate Board," *New York Times*, November 9, 1984.

111. Ronald Reagan. Quoted in Petersen and Hefner, *The Century of Sex*, 410.

112. Robert Scheer, "Inside the Meese Commission: How a Group of Zealots Took Aim at Pornography and Ended up in a War Against Sex Itself," *Playboy*, August 1986.

113. Anonymous letter submitted by Women Against Pornography to the Attorney General's Commission on Pornography, August 1984, in Attorney General's Commission on Pornography, *Final Report* (Washington, D.C.: U.S. Department of Justice, 1986), http://www.porn-report.com/401-victimization.htm (accessed August 11, 2006).

114. Goldstein and Friedman, *I, Goldstein*, 119.

115. Andrea Dworkin, "New York Hearing, Vol. II," in Attorney General's Commission on Pornography, *Final Report*, 129-51. http://www.porn-report.com/401-victimization.htm (accessed August 11, 2006).

116. Scheer, "Inside the Meese Commission..."

117. Scheer, "Inside the Meese Commission..."

118. Al Goldstein, "Pay Dirt, As It Were," editorial, *New York Times*, July 23, 1986.

119. Matthew L. Wald, "'Adult' Magazines Lose Sales as 8,000 Stores Forbid Them," *New York Times*, June 16, 1986.

120. Seka. Quoted in Goldstein and Friedman, *I, Goldstein*, 7.

121. Goldstein and Friedman, *I, Goldstein*, 5.

122. Nicholas Kristof, "X-Rated Industry in a Slump," *New York Times*, October 5, 1986.

123. Reichl, *Reconstructing Times Square*, 143.

124. Robert A.M. Stern Architects, "42nd Street Now! for Empire State Development Corporation, 1992," http://www.ramsa.com/project.aspx?id=5 (accessed August 11, 2007).

125. Jerry Adler, "Theme Cities," *Newsweek*, September 11, 1995.

126. Robin Pogrebin, "From Naughty and Bawdy to Stars Reborn: Once Seedy Theaters, Now Restored, Lead the Development of 42nd Street," *New York Times*, December 11, 2000.

127. Frank Rose, "Can Disney Tame 42nd Street?," *Fortune*, June 24, 1996.
128. Disney executive. Quoted in Eliot, *Down 42nd Street*, 247.
129. Eliot, *Down 42nd Street*, 249.
130. Thomas J. Lueck, "Hold the Neon: One More Battle on 42nd Street," *New York Times*, May 1, 1994.
131. Disney executive. Quoted in Eliot, *Down 42nd Street*, 249.
132. Rose, "Can Disney Tame..."

8. DISNEY VS. THE DIRTY DEBUTANTES

1. A.J. Lobbia, "Silent Rivals," *The Village Voice*, November 2, 1993.
2. Celia W. Duggar, "New York Rivals Differ Strikingly on Dealing with City's Poorest," *New York Times*, October 2, 1993.
3. Lobbia, "Silent Rivals."
4. Michael Winerip, "High-Profile Prosecutor," *New York Times Magazine*, June 9, 1985.
5. Winerip, "High-Profile Prosecutor."
6. Arnold H. Lubasch, "U.S. Jury Convicts Eight as Members of Mob Commission," *New York Times*, November 20, 1986.
7. Winerip, "High-Profile Prosecutor."
8. Winerip, "High-Profile Prosecutor."
9. Alison Mitchell, "Taking Oath, Giuliani Urges 'Courage,'" *New York Times*, January 1, 1994.
10. James Q. Wilson and George L. Kelling, "Broken Windows: The Police and Neighborhood Safety," *Atlantic Monthly*, March 1982.
11. John Tierney, "The Holy Terror," *New York Times Magazine*, December 3, 1995.
12. Tierney, "The Holy Terror."
13. Garry Pierre-Pierre, "Fewer Killings Tallied in '93 in New York," *New York Times*, January 2, 1994.
14. Clifford Krauss, "Study Suggests it is Easy to Banish Squeegee Men," *New York Times*, February 7, 1994.
15. Jane Fritsch, "Mayor Orders Jail Reopened in Brooklyn," *New York Times*, September 30, 1994.
16. Joseph B. Treaster, "Crime Rate Drops Again in New York, Hastening a Trend," *New York Times*, June 2, 1994.
17. James Barron, "Operation Losing Proposition: 2 Years and 90 Cars Later," *New York Times*, December 4, 1992.
18. Barron, "Operation Losing Proposition."
19. Garry Pierre-Pierre, "Police Focus on Arresting Prostitutes' Customers," *New York Times*, November 20, 1994.
20. Pierre-Pierre, "Police Focus on Arresting..."
21. Philip Elmer-Dewitt, "The Battle for the Soul of the Internet," *Time*, July 25, 1994, http://www.time.com/time/magazine/article/0,9171,981132,00.

html (accessed August 23, 2007).

22. Insight Associates, "Report on the Secondary Effects of the Concentration of Adult Use Establishments in the Times Square Area," prepared for the Times Square Business Improvement District (April 1994), http://hellskitchen.net/issues/bids/tsbidsex/title.html (accessed September 6, 2007).

23. Insight Associates, "Report on the Secondary Effects..." 4.

24. Insight Associates, "Report on the Secondary Effects..." 11.

25. Insight Associates, "Report on the Secondary Effects..." 24.

26. Insight Associates, "Report on the Secondary Effects..." 24.

27. Todd Seavey, "Erogenous Zones: New York Porn Shops Say Goodbye to Broadway," *Reason*, March 1997.

28. Steven Lee Myers, "Giuliani Proposes Toughening Laws on X-Rated Shops," *New York Times*, September 11, 1994.

29. Myers, "Giuliani Proposes Toughening..."

30. Myers, "Giuliani Proposes Toughening..."

31. Zoning Resolution of the City of New York. Section 12-10, Definitions.

32. Myers, "Giuliani Proposes Toughening..."

33. Tom Redburn, "Putting Sex in Its Place," *New York Times*, September 12, 1994.

34. Charles Lane, "Titillation: Rudy Giuliani's Victorian Crusade," *The New Republic*, October 24, 1994.

35. Ashley Dunn, "The Owner and the Neighbors: Opposite Views of the Pornography Issue," *New York Times*, September 11, 1994.

36. Jonathan P. Hicks, "Plan to Change Sex Zoning Rules Draw Vocal Opposition," *New York Times*, July 27, 1995.

37. Vivian S. Toy, "Council Approves Package of Curbs on Sex Businesses," *New York Times*, October 26, 1995.38. Seavey, "Erogenous Zones..."

39. Hicks, "Plan to Change Sex Zoning..."

40. Hicks, "Plan to Change Sex Zoning..."

41. David Firestone, "In Land of Topless Bars, a Ho-Hum," *New York Times*, September 25, 1994.

42. Jonathan P. Hicks, "Giuliani in Accord with City Council on X-Rated Shops," *New York Times*, March 14, 1995.

43. Toy, "Council Approves Package..."

44. Seavey, "Erogenous Zones..."

45. Toy, "Council Approves Package..."

46. Hicks, "Giuliani in Accord..."

47. Thomas J. Lueck, "Sex Shops and Patrons Join in Suits Challenging Zoning," *New York Times*, February 28, 1996.

48. Dan Barry, "The Fading Neon of Times Square's Sex Shops," *New York Times*, October 28, 1995.

49. Sagalyn, *Times Square Roulette*, 598-9.

50. Vivian S. Toy, "New York Zoning Against Sex Shops is Upheld as Fair," *New York Times*, October 24, 1996.

51. Toy, "New York Zoning Against..."

52. Vivian S. Toy, "Sex Shop Law is Postponed by State Judge," *New York Times*, October 25, 1996.

53. Bruce Weber, "Disney Unveils Restored New Amsterdam Theater," *New York Times*, April 3, 1997.

54. Archives of the Mayor's Press Office, "Press Release #554-97: Adult Video Store in Residential Area Ordered to Close under Mayor Giuliani's Adult-Use Zoning Moratorium," September 19, 1997.

55. Raymond Fernandez, "Court, 6-0, Backs New York Statute Limiting Sex Shops," *New York Times*, February 25, 1998.

56. Benjamin Weiser, "Judge Blocks Zoning Limit on Sex Shops," *New York Times*, February 28, 1998.

57. Mike Allen, "Mayor Urges Photos to be Taken of Patrons Entering Sex Shops," *New York Times*, May 16, 1998.

58. Benjamin Weiser, "Supreme Court Denies Sex Shops' Plea to Halt New York Law," *New York Times*, July 29, 1998.

59. Mike Allen, "New York Begins to Raid and Close Adult Businesses," *New York Times*, August 2, 1998.

60. Elizabeth Kolbert, "The Last Peep for Smutland in Times Sq.?," *New York Times*, June 4, 1998.

61. Charles V. Bagli, "Corporation Walks Away from Tax Deal," *New York Times*, September 5, 1999.

62. Charles V. Bagli, "Reuters Given Big Tax Deal for its Project in Times Square," *New York Times*, November 1, 1997.

63. Times Square Alliance, "Pedestrian Projections." n.d. (2003?) http://timessquarenyc.org/facts/documents/OfficeWorkerGrowthDevelopment.pdf (accessed December 18, 2007).

64. Times Square Alliance, "Pedestrian Projections: Pedestrian Growth 1982-2030." n.d. (2003?) http://timessquarenyc.org/facts/documents/PedIncreases19822030.pdf (accessed December 18, 2007).

65. *Broadway Magazine*, "Media Kit," http://broadwaymag.com/files/Broadway_Magazine_Media.pdf (accessed December 19, 2007).

66. Frank Mastrangelo, interview with author, December 2001.

"THE WICKEDEST CITY"

1. Kurt Andersen, "Can 42nd Street Be Born Again?," *Time*, September 27, 1993.

BIBLIOGRAPHY

AIDS Coalition to Unleash Power (ACT UP). First demonstration flyer,http://www.actupny.org/documents/1stFlyer.html (accessed July 28, 2007).

AIDS Coalition to Unleash Power (ACT UP). "Reagan's AIDSgate," http://www.actupny.org/reports/reagan.html (accessed August 18, 2006).

Allen, Frederick Lewis. *Only Yesterday: An Informal History of the 1920's.* New York: Harper & Row, 1931.

Allen, Frederick Lewis. *Since Yesterday: The 1930s in America, September 3, 1929-September 3, 1939.* Harper & Row, 1939, 1940.

Allyn, David. *Make Love, Not War: The Sexual Revolution: An Unfettered History.* New York: Little, Brown and Co., 2000.

American Social Health Association. "ASHA Background." http://www.ashastd.org/about/about_history.cfm (accessed July 13, 2007).

American Social Hygiene Association. *Keeping Fit to Fight.* Washington, D.C.: The War Department Commission on Training Camp Activities, n.d.

Archives of the Mayor's Press Office, Press Release #554-97, "Adult Video Store in Residential Area Ordered to Close under Mayor Giuliani's Adult-Use Zoning Moratorium," September 19, 1997.

Asbell, Bernard. *The Pill: A Biography of the Drug that Changed the World.* New York: Random House, 1995.

Bannon, Ann. *The Beebo Brinker Chronicles.* New York: Quality Paperback Book Club, 1995.

Bad Girls Go To Hell, videocassette. Directed by Doris Wishman (1965; Seattle, WA: Something Weird Video, 2002).

Barnet, Andrea. *All Night Party: The Women of Bohemian Greenwich Village and Harlem, 1913-1930.* Chapel Hill, NC: Algonquin Books, 2004.

Beisel, Nicola. *Imperiled Innocents: Anthony Comstock and Family Reproduction in Victorian America.* Princeton, NJ: Princeton University Press, 1997.

Berube, Allan. "A History of the Gay Bathhouses." In *Policing Public Sex: Queer Politics and the Future of AIDS Activism,* edited by Dangerous Bedfellows (Ephen Glenn Coulter, Wayne Hoffman, Eva Pendleton, Alison Redick, David Serlin), 200. Boston: South End Press, 1996.

Bianco, Anthony. *Ghosts of 42nd Street: A History of America's Most Infamous*

Block. New York: William Morrow, 2004.

Brace, Charles Loring. *The Dangerous Classes of New York; and Twenty Years' Work Among Them.* New York: Wynkoop and Hallenbeck, 1872.

Brandt, Allan M. *No Magic Bullet: A Social History of Venereal Disease in the United States Since 1880.* Expanded Edition. New York: Oxford University Press, 1987.

Broun, Heywood and Margaret Leech. *Anthony Comstock: Roundsman of the Lord.* New York: Albert and Charles Boni, 1927.

Brownmiller, Susan. *In Our Time: Memoir of a Revolution.* New York: Dial Press, 1999.

Brownmiller, Susan. "Let's Put Pornography Back in the Closet." http://www.susanbrownmiller.com/html/antiporno.html (accessed July 22, 2006).

Bureau of Social Hygiene. *Commercialized Prostitution in New York City: A Comparison Between 1912, 1915, 1916 and 1917.* New York: The Century Company, 1917. http://pds.harvard.edu:8080/pdx/servlet/pds?id=2581290 (accessed February 18, 2007).

Burstyn v. Wilson, 343 U.S. 495 (1952).

Caldwell, Mark. *New York Night: The Mystique and its History.* New York: Scribner, 2005.

Caro, Robert A. *The Power Broker: Robert Moses and the Fall of New York.* New York: Vintage, 1974.

"Carol" and "Tim." *The Swinger's Handbook: The Definitive How-To Guide to Group Sex.* New York: Pocket Books, 1974.

Chambré, Susan M. *Fighting for Our Lives: New York's AIDS Community and the Politics of Disease.* New Brunswick, NJ: Rutgers University Press, 2006.

Chauncey, George. *Gay New York: Gender, Urban Culture, and the Making of the Gay Male World, 1890-1940.* New York: Basic Books, 1994.

Christianson, Scott. "Criminal Punishment in New Netherland." In *A Beautiful and Fruitful Place: Selected Rensselaerswijck Seminar Papers,* edited by Nancy Anne McClure Zeller. Albany, NY: New Netherland Publishing, September 1991. http://www.nnp.org/nnp/publications/ABAFB/1001.pdf (accessed March 25, 2007).

Cooney, John. *The American Pope: The Life and Times of Francis Cardinal Spellman.* New York: Times Books, 1984.

Costello, Augustine. *Our Police Protectors, History of the New York Police, Published for the benefit of the Police Pension Fund,* n.p., Published by Author, 1885. http://www.usgennet.org/usa/ny/state/police/ch13pt1.html (accessed November 21, 2006).

Costello, John. *Virtue Under Fire: How World War II Changed Our Social and Sexual Attitudes.* New York: Fromm International Publishing Corporation, 1987.

Crane, Stephen. *Maggie: A Girl of the Streets and Other New York Writings.* New York: Modern Library, 2001.

Deep Throat, videocassette, directed by Gerard Damiano (1973; Aquarius Releasing, Inc., n.d.).

De Grazia, Edward. *Girls Lean Back Everywhere: The Law of Obscenity and the Assault on Genius.* New York: Random House, 1992.

De Grazia, Edward. "I'm Just Going to Feed Adolphe." *Cardozo Studies in Law and Literature,* Vol 3, No. 1 (Spring-Summer, 1991), 127-51.

Delany, Samuel F. *Times Square Red, Times Square Blue.* New York: New York University Press, 1999.

D'Emilio, John, and Estelle B. Freedman. *Intimate Matters: A History of Sexuality in America.* New York: Harper & Row, 1988.

D'Emilio, John. *Sexual Politics, Sexual Communities: The Making of a Homosexual Minority in the United States, 1940-1970.* Second edition. Chicago: University of Chicago Press, 1983, 1998.

Douglas, Ann. *Terrible Honesty: Mongrel Manhattan in the 1920's.* New York: Farrar, Straus and Giroux, 1995.

Duberman, Martin. *Stonewall.* New York: Plume, 1993.

Dworkin, Andrea. "The Lie." In *Letters from a War Zone: Writings 1976-1989.* Chicago: Lawrence Hill Books, 1993. http://www.nostatus-quo.com/ACLU/dworkin/WarZoneChaptIa.html (accessed July 23, 2006).

Dworkin, Andrea. "The Root Cause." In *Our Blood: Prophecies and Discourses on Sexual Politics.* New York: Harper & Row, 1976.

Eliot, Marc. *Down 42nd Street: Sex, Money, Culture and Politics at the Crossroads of the World.* New York: Warner Books, 2002.

Ellis, Edward Robb. *The Epic of New York City: A Narrative History.* New York: Carroll & Graf, 1966.

Ernst, Morris L. and David Loth. *American Sexual Behavior and the Kinsey Report.* New York: Bantam, 1948.

Federal Writers Project, *The WPA Guide to New York City: A Comprehensive Guide to the Five Boroughs of the Metropolis—Manhattan, Brooklyn, the Bronx, Queens, and Richmond—Prepared by the Federal Writers' Project of the Works Progress Administration in New York City.* New York: Random House, 1939.

Ford, Luke. *A History of X: 100 Years of Sex in Film.* Amherst, NY: Prometheus Books, 1999.

Friedan, Betty. *Life So Far: A Memoir.* New York: Simon & Schuster, 2000.

Friedman, Andrea. *Prurient Interests: Gender, Democracy, and Obscenity in New York City, 1909-1945.* New York: Columbia University Press, 2000.

Friedman, Josh Alan. *Tales of Times Square*. Portland, Oregon: Feral House, 1993.

Garber, Eric. "A Spectacle in Color: The Lesbian and Gay Subculture of Jazz Age Harlem." In *Hidden From History: Reclaiming the Gay and Lesbian Past*, edited by Martin Bauml Duberman, Martha Vicinus, and George Chauncey Jr., 318-331. New York: New American Library, 1989.

Gardner, Charles W. *The Doctor and the Devil, or, Midnight Adventures of Dr. Parkhurst*. New York: Gardner, 1894.

Garrett, Charles. *The La Guardia Years: Machine and Reform Politics in New York City*. New Brunswick, NJ: Rutgers University Press, 1961.

Gilfoyle, Timothy. "From Soubrette Row to Show World: The Contested Sexualities of Times Square, 1880-1995." In *Policing Public Sex: Queer Politics and the Future of AIDS Activism*, edited by Dangerous Bedfellows (Ephen Glenn Coulter, Wayne Hoffman, Eva Pendleton, Alison Redick, David Serlin), 263-94. Boston: South End Press, 1996.

Ginzburg, Ralph. *An Unhurried View of Erotica*. New York: Ace Books, 1958.

Ginzburg, Ralph. *Eros*, Volume 1, No. 1, Spring 1962; No. 2, Summer 1962; No. 3, Autumn 1962; No. 4, Winter 1962.

Ginzburg, Ralph. "Eros Unbound." n.p., 1999. http://www.evesmag.com/ginzburg.htm (accessed May 1, 2007).

Ginzburg. V. United States, 383 U.S. 463 (1966).

Goldstein, Al and Josh Alan Friedman. *I, Goldstein: My Screwed Life*. New York: Thunder's Mouth Press, 2006.

Hay, Harry. *Radically Gay: Gay Liberation in the Words of its Founder*. Edited by Will Roscoe. Boston: Beacon Press, 1996.

Heins, Marjorie. "*The Miracle*: Film Censorship and the Entanglement of Church and State." Lecture given at University of Virginia Forum for Contemporary Thought, October 28, 2002.

Henry, George W., M.D. *All the Sexes: A Study of Masculinity and Femininity*. New York: Rinehart and Co., Inc., 1955.

Henry, George W., M.D. *Sex Variants*. New York: Paul B. Hoeber, 1941.

Humphreys, Laud. "Tearoom Trade: Impersonal Sex in Public Places." In *Public Sex/Gay Space*, edited by William L. Leap. 24-54. New York: Columbia University Press, 1999.

Hutchinson, E.R. *Tropic of Cancer on Trial: A Case History of Censorship*. New York: Grove Press, 1968.

Insight Associates for the Times Square Business Improvement District. *Report on the Secondary Effects of the Concentration of Adult Use Establishments in the Times Square Area*. April 1994. hellskitchen.net/issues/bids/tsbidsex/title.html (accessed September 6, 2007).

Kaiser, Charles. *The Gay Metropolis: 1940-1996*. New York: Houghton-

Mifflin, 1997.

Katz, Jonathan Ned. *Gay American History: Lesbians and Gay Men in the USA*. Revised edition. New York: Meridian, 1976, 1972.

Keire, Mara L. "The Committee of Fourteen and Saloon Reform in New York City, 1905-1920." In Business and Economic History, vol. 26, no. 2 (Winter 1997). http://www.h-net.org/~business/bhcweb/publications/BEHprint/v026n2/p0573-p0583.pdf (accessed November 26, 2006).

Kinsey, Alfred C., Wardell B. Pomeroy and Clyde E. Martin. *Sexual Behavior in the Human Male*. Philadelphia: W.B. Saunders Company, 1948.

Kornblum, William and Terry Williams, "West 42nd Street: The Bright Lights Zone," unpublished study, City University of New York Graduate Center, 1978.

Kramer, Larry. *Reports from the Holocaust: The Story of an AIDS Activist*. New York: St. Martin's Press, 1994.

Kyvig, David E. *Daily Life in the United States, 1920-1940*. Chicago, Ivan R. Dee, 2002.

Lankevich, George J. *American Metropolis: A History of New York City*. New York: New York University Press, 1998.

Lewis, David Levering, ed. *The Portable Harlem Renaissance Reader*. New York: Viking, 1994.

Lord, Sheldon. *21 Gay Street*. New York: Midwood, 1960.

Lovelace, Linda, with Mike McGrady. *Ordeal: An Autobiography*. New York: Bell Publishing, 1980.

Mackey, Thomas C. *Pursuing Johns: Criminal Law Reform, Defending Character, and New York City's Committee of Fourteen, 1920-1930*. Columbus, OH: Ohio State University Press, 2005. http://www.ohiostatepress.org/Books/Book%PDFs/Mackey%20Pursuing.pdf (accessed November 26, 2006).

Marsh, Marguerite. "Prostitutes in New York City: Their Apprehension, Trial, and Treatment, June 1939-June 1940." New York: Research Bureau, Welfare Council of New York City, 1941.

McCabe Jr., James D. *Lights and Shadows of New York Life; Or, The Sights and Sensations of the Great City*. Facsimile edition. New York: Farrar, Straus and Giroux, 1970.

McCabe Jr., James D. *New York by Gaslight*. Facsimile of 1882 Edition. New York: Greenwich House, 1984.

Miller v. California, 413 U.S. 15 (1973).

Morrow, Prince A. "Sanitary Aspects of Clause 79 of the Page Law." In *Social Diseases 1* (October 1910).

National Board of Review of Motion Pictures Collection, Rare Books and Manuscripts Division, New York Public Library, Astor, Lenox and Tilden Foundations.

New York City Department of Health and Mental Hygiene. *New York City HIV/AIDS Annual Surveillance Statistics.* 2006. Updated December 4, 2006. http://www.nyc.gov/html/doh/html/ah/hivtables.shtml (accessed July 12, 2006).

New York State Senate. *Report and Proceedings of the Senate Committee Appointed to Investigate the Police Department of the City of New York,* Vol. III, January 18, 1895 ("Lexow Report"). Albany, NY: James B. Lyon, State Printer, 1895.

New York State Youth Commission, *Blueprint for Delinquency Prevention.* Albany, NY, 1953.

Nugent, Richard Bruce. "You See, I Am a Homosexual" (Interview by Thomas H. Wirth). Tape recording, June 19, 1983, Collections of Thomas H. Wirth and the Schomburg Center. In *Gay Rebel of the Harlem Renaissance,* edited by Thomas H Wirth, 268. Durham, NC: Duke University Press, 2002.

Office of Midtown Planning and Development, Office of the Mayor, Times Square Development Council. Times Square Vice Map (1973). Shubert Archives collection.

Peale, Norman Vincent. *Sin, Sex and Self-Control.* New York: Fawcett Crest, 1965.

Petersen, James R. and Hugh M. Hefner. *The Century of Sex: Playboy's History of the Sexual Revolution, 1900-1999.* New York: Grove Press, 1999.

Post, Emily. *Etiquette in Society, in Business, in Politics, and at Home.* New York: Funk & Wagnalls, 1922, Bartleby.com, 2000. http://www.bartleby.com/95/ (accessed November 4, 2006).

Powell, Adam Clayton. *Against the Tide: An Autobiography.* Reprint Edition. New York: Arno Press, 1980.

Rechy, John. *City of Night.* New York: Grove Press, 1963.

Reichl, Alexander. *Reconstructing Times Square: Politics and Culture in Urban Development.* Lawrence, Kansas: University Press of Kansas, 1999.

Rembar, Charles. *The End of Obscenity: The Trials of Lady Chatterley, Tropic of Cancer, and Fanny Hill.* New York: Random House, 1968.

Riis, Jacob. *How the Other Half Lives.* New York: Penguin Classics, 1997.

Sagalyn, Lynne B. *Times Square Roulette: Remaking the City Icon.* Cambridge, MA: MIT Press, 2001.

Salvato, Richard and Cherie Myers. "National Board of Review of Motion Pictures Records, 1907-1971." The New York Public Library, Humanities and Social Sciences Library, Manuscripts and Archives Division, 1984.

Samuel Roth vs. the United States of America, 354 U.S. 476 (1957).

Sanger, Margaret. "The Aim." In *The Woman Rebel,* Vol. 1, Issue 1 (March

1914).http://adh.sc.edu/dynweb/MEP/ms/@ebtlink;td=2;hf=0?targ
et=%25N%15_48534_START_RESTART_N%25#X (accessed December 2, 2006).

Sanger, Margaret. "The Case for Birth Control." In *The Woman Citizen*, Vol.
8 (February 23, 1924). http://womenshistory.about.com/library/etext/
bl_sanger_1924.htm (accessed December 2, 2006).

Sanger, Margaret. *What Every Girl Should Know*. Girard, KS: Haldeman-Julius Company, 1922. http://archive.lib.msu.edu/AFS/dmc?radicalism/
public/all/whateverygirl1922/AEZ.pdf?CFID=577301&CFTOKEN
=48590189 (accessed December 2, 2006).

Sanger, Margaret. *Woman and the New Race*. New York: Brentano's
1920, Bartleby.com, 2000. http://www.bartleby.com/1013/ (accessed
November 4, 2006).

Sante, Luc. *Low Life: Lures and Snares of Old New York*. New York: Vintage,
1991.

Saturday Night at the Baths, DVD, directed by David Buckley (1975; Charlottesville, VA: Water Bearer Films, 2006).

Selenick, Laurence. "Private Parts in Public Places." In *Inventing Times
Square: Commerce and Culture at the Crossroads of the World*, edited by
William R. Taylor, 329-353. Baltimore, MD: Johns Hopkins Univer-
sity Press, 1996.

Social Protection Division, Office of Community War Services, Federal
Security Agency. "Meet Your Enemy: Venereal Disease." Washington,
D.C.: U.S. Government Printing Office, 1944.

Stansell, Christine. *American Moderns: Bohemian New York and the Creation
of a New Century*. New York: Metropolitan Books, 2000.

Stevenson, Jack. "From the Bedroom to the Bijou: A Secret History of
American Gay Sex Cinema." *Film Quarterly* 51, no. 1 (Autumn 1997):
24-31.

Stopes, Marie. *Married Love*. Edited and with an introduction by Ross
McKibbin. New York: Oxford University Classics, 2004.

Stryker, Susan. *Queer Pulp: Perverted Passions from the Golden Age of the Paperback*. San Francisco: Chronicle Books, 2001.

Summers, Claude J. ed. *The Queer Encyclopedia of Music, Dance and Musical
Theater*. San Francisco: Cleis Press, 2004.

Talese, Gay. *Thy Neighbor's Wife*. Garden City, NY: Doubleday and Co.,
1980.

Temporary State Commission on Youth and Delinquency, *Report*. New
York, NY, 1955.

United States Bureau of the Census. *U.S. Census of Population, 1920*. Ab-
stract of the Census – Population. Washington, D.C.: Government
Printing Office, 1923.

United States Bureau of the Census. *U.S. Census of Population, 1940.* Vol. 2, Part 5: New York-Oregon. Washington, D.C.: Government Printing Office, 1943.

United States Bureau of the Census. *U.S. Census of Population, 1950.* Vol. II, Part 32: New York. Washington, D.C.: Government Printing Office, 1952.

United States Bureau of the Census. *U.S. Census of Population, 1950.* Vol. IV, Special Reports, Part 3, Chapter D, Puerto Ricans in Continental United States. Washington, D.C.: Government Printing Office, 1953.

United States Bureau of the Census. *U.S. Census of Population, 1960.* Vol. I, Part 34: New York. Washington, D.C.: Government Printing Office, 1963.

United States Constitution. Eighteenth Amendment, Sec. 1.

United States War Department. "Sex Hygiene and Venereal Disease." Washington, D.C.: U.S. Government Printing Office, 1940.

Vining, Donald. *How Can You Come Out if You've Never Been In?: Essays on Gay Life and Relationships.* Trumansburg, NY: The Crossing Press, 1986.

Watkins, Elizabeth Siegel. *On The Pill: A Social History of Oral Contraceptives, 1950-1970.* Baltimore, MD: Johns Hopkins University Press, 1998.

Watson, Steven. *The Harlem Renaissance: Hub of African-American Culture, 1920-1930.* New York: Pantheon Books, 1995.

Weisbrod, Carl. "Transforming Times Square." In *New York Comes Back: The Mayoralty of Edward I. Koch,* edited by Michael Goodwin, 76-80. New York: Powerhouse Books, in association with the Museum of the City of New York, 2005.

Williams, Colin J., and Martin S. Weinberg. "Homosexuals in the Military: A Study of Less than Honorable Discharge." New York: Harper & Row, 1971.

Wojnarowicz, David. *Close to the Knives.* New York: Serpent's Tail, 1991.

Zoning Resolution of the City of New York. Section 12-10, Definitions.

INDEX

Numbers in italics indicate photos.